Bon Voyage!

The Cruise Traveler's Handbook

By Gary Bannerman

PASSPORT BOOKS

Trade Imprint of National Textbook Company
Lincolnwood, Illinois U.S.A.

Cover Photo: Sitmar Cruises

This edition first published in 1984 by Passport Books, Trade
Imprint of National Textbook Company, 4255 West Touhy
Avenue, Lincolnwood, Illinois 60646-1975 U.S.A.

4 5 6 7 8 9 0 TS 9 8 7 6 5 4 3 2 1

This book is dedicated to my grandparents.

It is in memory of Jack and Jesse Bannerman, the fifth generation of Bannerman Scots in Canada's Nova Scotia; and of Thomas Scobie of Paisley, Scotland, Sydney, Nova Scotia and, at the time of his death, Toronto.

It is a special tribute to my maternal grandmother who, at age 86, enjoys an active life and good health in Toronto. Margaret (Maggie) Scobie, her husband, Tom, and their small baby in arms crossed the Atlantic in *Athenia* in 1923, to build a new life in Canada. The voyage offered none of the comforts outlined in this book.

Contents

Acknowledgments

From my first tentative cruise and through this new book, my wife has been a partner in every sense of the word. Patricia has been responsible for photography, research, filing, bulk mailings and communication with the cruise industry. This book is as much hers as it is mine.

My friend Charlie White of Victoria, British Columbia, not only assigned me to investigate cruise ships many years ago, but he helped with the research and put it all into print. Christine and Duncan Howatson shared many of their experiences at sea, and Judi Sallay helped convince her company that this book might be worthwhile undertaking.

This book will serve as lasting tribute to two outstanding P&O captains who died suddenly at sea during 1982; John Crichton, who introduced me to this industry, and Brian Biddick, a personal friend who had been of immense assistance. Hundreds of seamen, from captains to dishwashers, and their corporate masters, were generous with both their time and knowledge. There are just too many names to mention.

I am grateful to all these people.

Introduction

It's always an honor to have the opportunity of introducing a fine book. *Bon Voyage* by Gary Bannerman is an exceptional effort, well-rounded and informative enough for first-time cruise travelers as well as veterans.

A cruise is the best vacation you can take, regardless of age or sex. A strong statement? Of course, but one easily proven.

Think over your past vacations. When was the last time you returned home having made a dozen or so new friends, nice folks that you want to keep in touch with by letter and phone? When did you last visit three to five new countries and experience a variety of cultures, with no packing and unpacking of luggage or switching trains and planes? Where have you enjoyed a totally prepaid (except for drinks and tips) environment in which you were waited upon day and night, served up to six fine meals per day, provided with fine evening entertainment, and made to feel relaxed and special? A cruise easily accomplishes all this and much more.

A cruise is a floating holiday. It underscores our fascination with the sea. It is romantic. It is fun. And this book will assure you a successful trip. It includes everything you need, from selecting a cruise, choosing accommodations, preparing for the trip, selecting your wardrobe, planning your time on ship and visits to ports of call.

Today's modern stabilized ship is literally a self-contained, total-services environment in which you are made to feel as comfortable as possible. A cruise vacation is truly care free, but it is never boring. As you will find throughout the following pages, there are abundant activities and programs to satisfy all but the most jaded of personalities. Fascinating ports of call, varied and energetic entertainment, fine, relaxing days on deck all add up to a wonderful floating holiday.

So, all you first-timers out there, start discovering that magic ingredient missing from most vacations—relaxation. Bon Voyage!

Robert Meyers
Editor/Assoc. Publisher
Cruise Travel Magazine

Prologue

"Never a ship sails out of the bay
But carries my heart as a stowaway."

Roselle Mercier Montgomery

One's life can often take peculiar turns from its so-called charted path; my own interest in cruise ships is a product of circumstance and not design. While I was developing a journalism career that focused on investigative reporting, hard news and politics, travel writing was not even a passing fantasy.

Many years ago, the idea of a cruise as a holiday was proposed to me. The notion was greeted with the utmost reluctance; there was a fear of being trapped among a horde of bingo players and with no avenue of escape, a worry about claustrophobia, and uncertainty about food, language, and customs. Not only was that first cruise a success, it led to many other cruises—and along the way an obsessive interest in the cruise ship industry was generated.

An earlier version of this book was published in 1976, a period of both optimism and anxiety in the passenger shipping business. In the transportation war, aircraft had emerged victorious. The passenger ships that survived had adapted to cruising. Gone were the great ocean liners. The intelligent companies had built sparkling 15,000 to 20,000-ton cruise ships, and the larger, older tonnage had been adapted to serve the holiday trade. Significant numbers of people who had never been on a ship were discovering a most delightful mode of vacation travel.

The industry had finally found its role and the first sparks of public interest were apparent; and so in 1976, there was a degree of optimism. But the period was also one of anxiety. Most companies were losing money; ship occupancy rates were about 75 per cent, and the first bombshell of Arab oil increases had fallen. There were no ships under construction in 1976.

The intervening years have proven that the optimism of the mid-seventies was well placed. Fuelled in part by the phenomenal success of ABC's "The Love Boat" on television, the last decade brought a boom unprecedented in the history of passengers at sea. All cruise ship companies boasted 100 per cent capacity most of the year, and some managed annual occupancy rates of as high as 107 percent, a bizarre figure developed when third and fourth bunks are added to cabins that normally carry only two passengers.

The present period signals tremendous excitement within the industry. The illustrious *S.S. France* has resailed as *S.S. Norway*, a Seattle group is attempting to relaunch *S.S. United States*, a San Diego businessman has the fantastic idea of building three replicas of *Titanic*, and the first American cruise line in two decades is operating a ship in Hawaii.

This book is the result of numerous cruises, visits to scores of ships, hundreds of interviews and the conscientious assembly of exhaustive files of printed matter. It is intended to be a handbook for veteran cruisers as well as for anyone who is thinking of taking a first cruise. It offers some shipping history, provides who's who of the cruising world, explains the roles of a ship's personnel, and passes along useful information to assist passengers in planning for and enjoying a cruise—their first, second or tenth. A cargo of anecdotes, scattered throughout the chapters, should make the book, we hope, an entertaining read.

No book can replace the sheer tranquility and pleasure of watching the sea go by from the viewpoint of a deck chair. Cruising is the most relaxing of vacations, a package deal of transportation, gourmet dining, comfortable accommodation, recreation and entertainment. The pay-in-advance fare may seem high, but it can prove a pure bargin when the combined costs of a land-based holiday are compared.

If this book convinces the reader to try a cruise, it will have served a useful purpose.

1

The Duty
and the Majesty

A BRIEF HISTORY

The steamship era of the North Atlantic Blue Riband was more than a golden age of transportation. The huge, powerful and luxurious vessels of the early twentieth century reflected a country's pride. Their sail-driven forebears had represented the epitome of discovery. Now, passenger liners — bold and brash — carried the multitudes to populate a new world.

Nations competed to build the biggest, the fastest and the most lavish vessels. After all, steamers carried the captains of international industries in the elegant suites. To the nobility and the global society set, the reigning monarch of the seas was the most important ballroom, banquet hall and hotel on the planet. There may never again be an industry that so carries with it such a powerful combination of glory, aspirations and romance — together mirroring the strength of a nation.

THE CATTLE CARS

That industry started, as all things do, by necessity. Early man understood that water was the simplest highway between two points, and it took little imagination for him to launch our first mode of transportation.

Viking and Nordic accomplishments are fabled. Thor Heyerdahl has presented his hypothesis of early Egyptian seamanship. We've heard much about the early British and European navies. And then, in the fifteenth and sixteenth centuries, the voyages of Columbus, Cabot, Cartier — and the many explorers who were to follow — changed the "earth" to the "globe," with the sea as its circulatory system. The Spaniards, following in the wake of Columbus, dominated the southern half of the Western Hemisphere. The French and the British shared and sometimes fought for the north. Captain James Cook and his British seamen charted the South Pacific.

The first passenger vessels were not much more than cattle boats, transporting the adventurous pilgrims to settle the New World. Total discomfort, disease and often death, were ever-present companions during those first days of the passenger liner industry. But refugees from persecution faced the perilous and uncomfortable journey with anticipation.

Many of the early vessels were to occupy a proud place in later history books. *Mayflower*, which sailed from Plymouth in 1620, carried the hardy who were to lay the cornerstone of American history. *Hector*, which sailed from Scotland in 1773, carried the 33 families plus 25 unmarried men who were to establish New Scotland: Canada's Nova Scotia.

The ships improved as the New World took shape. The discomforts were no longer so great as to make a would-be settler think twice, and for the colonial leaders there were definite touches of luxury.

THE AGE OF STEAM

When Robert Fulton demonstrated his steam-powered paddle-wheeler *Clermont*, on the Hudson River in 1807, the age of sail was reaching its most glorious moments. The beautiful squareriggers, brigantines, barquentines and schooners were dotting every coastline of the world. They were to remain a factor for another century, but for practical purposes, James Watt's steam engine had rendered them anachronisms.

Shipbuilders around the world were soon experimenting with steam. An American vessel, *Savannah*, supplementing her sails with a steam-driven paddle wheel, crossed the Atlantic in 1819. Sighted off the coast of Ireland, soot spewing from her stack, she was thought by onlookers to be on fire. In 1831 a Canadian firm constructed *Royal William*, a paddle-wheeler equipped with two 300-horsepower side-lever engines. In 1833, the 1,370-ton vessel became the first to cross the Atlantic mostly by steam; *Royal William* reverted to sail only when her engines had to be stopped for cleaning.

The true patriarch of steam on the North Atlantic was railway engineer Isambard Kingdom Brunel, whose three ships — *Great Western* (1837), *Great Britain* (1845) and *Great Eastern* (1859) — dominated the industry.

The steam-and-sail *Great Western* was to carry passengers on 64 crossings of the Atlantic, but it was *Great Britain*, the first steel-hulled and propeller-driven ship in the world, that in many ways represented the first true ocean liner. After several trips to New York, *Great Britain* ran aground on the Irish coast and sat idle for 11 months. Finally lifted from the sand, she made numerous runs to Australia. In her last years of service, *Great Britain* carried grain, before being beached once again in the late 1880s. She sat abandoned in the Falkland Islands, in the South Atlantic, for 80 years before being resurrected in 1970. Returned to Bristol, England, she is now a maritime museum.

Brunel's crowning achievement was, however, *Great Eastern*: 18,915 tons and designed for 3,000 passengers and 6,000 tons of cargo. Sadly, the extravagances of the ship were also to lead to the premature death of the innovative designer. Her $5 million cost bankrupted the owners before she sailed. Suffering through the economic and technical strains of the vessel's development, Isambard Kingdom Brunel became ill and died before *Great Eastern* ever carried a paying passenger. Her luxury was unparallelled, but the high cost of technology and crewing made her a business disaster through all her days. But while *Great Eastern* earned only a rare profit, she did also earn a place in history when she laid the first trans-Atlantic cable in 1866. *Great Eastern* ended her days as a shoreside amusement centre, festooned with advertisements and billboards. Yet not for 50 years was she surpassed in size. In 1906, Cunard's *Lusitania* was able to claim the honor of largest passenger vessel ever built.

While Brunel and other pioneers in technology were losing money, companies who held profitable mail contracts — toiling with unspectacular ships — were generally successful. Among these firms, Cunard, P&O Lines, White Star and American Collins Line dominated the market.

Actually, the ships of E. K. Collins of Miami were not entirely profitable. *Atlantic, Arctic, Baltic, Pacific* and, later,

Adriatic, were all subsidized by the United States government, and were leaders in comfort and speed. But two vessels were to sink — part of a series of misfortunes that led to the collapse of Collins Line in 1858. (When *Arctic* went down, E. K. Collins lost his wife, son and daughter.) The failure in shipping was ironic: Collins was vastly more wealthy than any of his competitors, and his immortality has been assured. The plush hotel resort strip of Miami Beach — Collins Avenue — has become an international landmark.

P.O.S.H.

In 1837, the Peninsular Steam Navigation Company successfully obtained a contract to carry mail from England to Spain and Portugal. Two years earlier, one of the company's co-founders, Arthur Anderson, had been promoting passenger cruises, but it was the mail contract that finally established the firm. By 1842, the growing steamship company had added Egypt and India to its routes.

The trip to India, as devised by Anderson and associates, was only for the rugged: ship from Southampton to Alexandria; camel train and horse carriage across Egypt to the Red Sea; and finally ship to the destination. (The alternative to that pilgrimage would have been an 80-day voyage around the Cape of Good Hope.)

By 1874, the Peninsular Steam Navigation Company had more than 50 ships covering greater than 1.5 million miles yearly — from Britain to the Iberian Peninsula, India, China, Australia and Japan. Absorbing the British India Steam Navigation Company in 1914, the firm doubled its size, only to lose 85 vessels during the first world war. The second world war claimed 182 more ships; but construction between the conflicts and following 1945 reached dramatic heights.

The year 1960 saw the purchase of the Orient Line. Today, with 120 companies involved in shipping, air transport, general cargo and passenger liners, the corporate realm of P&O is one of the largest and most distinguished in the seafaring world.

P&O contributions extend beyond the shipping industry and into the English language, the word "posh" being a P&O

invention. During the mid-nineteenth century, the passenger industry donned more gracious apparel but the voyage to India remained a long, hot and arduous ordeal. The heat, at least, was partially manageable. En route to India, the shaded cabins were on the port (left) side. During the return voyage, the starboard (right) accommodation offered the most comfort. Prestige passengers — those who could wield the most influence with ticket agents — won the best sides both ways. Their tickets were smartly stamped: P.O.S.H. (Port Out, Starboard Home.)

THE LAD FROM HALIFAX

The name Cunard is to shipping what Einstein is to physics. Born in Halifax, Nova Scotia, in 1787, Samuel Cunard, the son of a merchant, demonstrated his business ability at a young age. His personal wealth totalled 200,000 pounds sterling by 1830.

When the British Colonial Office expressed an interest in establishing a regular mail service between Great Britain and Nova Scotia, Cunard was ready to act. There were 40 sailing ships in his fleet, and as a former shareholder in the company that had built *Royal William*, he had some experience with steam. Cunard sailed to Britain in 1839 to secure the contract. With British partners, he created the cumbersome corporate title: British and North America Royal Mail Steam Packet Company. Mercifully, it soon became known as The Cunard Line.

The founder was aboard when his paddle-steamer *Britannia* embarked for Halifax on July 4, 1840. She chugged into his native harbor on the 17th. The following day, the ship docked at Boston. The company grew and prospered with the Liverpool, Halifax and Boston mail run and soon competed vigorously in the passenger market. As competition increased, Halifax was dropped as a port of call and the Cunard ships steamed directly for New York.

Sir Samuel Cunard spent his later life in Britain. He died in London in 1865. Through numerous corporate changes, and through a long succession of famous ships — *Mauretania, Lusitania, Acquitania, Saxonia, Queen Mary, Queen Elizabeth 2* —

the name Cunard has remained high on the company's masthead

POMP, CIRCUMSTANCE AND TRAGEDY

As the new century dawned, the passenger liner was at the focal point of international glamor. Newspapers and magazines would herald the latest new wonder to roll down the slips. Monarchs, assorted members of the nobility, ladies in their finery, the cream of society and the best bands in the land would gather at the shipyards to crown the finest new symbol of national pride. The champagne bottle would crash and, with a lurch, the vessel would roll into the sea.

She would occupy the spotlight during her maiden voyage, most frequently to New York, or from there to Southampton. At each new port, the gleaming and elegant ship would again be the headlined story of the local press. After the fame, the ship would drift out of the spotlight, to be replaced there by a more lavish successor. As the years passed, the suites, the panelling and the public rooms would become more and more dignified, and the cuisine would become increasingly elegant.

Britsh complacency was somewhat rocked in 1897, when the Germans launched the luxurious 14,000-tonner *Kaiser Wilhelm der Grosse*. The North German Lloyd ship set all standards for first-class opulence in her day. And though the British were slow to react, the German competitor Hamburg-Amerika launched an almost immediate challenge with *Deutschland*, a ship that emphasized speed over glamor. Although she was the fastest ship afloat, *Deutschland* had a severe vibration problem. Cartoonists of the day were not kind to her.

The German successes forced Cunard to improve and, in 1907, the sister ships *Lusitania* and *Mauretania* dominated world news. Subsidized by the British government, the two ships instantly restored the national ego: they were the fastest, the most lavish and the largest vessels afloat. Both ships are firmly etched in history. They were the first to travel the North Atlantic in less than five days, with *Mauretania* holding the time record for 22 years. *Lusitania's* name is connected with tragedy. It was torpedoed off the coast of Ireland in 1915. The 114 Americans killed — the death toll exceeded one thousand —

prepared the way for the United States' entry into the first world war.

Through this period, Britain's White Star Line competed successfully with Cunard and the foreign firms. White Star emphasized comfort over speed, and with this in mind it commissioned the construction in Belfast of *Olympic* and *Titanic*. The 46,000-ton vessels offered a degree of luxury that stunned the shipping world. One writer called the maiden voyage of *Titanic*, "the millionaires' special."

More than two thousand *Titanic* passengers and crew partied their way into the North Atlantic, envied by all for their good fortune. Only 483 were to survive the voyage. The "unsinkable ship" crashed into an iceberg, shattering five watertight compartments. *Titanic's* engineers had boasted that she could float if two compartments were filled with water. Excessive speed in fog conditions and a smug sense of security among the crew were major factors in the tragedy. *Titanic* carried only enough lifeboats for half the number of people aboard, and April 14, 1912 has perhaps become the most famous date in the history of passenger shipping. Overshadowed by the tragedy, *Titanic's* beautiful sister, *Olympic*, served with anonymous distinction until retired from service more than two decades later.

THE BLUE RIBAND

The Blue Riband (blue ribbon) has traditionally been worn as a badge of honor; specifically by members of the Order of the Garter of the British knighthood, and in general by the winner of any highly coveted prize. On the high seas, the Blue Riband championship turned into one of the fiercest competitions in history, as ships crossed the north Atlantic Ocean at faster and faster speeds.

The 3,044 nautical miles of the Blue Riband competition extended from Bishop's Rock, just off Cornwall, to Ambrose Light Ship at the entrance to New York Harbor. Prior to *Mauretania's* triumph over *Deutschland* in 1907, such unremembered ships as *Persia*, *Arizona*, *City of New York* and *Tautonic* had held the time record.

The decade of the thirties brought the competition to the centre of the world stage. In 1933, British Member of Parliament Harold K. Hales dedicated a huge and expensive trophy for the Blue Riband competition. And though most of the companies in the industry toiled vigorously to win the cup, each denied publicly that it was in a race. The title was successively held by Germany's *Bremen*, Italy's *Rex* and France's *Normandie* before the sweepstakes ended, temporarily, in 1938 as *Queen Mary* steamed the Riband in three days and 21 hours.

After *Queen Mary* captured the Hales Trophy, Cunard issued this curious announcement:

> We are only interested in having the liner officially designated the fastest. We deprecate record breaking voyages and we do not recognise the Blue Riband Trophy, which we shall not claim from the French liner *Normandie*.

Despite the denials, every ship that won the Riband immediately enjoyed popularity and profitability. *Queen Mary* remained unchallenged until 1950, when the American government awarded United States Lines a $48 million subsidy to build the fastest ship in the world. The total cost of *S.S. United States* was $75 million, and to this day, many aspects of her engine room design remain secrets of the United States Department of Defense. Said to be capable of top speeds in excess of 40 knots, *United States* established the permanent Blue Riband mark of three days and 11 hours in 1952.

She did it twice — once each way. But never again could *S.S. United States* achieve such glory. The truth has never been told, but it is believed in the industry that her punishing record voyage caused significant engine damage. She was never a profitable ship, plagued by both mechanical and marketing difficulties. Veteran Cunard employees, many of whom still toil on *Queen Elizabeth 2*, cheerfully recount the scores of times *Queen Mary* left the American upstart sitting in her wake. *Mary* handled a speed of 30-knots-plus consistently for 30 years.

THE GIANTS

When Germany launched the 60,000-ton behemoth *Vaterland* in 1914, global warfare obscured the new era in shipping she represented. It was only at the conclusion of the conflict, when the Allies seized the German passenger liners, that the enormity of the ship was rightly appreciated. Under American control and renamed *Leviathan*, she sailed for years — known affectionately by the public as "The Levi Nathan."

Many countries played significant roles in the development of ocean liners. Holland America Line, with a century of involvement in the industry, has put 134 ships to sea in the passenger trade. Perhaps the most famous of these was *Nieuw Amsterdam II*, launched in 1938, which saw distinguished wartime service. At the same time, the many Canadian Pacific "Empresses" were familiar sights around the world. The 42,000-ton *Empress of Britain* was the largest ship of any kind sunk during the second world war. Although capable of carrying 8,000 troops, she was carrying but a few hundred when bombed by the *Luftwaffe* in 1940. The Greeks and Scandinavians have been active in shipping from the earliest days of the passenger liners. But generally most of the headlines were dominated by the Germans, the Italians, the French and the British.

When the French launched the 43,000-ton *Île de France* in 1927 — the final word in elegance — even grander ships were on the drawing boards. Germany's 51,000-ton Blue Riband champion *Bremen* sailed for the first time in 1929. In Italy, Benito Mussolini was not to be outdone. He commissioned on behalf of his government two magnificent 51,000-ton sister ships: *Conte di Savoia* and *Rex*. Famed especially for their opulent lounges, they were without parallel.

Their moment of glory was soon over, for the French were wasting little time. Rising in the shipyards of Saint Nazaire was a 79,000-ton titan which many claim to this day was the finest ship ever to sail the seas. *Normandie* featured broad fan-shaped staircases that opened into the elegant public rooms. No luxury was left out. One of her three smokestacks was a fake, placed for appearance only. (The ship's kennels were housed inside it.) *Normandie* captured the Blue Riband from *Rex* and held it for three years, when it was taken by *Queen Mary* in 1938. So sensitive were the French that when the British proudly announced their 81,000-ton giant, *Normandie* was expanded to 82,700 tons. Following this decision, Cunard White Star increased the specifications for *Queen Elizabeth*. When *Mary's* sister finally sailed in 1940, her tonnage was recorded at 83,673.

The construction of the *Queens* brought the era of romance, glamor and majesty to its zenith. To the casual onlooker, the sisters differed only in smokestacks: *Mary* had three, her sister two. There were many differences, however; some significant, most merely cosmetic.

Cunard's plans for building the greatest vessels that had ever sailed the seas were prompted by simple business economics. Prior to the construction of the sisters, the company required several ships to service the New York-Southampton route. By increasing the size of the ships substantially, and by making them faster, the company could handle its trade by a two-ship shuttle.

In December 1930, the keel of ship number 534 was laid at the Clydeside shipyard of John Brown, just outside Glasgow. As construction reached high gear, nearly four thousand workers were laboring full time at the site, while tens of thousands toiled in components factories throughout Britain. A year later, the Great Depression brought the world to its knees, and the Cunard executives were forced to suspend work on their massive Glasgow project.

The towering skeletal hull of the great vessel 534 became Britain's monument to the gloom of the Depression. It was the focal point of lengthy debates at Westminster. The Cunard people were inundated with offers of financial help from all over the world, but it finally took a major shipping merger with White Star Line, plus significant government assistance, before work was again started on April 3, 1934. Ship 534 was christened by Queen Mary, the wife of British Monarch King George V, on September 26, 1934, and the hull went down the slip into the Clyde.

After a further year and a half of work, the monarch of the seas set forth on her maiden voyage, sailing from Southampton in May 1936. And although her size was exceeded slightly when her younger sister *Queen Elizabeth* was launched in 1940, her speed was not. No two ships that ever sailed have carried a prouder history, never so fine as during their troop movements, in every corner of the globe, through the second world war. Unlike other carriers, which travelled with the protection of convoy, the *Queens*, sporting dull naval grays, sailed on their own. The *Gray Ghosts*, as they became known, were faster than anything else at sea. Each ship carried up to 17,000 soldiers on a trip (peacetime passenger capacity was 2,000), with tiers of bunks covering every square inch of deck space. Fully loaded with soldiers at New York, the ships could clear the passage over the Hudson River car tunnel only if every person aboard remained rigidly still. *Queen Mary* carried Churchill to North America for his historic wartime meetings with Roosevelt.

The Cunard Line was unable to establish the two-ship shuttle between Britain and the United States until after the war, when the industry began to decline, and the *Queens'* place in history comes from distinguished wartime service. At one point in the war, Adolph Hitler, so frustrated by the incredible good fortune of the *Queens*, offered a huge cash reward to any Nazi captain who could sink one of them. And despite substantial anti-aircraft armaments on board, not one shot had to be fired throughout the war. There were many people who believed the ships to be navigated by Divine Providence.

Other great ships did not fare so well. *Bremen* was officially reported as lost to Allied bombs while in port during the war (there are many who believe she was scuttled by her crew), and both *Conte di Savoia* and *Rex* were sunk by Allied bombers. *Normandie* stood idle in New York for two years; when the Americans entered the war, she was confiscated for the Allied cause. Renovations to *Normandie* were under way when sparks from a welding torch ignited a major fire. Some three thousand tons of water were pumped aboard in an effort to douse the flames — and *Normandie* capsized under the weight of the water. Finally lifted from the harbor bed in 1943, she was sold for scrap, fetching a meagre $161,680. *Normandie* had cost the French $48 million to build.

The demise of the venerable *Île de France* was also one of great sorrow. Screams of shame and scandal came from the people of France when their government sold the great ship to Hollywood for the making of a motion picture. The disaster film, "The Last Voyage," used a blazing *Île de France* as a prop.

Queen Mary was allowed to rest with dignity, and today is an exciting hotel and museum complex in Long Beach, California. *Queen Elizabeth* perished in a deliberately set Hong Kong harbor fire. A construction crew working on the ship, hoping to extend their employment for a few weeks, started what they had thought would be a small blaze.

The January 1972 demise of *Queen Elizabeth* ended an age when ships were the dreams of mankind.

PROSPERITY AND DELUSION

The years immediately following the war, with hundreds of thousands of returning soldiers and displaced persons moving across the Atlantic, were among the most prosperous in the history of shipping. Restored to prewar splendor, the *Queens* were earning an annual profit of $50 million. Anything that could float and offered a modicum of safety was used in the brisk trade.

Italy was soon back in the luxury sweepstakes, launching the breathtaking 29,000-ton *Andrea Doria* in 1952 and her younger sister, *Cristoforo Columbo*, in 1953. For a period, until a foggy night off Nantucket Island in 1956, these were among the most admired ships in the world. That night, a smaller Swedish ship, *Stockholm*, rammed into the side of *Andrea Doria*. There was fault on both sides. Each had watched the other on radar — right to the point of impact — and a last-minute desperation turn of *Andrea Doria* only served to create a more ideal target for *Stockholm*. Only the fast arrival of *Île de France* prevented one of the greatest tragedies of all time. There were 51 deaths: 46 passengers from *Andrea Doria* and five crewmen from *Stockholm*. With her bow crushed severely, the Swedish ship not only managed to stay afloat but to limp back to New York on her own steam. *Andrea Doria* remains 226 feet below the ocean surface.

The high drama on the water was, from a business perspective, insignificant compared with the challenge from the sky. While everyone else in the world was dancing above in silvery birds, the shipping executives seemed to suffer from a curious inability to look up. The jet age was ascending and every long-distance need was being handled by the aviators.

Unwilling to adapt to the new era, the shipping magnates clung to their glorious past. Despite the waning fortunes of the industry by the late 1950s and the awesome competition from the sky, contracts were let to build massive, elegant ships, best suited to trans-Atlantic travel.

In 1959, P&O welcomed the 42,000-ton *Oriana* to its fleet, offering accommodation for 2,100 passengers. A year later, the 45,000-ton *Canberra* joined P&O to carry 2,200 guests and a crew of a thousand. It was a great occasion in France in 1962, when government leaders and dignitaries from all walks of life watched the stunningly beautiful 1,035-foot, 67,000-ton *S.S. France* depart with her 2,200 passengers. Italy followed in 1965 with the 46,000-ton sister ships *Michelangelo* and *Raffaello.*

In England, Cunard lobbied Parliament for assistance in the development of a ship known only as *Q3.* The company was looking for a 70,000-ton replacement for *Queen Mary* and managed to win a subsidy of $18 million from the government. The idea was scrapped, however, when wiser minds decided to build a multi-purpose vessel capable of both cruising and trans-Atlantic sailing, but narrow enough to fit through the Panama and Suez Canals. That ship was the 66,000-ton *Q4,* christened *Queen Elizabeth 2* in 1969.

The large ships were a business nightmare from the first day they sailed. They gobbled fuel in staggering quantities and, in most cases, were designed for a transportation market that had evaporated. After averaging annual losses of $20 million over several years, *S.S. France* was put into mothballs in 1972. And so ended the distinguished Compagnie Générale Transatlantique, known in the English-speaking world as the French Line.

The Italian Line lost $320 million in 1974, attempting to operate *Michelangelo, Raffaello, Leonardo da Vinci* and the aging *Cristoforo Columbo.* That loss signalled the end of the Italian Line.

P&O Line and Cunard were more fortunate, or more shrewd, than the French Line and the Italian Line. They continued to pilot their large ships through several bad years, taking losses but investing heavily in modernizations. When the boom arrived in the late 1970s, *Queen Elizabeth 2, Oriana* and *Canberra* turned profitable once again.

THE CRUISE ERA

In the 1960s, the companies that had dominated the shipping market began building 15,000- to 20,000-ton cruise ships, geared toward holidays, not transportation. Most of these vessels were designed with economy diesel motors.

The ships became the purpose of the holiday, not the means to a destination. Through the 1970s, as public demand increased and fuel and crew costs soared, the ships became larger. In 1975, the ideal cruise ship was 20,000 tons with a passenger capacity of 750. By 1982, the ideal ship had grown to 30,000 tons, with accommodation for 1,100 passengers.

The shipping industry is once again happy and affluent. From the ashes of a devastated Blue Riband market, ships are rising to the top of the travel trade.

2

The Fleet

THE INDUSTRY TODAY

In the cruise industry, where the most infinite details are cautiously and meticulously calculated, there are few surprises. When the news emerged in 1979 that Knut Kloster of Oslo and his backers had purchased the aging and long-abandoned giant *S.S. France,* the corporate boardrooms of cruising were rocked to their very foundations. A deal had been struck to buy the ship from the French government for $16 million, and $60 million had been set aside for renovations.

If the announcement had come from a wealthy Arab or some naive billionaire, the level of astonishment would have been minor. It is a relatively common and amusing occurrence to hear of major ships being brought from retirement with fantastic plans for floating museums, hotels, condominiums or even cruising. After much fanfare, these deals usually amount to nothing.

When the *S.S. France* announcement was made in Norway, it was a different matter. The Norwegians in general, and the firm of Klosters-Rederi A/S in particular, have been among the most proficient, innovative and successful in the field of passenger shipping. Klosters' Norwegian Caribbean Lines has been a dominant force in cruising since the mid-1960s.

By the time the renovations were completed, *S.S. France*—rechristened *S.S. Norway*—was more beautiful than ever. The budget for the work had been shattered, exceeding $110 million. *Norway* sailed in the fall of 1980 with a carefully constructed plan of action. She would not compete in the fuel-thirsty and waning trans-oceanic and world cruise market, but would operate in a set pattern of seven-day, slow-speed cruises out of Miami. Half her engine room was removed, and many fuel-saving techniques were put to use. *France* had skipped over the oceans at 35 knots. *Norway* would cruise at 16 knots, capable on her two remaining engines of an absolute maximum of 25 knots.

There was similar shock and excitement during 1983 in Britain, when two of the venerable names in shipping—Cunard and P&O—opened a very public corporate war. Sensing financial vulnerability at P&O, Cunard's parent company, the predatory conglomerate Trafalgar House, launched a takeover bid through the stock market. A fascinated British public sat on the sidelines surveying the fight through millions of dollars worth of newspaper advertising. Each company used the newspapers to deprecate the other. Trafalgar condemned P&O for its debt load and lack of profitability. P&O newspaper ads, complete with skull and crossbones, accused Trafalgar and its chairman, Sir Nigel Broakes, of piracy. P&O went so far as to ridicule the mechanical reliability of *Queen Elizabeth 2* and the competence of Cunard as ship managers.

The battle was finally shifted indoors to the chambers of the British government's monopolies commission, where it is likely to remain through much of 1984. As the dust settled in The City—London's renowned financial district—most brokers seemed convinced that P&O has had a superior track record managing ships, but that Trafalgar were better financiers. And the government was pondering moves to control slanderous extremes in future corporate takeover battles.

THE MONARCHS

In every era of shipping, one vessel—usually the largest afloat—sailed proudly as the monarch of the seas. Sometimes there were battles for the crown, such as the one between *Queen Mary* and *Normandie* before the second world war, or in postwar years, the rivalry between the two *Queens*. For most of the 1970s, *R.M.S. Queen Elizabeth 2* was without challenge or parallel. Today she shares the throne with *S.S. Norway.*

The Norwegian ship, with extra-deluxe cabins added in the refit, is both the longest and largest liner (1,035 feet, 70,202 tons). She is even more elegant than the majestic *Queen Elizabeth 2* (963 feet, 67,140 tons). But the British claim to the throne gains significantly through *QE2's* strict adherence to tradition: two dozen trans-Atlantic crossings a year, one major annual world cruise, two classes of accommodation and fuel-gobbling speeds of up to 30 knots. (P&O's *Oriana* is the fastest passenger liner still in service, though her peak speed of 35 knots is rarely used.) One more plus: *Queen Elizabeth 2,* one of the most luxurious ships in the world, is, by a substantial margin, the most expensive to travel on.

THE PORT OF MIAMI

The incredibly blue waters of the Caribbean play host to a great proportion of the world's ships at any time of the year, and in peak periods as many as 50 ships—representing half the global industry—will be darting from island to island. Many use San Juan, Puerto Rico, as home base and a few embark from Port Everglades, near Fort Lauderdale, Florida. But the Port of Miami is the point of embarkation for and the headquarters of about one-third of the international industry.

On a busy winter weekend, with ship after ship steaming for the Caribbean, the scene resembles the evacuation of Dunkirk. The people of Miami can be justly proud of their port facilities—the most modern, most efficient and most profitable in the world. The port is governed by an appointed commission, independent of politics and the shipping industry, and in appearance, comfort and functionability of facilities, it rivals the most modern international airports. There is also plenty of room for parking.

A ship's crew welcomes a visit to Miami, where a swimming pool, recreational centre and playing fields are provided for their exclusive use. Rather stark is the comparison to the waterfront sheds and warehouses found in most of the world's ports. The Port of Miami has dramatically pulled ahead of its competing neighbor, Port Everglades, largely because of the former's politically independent port commission.

None of the companies operating out of Miami can be considered a luxury leader in the industry (the *S.S. Norway* is the only luxury vessel sailing out of Miami.) One stuffy competitor describes the entire Miami scene as "the beer and pretzels crowd.'' The remark is not completely without substance, but it distorts reality. The Miami companies offer a product that ranges from good to superb. And without question, they offer the most outstanding dollar value in the business. The competition is fierce, which means that prices are from 25 to 40 per cent lower than for equivalent cruises out of other ports. Miami's target is the mass market, with just as much emphasis placed on attracting secretaries as corporate presidents.

The United States marketplace provides greater than 70 per cent of the cruise industry's annual revenue, yet only two cruise ships are American registered. The combined factors of crew salaries and taxes have, over the years, made it far more desirable to register ships elsewhere.

THE FLEET

Passenger ships are measured in Gross Registered Tons (G.R.T.), a calculation that has little to do with weight. To determine the G.R.T., revenue areas of the ship are precisely measured, then multiplied by a set tonnage factor. (Cargo ships are recorded in Deadweight Tons, the actual weight of the vessel when fully loaded with cargo.)

Today, there are about a hundred cruise ships in operation or under construction, having a combined weight of just under two million G.T.R. To put that figure in perspective, this tonnage is equivalent to 24 ships the size of *Queen Mary* or *Queen Elizabeth*. Despite the very high profile of cruise ships, the industry represents a very small arena of commercial activity. The gross revenue of the business is less than that of Waikiki Beach in Hawaii—just one of hundreds of major resorts.

The profiles of the cruise companies that follow are arranged according to tonnage. Addresses, ships' statistics and countries or registry are found in Appendix B.

Costa Cruises (196,039 tons, 11 ships)

The largest cruise company in the world is operated by a remarkable Italian family whose 11 ships around the globe sport a distinctive "C" on their smokestacks. The family Costa of Genoa became active in cruising in 1948, competing for most of its years against the government's Italian Line which, despite spectacular vessels and bottomless subsidies sank into bankruptcy and oblivion. Costa Line on the other hand, was a thriving concern.

There are 20 members of the family engaged in a corporate realm that also includes a Spanish oil refinery, cargo ships and real estate holdings from South America to Saudi Arabia. The company has remained totally private. There are no outside investors and no published annual reports.

Until moving on to other areas of the family business late in 1981, the chief executive officer of Costa Cruises was Dr. Piergeorgio Costa, 40, based in the New York office. Enigmatic, enthusiastic and one of the shrewdest executives in the business, Dr. Costa says the major decision facing his company is whether or not to go public. With outside investors, the Costa empire could enter a period of significant growth. Dr. Costa says that family capital is currently strained to its limit. If the firm remains private, it will become a more compact operation.

The Costa fleet is not only the largest, but the most diverse. The ships range in size from the 8,600-ton *Andrea C* to the flagship—the 30,500-ton *Eugenio C.* Eight ships are company owned, and three are under charter from firms that were unsuccessful. Nine ships are crewed by Italians, two by Greeks. The latter vessels, all operated by Costa under charter, provide a hedge against the unpredictable nature of Italian shipping unions.

Costa offers ships that cater to the complete cruise market, from economy to luxury. During the mid-1970s, the Greek company Carras commissioned the lavish conversion of two cargo liners, *Port of Sydney* and *Port of Melbourne,* into the opulent 16,000-ton cruise ships *Danae* and *Daphne.* The space-per-passenger ratio on these vessels is the most generous in the industry. When Carras Cruises failed as a company, the first call was to Costa—standard practice in the business. A similar story involves perhaps the most elegant small ship ever built, the 12,000-ton *Italia.* Her original owner, completely obsessed with luxury, went bankrupt during the construction period. Ownership reverted to the Banco del Lavoro, which then chartered out *Italia* to other operators. Renamed *Princes Italia,* she became one of the early ships of the now famous Princess Cruises fleet. Later, Costa purchased *Italia* outright from the bankers.

The Costa fleet tends to be older than its major competitors and as of 1981, no new construction was planned. Piergeorgio Costa is resisting many of the trends in the industry. He remains unconvinced that the new wave of 30,000-ton-plus ships will be successful. The passenger-to-crew ratios have been miscalculated, he feels, and a larger crew will be required to maintain service standards. About fuel costs, Dr. Costa is not as worried as his competitors are. Most of Costa's vessels have expensive fuel-intensive turbines, but he thinks that the highly refined fuel required by the new ships will be even more costly—significantly so—than the heavier bunker that the older ships use.

Dr. Costa is gambling that other companies will be unsuccessful with their new ships. "I wouldn't be surprised," he says, "if in one or two years some very good ships are for sale." He claims to be unsuperstitious, but when asked why, as Italy's prime shipping company, Costa has not made an offer for the retired *Michelangelo* and *Raffaello,* both 46,000-tonners, he replies simply, "These are ships with a bad spell." He says much the same about *S.S. France/S.S. Norway.*

With operations in South America, the Caribbean, the Mediterranean, Alaska and, soon, in South Africa and South Pacific, Costa is among the most international companies in the industry. The diverse range of the ships—in the market area, in crew nationality, in size and in levels of luxury— creates managerial nightmares. The one tremendous asset is that the firm can cater to every requirement, to every taste.

P&O Inc. (178,040 tons, 8 ships)

Amid the efforts to defeat Trafalgar House's takeover bid, P&O continues to forge ahead with enthusiasm. A state-of-the-art $150-million 40,000-ton luxury ship *Royal Princess* is rising in the Wartsila Shipyard at Helsinki, Finland. P&O hopes to have her christened by Princess Diana in late 1984. The company also recently acquired Swan Hellenic Cruises, which markets exotic cruise packages from the middle east to the Dardanelles, with as much emphasis on education as relaxation. Swan Hellenic features a 6,000-ton Greek ship *Orpheus,* leased from the Epirotiki Line, and several smaller vessels for river cruising.

In 1970 the British shipping leader had a fleet of 13 ships (343,000 tons), most of them getting on in years and showing signs of wear. Over the next decade, P&O was to present one of the most dramatic illustrations of corporate fat-trimming, modernization and market penetration—anywhere in the international business sphere. Of the 13 ships sailing in 1970, only the huge *Canberra* and *Oriana* remain.

Cruise ships represent only one segment of the P&O conglomerate's business activity, but they provide the company with a public profile. The new era of P&O was launched in 1972 with the purchase from the Norwegians of a new cruise ship, christened *Spirit of London.* This 17,000-ton sporty vessel is the nearly identical twin of Norwegian Caribbean Lines' *Southward. Spirit* was dispatched to Los Angeles to begin a career of Mexican and Alaskan cruising. In 1974, P&O purchased Princess Cruises of Seattle and Los Angeles, best know for its extremely popular and beautiful ship, *Island Princess.* The British company then bought the *I.P.'s* twin sister *Sea Venture,* now calling her *Pacific Princess. Spirit of London* was renamed *Sun Princess,* and the three-ship, wholly-owned P&O subsidiary of Princess Cruises began sailing from the company's Los Angeles headquarters. Princess Cruises operates under the slogan, ''Part of the growing world of P&O.''

With the success of the television series ''The Love Boat,'' the three *Princesses* were to join the ranks of the world's most famous ships. Princess Cruises, with its independent management has become an example of ''the tail wagging the dog.'' P&O provided the money, but the Princess people offerred the dynamic marketing and service skills necessary in today's industry. ''The P&O Line'' masthead has been changed to read, ''P&O Cruises.''

The Princess Cruises division of P&O caters to the Alaska, Mexico, trans-canal and Caribbean markets, with occasional sailings to the South Pacific. P&O Cruises serves the Australian, South Pacific and Mediterranean areas, as well as offering annual world cruises. With the demise of Swedish American Line in 1978, P&O Cruises purchased the 27,670-ton *Kungsholm*. After extensive renovations, the ship was renamed *Sea Princess*. Her name notwithstanding, she is part of the P&O Cruises fleet, not the Princess division.

P&O is sufficiently large to feature one ship for the sole purpose of the training of seamen and officers.

The principal cruise executive with P&O in London is Len Scott, managing director of P&O Cruises and chairman of Princess Cruises. He is proud of the modernization of his own fleet, but concerned about companies that are stretching the life of old ships beyond a healthy span.

"The exploitation of old tonnage is not without risk...and in the competitive arena, when business is difficult, there is a tendency to cut corners, reducing standards of maintenance, safety and hygiene. This," Scott says, "can be dangerous."

The cruises division of P&O has shown a happy profit picture in recent years, while the company was suffering heavy losses on oil tankers and other subsidiaries. Scott's principal concern today is the eventual replacement of *Oriana* and *Canberra*. Industry observers are speculating that soon after *Royal Princess* first sails, *Oriana* will be retired from service.

Cunard Line Limited (151,130 tons, 5 ships)

High on the superstructure of each of Cunard's ships, bold red letters spell out the most revered name in shipping. A Trafalgar House subsidiary, Cunard cruises are run by the energetic Ralph Bahna from the New York headquarters. A Trans World Airlines veteran, Bahna is known in the industry for his quick wit and a gift for the ad lib. Through the decade of the seventies, plagued by a series of difficulties within the firm, Bahna's sense of humor must have served him well. There were years of unprofitability, numerous mechanical breakdowns, one ship was lost in a Mississippi

River fire and the company's two 17,500 ton ships *Countess* and *Princess,* failed to win the respect enjoyed by many of their competitors.

At the outset of 1984, Cunard has, in fact, emerged as one of the most aggressive operations in the industry. In addition to the controversial P&O takeover attempt, Cunard has recently purchased outright one of the most respected companies in the cruise business, Norwegian American Cruises, with its two ships, the 24,000 ton *Sagafjord* and her 25,000-ton sister *Vistafjord* both the epitome of luxury. For the first time in her history, *RMS Queen Elizabeth 2* can boast of family members deserving to be in her presence.

Cunard plans to change little in the management structure of Norwegian American cruises. Independent offices will be maintained, ship registry stays in Norway, the Norwegian officers and excellent European catering crew remain on the ships and the appeal to the sedate uppercrust passenger will continue to be the market thrust.

An attempt was made during 1983 to sell *Cunard Princess* and *Cunard Countess* to American buyers who planned to register the ships in the United States, but the deal fell through. Asked if the ships are still for sale, a Cunard spokesman said that no negotiations were underway and that, in fact, Cunard wants more ships, not fewer.

Queen Elizabeth 2 emerged from drydock in late 1983 sporting a substantial face lift, a new personal computer laboratory where passengers can play with and learn about the new technologies, and a "Club Lido Magrodome" over one of her swimming pools. A dome with a retractable roof will make it possible for passengers to use the pool amid the blustery North Atlantic winters. The new facility is designed in such a way that it can also be used for theatre in the round. After an unsuccessful experiment with white paint, *QE2's* hull has been sandblasted down and returned to her original black.

When ships of the industry are discussed, senior Cunard executive Dennis Wong flatly states: "The Queen stands alone." And so she does. *QE2,* more computerized than any other ship at sea, was the first vessel to navigate by space satellite. The ship lacks nothing in comfort, facilities or elegance. Her Queen Mary and Queen Elizabeth penthouse suites, high on signal deck, are the most famous and the most sought-after hotel rooms in the world. The two-storey cabins rented in 1981 for $5,600 a day. Of course, food and entertainment are included.

The average daily fare on *QE2* is $200 for cruising, $300 for the world cruise and $350 for a trans-Atlantic crossing. There are four dining rooms, three of them for first-class passengers. The top restaurant is the Queen's Grill, high up on boat deck, but many passengers who know the ship well prefer the small Princess Grill, more isolated and more intimate. The offerings of the two rooms are the same: unlimited caviar, superb wines and a menu as long as the diner's imagination. The passenger eats what he wants: Beef Wellington, Chateâubriand, Peking Duck—whatever strikes the diner's fancy will be prepared. In the tourist class Tables of the World Restaurant, the menu is as outstanding as or better than the standard fare on most ships at sea.

Queen Elizabeth 2 is the most secure ship in the industry. Her high profile has made her a favorite target for the threats of terrorists. British registry encourages the I.R.A. Her steadfast determination to visit Israel every year angers the Palestinians. The ship is laced with complex technical security systems, and armed security men travel on every trip. The bridge and engine room are off-limits to nonauthorized personnel. The captain is admitted to the bridge only after being recognized through a peep hole.

All luggage that goes aboard *QE2* is x-rayed, and this regulation has resulted in amusing anecdotes. Recently in New York, a buzz was heard coming from one suitcase. Security people quickly ripped open the bag, ruining it in the process. A battery-operated electric razor was discovered with the switch in the "on" position. An employee was dispatched to a nearby store to purchase an identical Samsonite suitcase. Its owner was delighted.

Captain Bob Arnott, a wartime navy veteran, has been with *QE2* from the beginning. He was assigned by Cunard to supervise phases of her construction in Scotland and, after serving on other Cunard ships, he returned several years ago to become one of the *Queen's* masters.

He recalls vividly one of the most dramatic days in the ship's history. Arnott was staff captain (second-in-command) at the time. One overcast day in 1972 in the mid-Atlantic, a bomb threat came from New York. The caller, stating that a bomb was aboard and set to blow, was so exact in technical information about the ship that he was taken very seriously.

A team of British commandos and an army bomb disposal expert were sent from England in a Hercules aircraft. The army chap, subject to air sickness and seasickness, had used a parachute but once before. The team jumped blind into the clouds from a height of 800 feet, hitting the ocean almost as soon as they cleared the clouds. The mission commander jumped side-by-side with the army novice. Arnott recalls that the commander was out of his parachute almost before hitting the water, so as to help his partner.

"I have heard about people being green, but this army man actually was," Arnott remembers.

Meanwhile, when the commando captain arrived on the bridge, he went immediately to the ship's master, zipped open his frogman's suit, and pulled out a copy of the *London Times,* inquiring, "I don't suppose you've seen today's paper, sir?"

The bomb scare proved to be a hoax, and the New York shoemaker who called in the threat was sentenced to life in prison.

Norwegian Caribbean Lines (130,066 tons, 5 ships)

Sailing optimistically in the shadow of Norwegian Caribbean's new flagship, *Norway,* NCL's four "white ships" — *Southward, Skyward, Starward* and *Sunward II* — remain familiar sights throughout the Caribbean. Which is highly appropriate, for NCL played a major role in the development of the Caribbean market. In 1966, the Norwegian company Klosters-Rederi A/S formed a partnership with Miami businessman Ted Arison to market Miami cruises. Klosters provided the ships, and Arison provided the passengers. The partnership ended bitterly in the early 1970s and Ted Arison left to establish his own company, Carnival Cruises. Years of litigation followed; interestingly, the lawyer who handled the case for the Norwegians, Ron Zeller, emerged recently as the president of Norwegian Caribbean.

Although most executives of the industry believe the giant *Norway* could push NCL to the brink of ruin, Zeller speaks with excitement, enthusiasm and optimism. *Norway* is the greatest ship in the world, and he knows it. But she is also an enormous vessel. Zeller's staff is faced with the task of selling nearly five thousand beds every week. Nineteen hundred of them are on *Norway*.

The most striking features of *Norway* are the indoor promenades, known as Fifth Avenue on one side of the vessel and Champs Elysées on the other. The promenades represent the grandest deck of any ship at sea, and are lined with sidewalk cafes, cocktail lounges, an ice cream bar, assorted attractions and huge and magnificent plants. *Norway* offers cabins in a wide range of size and quality, two exquisite dining rooms, an ornate theatre (with balcony, numerous lounges and show rooms), a disco, indoor and outdoor pools, the largest retail store at sea, a gymnasium, a sauna, six-channel closed-circuit television and a bank of slot machines. Norwegian registry regulations prohibit a full scale casino, but NCL is attempting to have this situation changed.

NCL markets the flagship as "The Biggest Week in the World" and highlights the ship, not the ports of call. *Norway* departs each Sunday for a weekly package of five days at sea. One day is spent at anchor at Charlotte Amalie, St. Thomas (U.S. Virgin Islands), among the best freeports in the world and offering perhaps the cheapest liquor prices anywhere. *Norway* then sails for Little San Salvador, an uninhabited out-island of the Bahamas which is under lease to NCL. Ship passengers, rushed ashore on two 400-passenger launches designed similar to military LSTs with hugh bow doors that fall open to the beach, have a day of swimming, skindiving and other sports, and Calypso music, barbecues, and cocktails enjoyed under gaily colored umbrellas. When the time comes to leave the three-mile beach, it is not uncommon to hear the passengers chanting, like a chorus of protesters, "Hell No! We Won't Go!"

The beach parties are one of many NCL innovations. The extensive skindiving instruction program, with fully accredited teachers, is another. Passengers sign up for shipboard classroom instruction prior to a day of actual experience over beautiful coral reefs.

Competitors suggest that the executive offices of NCL lack a sufficient body of personnel with cruise experience. Zeller responds that this is not a weakness but a strength. He says that the industry has been the victim of in-breeding, that many industry executives know little other than cruising. Himself a lawyer, he has hired executives with banking, hotel, aviation and other corporate experience. NCL is in search of what Zeller calls "counter-cyclical diversification." He wants NCL to own businesses that will be bullish when cruising is sluggish and vice-versa. The company's food catering subsidiary, producing 18,000 meals a day for the ships, has plans to serve other customers. NCL has built a hotel resort in Jamaica.

Ron Zeller candidly admits that *Norway* is not yet profitable, and he lists a number of factors: the slight downturn in the market; the massive expansion of the fleet that *Norway* represents: and the rapid payoff program for *Norway's* $110 million cost. *Norway* fares, competitive with the Miami market, have been kept low to create demand. As the market expands, Zeller plans to raise the fares to a level more appropriate to her relative luxury.

The blunt reality of fuel costs is best illustrated by some comparative figures. Even at her slow speed with reduced engine capacity, *Norway's* turbines cost $28 per passenger per day at 100 per cent occupancy. The daily fuel costs of the smaller, diesel-powered 16,000-ton to 20,000-ton "white ships" in the NCL fleet are as low as $8 per passenger per day. (Daily fuel costs of Cunard's *Queen Elizabeth 2*, operating with full turbine power at high speed much of the year, are $50 per passenger per day.)

Norwegian Caribbean Lines offer three-, four-, and seven-day cruises that operate exclusively in the Caribbean. The single base of operations and single cruise area create tremendous efficiencies, but Zeller is exploring other regions. Planning for the 1990s, he is intrigued by the potential of the Japanese and German markets, and by the possibility of sailing ships off Alaska, the South Pacific and Mexico.

As for *Norway's* role as the years go by, Zeller explains that the fixed seven-day cruise is not necessarily permanent. "We

have an open mind with regard to the future of the *Norway*,"
he says.

Norway has suffered some embarrassing and costly interruptions of service. The first, shortly after she sailed in 1980,
was minor. The second, at the end of April 1981, made headlines in every newspaper of the world and shut down the ship
for a week. A blockage occurred in one of the boilers. When a
boiler is shut down, 50 hours are needed for cooling, and the
air conditioning and water supply are effectively eliminated.
Norway went on auxiliary power. During the two days of difficulty, the company distributed complimentary soft drinks.
Passengers brushed their teeth with bottled Perrier water.
Passengers were so warm that they slept in lifeboats. NCL
quickly emptied two of its smaller ships and sped them toward *Norway* in case evacuation of passengers would be required. This proved unnecessary; *Norway* was restarted, and
she limped to Miami two days late. Passengers dumped from
the small ships were given free airfare to Miami and discount
certificates for future cruises. *Norway* passengers were handed
more-than-proportionate cash refunds plus discount coupons
for future cruises. Most passengers left Miami in a happy
frame of mind. A good portion of the company's financial
loss was covered by business interruption insurance.

All cruise companies have had shutdowns, interruptions of
service, or other such incidents. But the fact remains that for
safety and consistency of performance, the record of the
cruise industry surpasses that of any other mode of
transportation.

For dining room and cabin service, Norwegian Caribbean
Lines employs, principally, natives of the Caribbean. It can
be argued that the European staffs of the competitors are
more skilled, but Zeller defends the competence of his people.
And, he says, the company earns an enormous amount of
goodwill throughout the Caribbean.

By special proclamation of the United Nations, and as an
NCL gesture in the interests of international peace and har-
mony, *S.S. Norway* flies the flag of the United Nations, in addition to that of its country of registry.

Carnival Cruise Lines (129,349 tons, 4 ships)

Carnival Cruise Lines has an image of being both brash and precocious, qualities made all the more irritating to the competitors by the very success of the firm. Its young president, Mickey Arison, the son of the founder, seems to take enormous delight whenever Carnival's aggressive nature shocks the industry. It is symbolic that Carnival Cruises uses a separate dock in Miami, hundreds of yards away from the competition. The no-nonsense nature of the Arison operation was best illustrated in 1981 when Honduran seamen went on strike. After a few weeks of confusion and misunderstanding, the strikers were fired, their U.S. Immigration cards were withdrawn, and the seamen were shipped home.

Following his parting with his Norwegian partners, Ted Arison went shopping for a ship. He struck a deal with Canadian Pacific for *Empress of Canada,* then in mothballs. The 27,250-ton ship, with her broad companion ways and attractive wooden bulkheads and fixtures, resailed in 1972 as *T.S.S. Mardi Gras.* Her identical sister, the last *Empress of Britain,* joined the company in 1975 and was renamed *Carnivale.* Both ships were trans-Atlantic, two-class vessels, and extensive renovations were required to turn them into cruise ships.

In October 1978, Carnival purchased a ship of great distinction, the former Union Castle liner *S.A. Vaal* (originally named *Transvaal Castle*). She had been built as a sister of *Windsor Castle* to carry passengers and cargo between England and South Africa. Launched in 1961, *S.A. Vaal* was celebrated for her public rooms of Victorian splendor. When Union Castle Line ceased operations in the 1970s, the newspaper ad for the last South African voyages featured a large photo of an aircraft wing and jet engines; the caption read, "Now this is the only view you will get en route to South Africa."

When she joined the Carnival fleet, following extensive renovations to make her suited to cruise purposes, *S.A. Vaal* became *Festivale,* the company's 38,175-ton flagship. The magnificent Victorian library remains intact.

Carnival Cruises, aimed directly at the young, economy-minded crowd, promotes a "Fun Ship" theme and offers the most informal settings afloat. Dining room waiters are prone to burst into song, the roulette wheel rarely stops in the full-scale riverboat casinos, and always —and in the least likely areas—a band seems to be getting underway. Passengers who search for subdued elegance, relaxation, or even spotless maintenance, may well be horrified.

The Arison success story has been nothing short of triumphant. In January 1982, the company welcomed the first ship it had built from the keel up. The 36,674-ton *Tropicale,* representing state-of-the-art engineering, was designed to move the company, for the first time, outside the Caribbean area. *Tropicale* competes in the Alaskan and Mexican markets, traditionally dominated by Princess and Sitmar Cruises.

Sitting at his desk beside the great ship's bell of *Empress of Canada,* an impish gleam in his eye, Mickey Arison says, "When we go into Los Angeles with a Miami-style operation and Miami prices, we will give those companies something to worry about."

This would appear to be just a beginning. Currently under construction is a $170 million, 45,000-ton ship, *The Holiday,* and contracts are planned for even further expansion of the fleet.

Holland America Cruises (117,000 tons, 4 ships)

In the New York headquarters of Holland America, it was hoped that the launching of the company's new 32,000-ton ship *Nieuw Amsterdam* (the third to carry the name in the Dutch firm's century-old history) would herald in a happy new era. Unfortunately, the vessel got off to a poor start. Upon completion at St. Nazaire, France, Holland America rejected her because of design defects, substantially delaying her first cruises. And when she finally did sail, a troublesome vibration emerged. Company engineers are currently dealing with the problem as a 32,000-ton identical sister, *Noordam* nears completion in France.

One of the truly great firms in the annals of passenger shipping, Holland America's current misfortunes seemed to begin when its popular little 9,000-ton ship *Prinsendam* caught fire and subsequently sank in the chilly waters off Alaska in 1980 (there was no loss of life.) However, there are few in the industry who doubt Holland America's ability to solve all of its current difficulties and to sail brightly into the future.

The flagship of the current Holland America fleet is one of the greatest ships at sea, *S.S. Rotterdam* (38,000 tons), which spends its year sailing from New York to the Caribbean and Alaska (since 1981), and offering one major world cruise. The company was among the first to offer speciality theme cruises (such as jazz specials), celebrity name entertainment and distinguished lecturers addressing an infinite variety of topics. Holland America and the Russian ships are the only vessels in the industry with a "no tipping required" policy.

The company has achieved success in New York marketing "honeymoon cruises" to Bermuda and other destinations. Ships have left New York with as many as 70 honeymoon couples aboard. Asked if this doesn't make newlyweds feel less special, Holland America's director of public relations, Oscar Kolb, chuckles, "That's not the way it works anymore. Honeymoon couples *like* to go with other honeymooners."

Industry speculation is that Holland America will sell its older tonnage, *Veendam* and *Volendam*, as soon as *Nordam* joins the fleet.

Sitmar Cruises (110,000 tons, 4 ships)

With the purchase in 1971 of the twin Cunard sisters *Sylvania* and *Carinthia*, a new cruise company, Sitmar Cruises, was launched. Beautifully rebuilt as *Fairsea* and *Fairwind,* and featuring impressive Italian cuisine, the two ships have captured an important market in Mexico. Recently joined by a stunning new $140 million flagship, the 36,000-ton *Fairsky,* Sitmar remains a dominant factor in the North American market.

Owned by the Vlasov group of Monaco (with interests in cargo shipping, a Swiss ski resort, textiles and ranching), Sitmar operates a 24,000-ton economy cruiser in Australia named *Fairstar.* The original 16,000-ton *Fairsky,* also nonluxurious, was retired from service after numerous difficulties.

Chandris Incorporated (106,293 tons, 7 ships)

Chandris, another of the venerable veterans of the industry, has had days of greater significance than it presently enjoys. Chandris is one of the biggest Greek names in the passenger field, but the average age of the company's ships in service is 40 years. And, while all have had periodic refits, none has undergone the kind of exhaustive rebuilding program that turns a senior vessel into a luxury ship. Chandris's ships range in size from the 3,500-ton *Fiorita* to the flagship, the 25,000-ton *Italis* (formerly named *America* and *Australis*). The company principally sails the Aegean, the Mediterranean and the Caribbean.

The Soviet Union (101,199 tons, 6 ships)

Where do great ships go to die? Many that disappear from the western market end up cruising the waters behind the Iron Curtain. Russia and its satellite countries construct their own ships, but they also purchase others that come available through brokers. The most famous of these vessels is *Maxim Gorki* (25,000 tons), which was the last great Hamburg America Line cruiser, *Hamburg*.

The Soviet Union, through several companies, sails some 75 passenger ships. Most never leave Communist bloc waterways, but some do visit ports in 25 countries. There are six ships that frequently sail in western waters: *Turkmenia* (5,035 tons), *Odessa* (14,000 tons), *Alexandr Pushkin* (19,860 tons), *Mikhail Lermontov* (19,860 tons), *Kazakhstan* (16,600 tons) and *Maxim Gorki*.

Until relatively recent times, the Soviets were significant participants in the North American market, with cruises of the St. Lawrence River, New England, the Caribbean, Mexico and Alaska, but repeated American sanctions over Afghanistan and Poland have effectively terminated the business. The Russian ships are now doing substantial trade in charters out of German ports.

When the Soviet vessels first sailed to western waters in the 1960s, the product was cheap, but positively dreadful. Food was inedible, entertainment almost non-existent and there was an inpenetrable language barrier. But the improvement was constant and by *Odessa's* final 1981 season on the Canadian and U.S. west coast, the ship offered excellent food, outstanding entertainment and one of the best fare bargains in the industry. Passengers also appreciated the "no tipping" policy. Yet service staff would accept small gratuities, and repay the passenger with a small gift purchased from the gift shop.

Royal Caribbean Cruise Line (96,164 tons, 4 ships)

Another of Miami's Caribbean success stories, RCCL was founded in 1970 by a consortium of Norwegian shipping companies. The company's three ships are the most easily identifiable in the seas: long and sleek, white with blue trim, and each dominated by a large and stylish smokestack near the stern. And high on the stack of each ship, affording panoramic views of the cruising area, is a Viking Crown Lounge.

Between 1970 and 1972, RCCL put into service its three identical 18,800-ton sisters: *Song of Norway, Nordic Prince* and *Sun Viking.* Over the years, the ships have enjoyed an occupancy record of 97.5 per cent. Recently, both *Nordic Prince* and *Song of Norway* have been "stretched," a process of sawing a ship in half and, in the case of the RCCL vessels, adding an 85-foot preconstructed section to each ship. The stretching increased the size of each ship to 23,000 tons.

The company has recently welcomed a new flagship into the fleet, *Song of America,* a 31,000 tonner featuring every modern innovation and fuel-economy system. Similar in style to her three smaller sisters, the ship also has a Viking Crown Lounge on the smokestack, but this one circles a full 360 degrees.

With a softened cruise market in 1981, and with significant expansion of the industry in progress, RCCL executive Rod McLeod remains optimistic about the new ship. "We have not lost one bit of enthusiasm for the decision that was taken," he states. The new breed of 30,000-tonners are costing their owners between $110 million and $140 million each, depending on degree of luxury.

Royal Caribbean ships are crowded; no company in the first-class industry packs in so many people. *Nordic Prince* and *Song of Norway* each routinely carries more than a thousand passengers. The new, larger *Song of America* carries 1,400.

It is a credit to the competence of this firm that the ships don't seem overcrowded. The cabins are compact, but they are well designed. The range of activities keeps the passengers in different parts of the ship, not concentrated in one section. Even some Miami competitors will acknowledge that the European galley and dining room staffs of RCCL produce the best food in the market area.

One of the companies involved in the Royal Caribbean ownership, Gotaas-Larsen, was co-founded by Harry Irgens Larsen in 1946. In 1942, Larsen and a companion escaped Nazi-occupied Norway in a small fishing boat. They arrived in New York 52 days later. The president of RCCL is Edwin Stephan, a veteran of the cruise industry.

Royal Caribbean ships are slow, minimizing fuel consumption, with top speeds of 16 knots. As Rod McLeod says, "We are not racing for the tea cup."

Royal Viking Line (84,000 tons, 3 ships)

Royal Viking ignores just about every trend in the industry. While other firms are trying to capture the young market, Royal Viking goes after the older, more affluent crowd. While most companies are dominated by short cruises, RVL still stresses 14-day, 35-day and longer itineraries (The company offered a seven day package for the first time in 1982.) Other ships offer two sittings for each meal, Royal Viking vessels seat everyone at once. And while the industry keeps increasing the number of slot machines and casinos, RVL thinks these are abominations.

If there is a leader in the luxury sweepstakes, it is most assuredly RVL. *Royal Viking Star, Royal Viking Sea* and *Royal Viking Sky* are floating art galleries. The space-per-passenger ratio is the most generous in the business, and the ships have an inordinately high proportion of deluxe cabins. In 1981, *Royal Viking Star* went into drydock to be stretched to 28,000 tons from 22,000 tons, increasing its capacity from 500 passengers to 725; deluxe verandah suites are being added to the top deck. The company has subsequently done the same with the other two ships.

Owned by a Norwegian shipping consortium, Royal Viking operates from San Francisco under Warren Titus, a veteran of American President Lines and P&O Lines. When he retires in two or three years, the loss to RVL will be significant. He joined the company before the first ship was constructed.

From his San Francisco office, Warren Titus enjoys a stunning view (the best in the business) of the harbor, Alcatraz and the Golden Gate Bridge. He thinks that many of his competitors, in ignoring the over-60 age group, are rather foolish. "Who else has the tiime and the money?" he asks. An average cabin on a Royal Viking ship will cost a couple $6,500 for two weeks. Only *Queen Elizabeth 2* is more expensive.

The ships cruise the world—Mexico, Central America, the Caribbean, the Mediterranean, Alaska, North Cape (Norwegian fjords), the Soviet Union, the South Pacific—and there is one annual world cruise.

Long an opponent of shipboard gambling, Titus finally gave in to the market demand and industry trend. The three Royal Viking ships now all offer fine casinos.

Home Lines Cruises Inc. (72,741 tons, 2 ships)

Home Lines' venerable flagship *Oceanic* (39,241 tons), launched in 1965, is the largest vessel ever built exclusively for cruising. Home Lines, with its famous ship of the 1950s, *Homeric,* was one of the first companies to understand that fine dining is an essential marketing feature. Today, *Oceanic* is served by an Italian crew that continues to recognize this fact.

Home Lines has just welcomed into service a 33,500-ton beauty, *M.V. Atlantic,* to cruise from New York to Bermuda. *Oceanic* will be based in Florida, to handle Caribbean operations. The company's respected 25,000-ton *Doric* was sold to Royal Cruise Line of San Francisco.

Paquet Cruises (62,400 tons, 4 ships)

As Holland America Lines progressed in its plans to renew the fleet with two grand ships under construction, Paquet Cruises, the last proud French entry in the industry, was presented with an opportunity. Paquet purchased Holland America's 24,500-ton *Statendam*. After a multi-million dollar rebuild and facelift in 1982, the ship now sails as the gleaming white Paquet flagship, *Rhapsody*.

The French company, noted for its haute cuisine, competes in most of the world's major markets. Other Paquet ships are *Dolphin* (12,500 tons), *Mermoz* (13,800 tons) and *Azur* (11,600 tons).

Epirotiki Lines Inc (56,700 tons, 7 ships)

Perhaps the dominant cruise line to operate from the historic port of Piraeus, Greece, Epirotiki has ships that range from the 4,000-ton *Neptune* to the 16,000-ton *Atlas*. For the Aegean Sea and Greek islands market, small ships are essential. The ships tend to be old. (Epirotiki has a history that dates back one hundred years.) Some vessels have been rebuilt through the years.

The president of Epirotiki, George A. Potamianos, is also a Greek recording star, known to the public as Yorgos.

Eastern Steamship Lines Inc. (44,458 tons, 2 ships)

Everything about Eastern Steamship Lines—its ships its low-rise office building on Miami's Biscayne Blvd., even its people—suggests a quality of relaxation. In marked contrast to the frenetic pace of its competitors, Eastern behaves in a calm and organized fashion. Not surprisingly, its flagship *S.S. Emerald Seas,* just "lopes along at eight knots," according to one company executive. All of which tends to hide the firm's business successes. Occupancy rates have been as high as 107 per cent per year.

Emerald Seas, in her thirty-eighth year of service, provides conclusive proof that an old ship can hold on to her greatness. She is a beauty, immaculately maintained. Commissioned as a troop ship *Richardson* in 1944, she later gained fame as *President Roosevelt,* then, successively, became *Leilani, La Guardia* and *Atlantis.* Eastern purchased the ship in 1972, rechristening her *Emerald Seas.*

The average cabin size of *Emerald Seas* is huge, and nearly all cabins are outside. The ship has every modern amenity, including closed-circuit television. She spends her time sailing three- and four-day cruises from Miami to Nassau and Freeport in the Bahamas. There is a full-scale casino.

Eastern Steamship Lines was the first company to offer regular cruises out of Miami to the Caribbean. Through a succession of ships—*Evangeline, Yarmouth, Bahama Star* and *Jerusalem*—Eastern has maintained its place in the market. The company was purchased ten years ago by Gotaas-Larsen of Norway, a shareholder in Royal Caribbean Cruise Line.

In 1980, Eastern Steamship Lines formed a subsidiary, Western Cruise Lines, and purchased *S.S. Calypso* a 20,000-ton cruiser well known in the Caribbean. Renamed *S.S. Azure Seas,* she was dispatched to the Los Angeles market for three- and four-day cruises to Ensenada, Mexico. There is a full-scale casino aboard. Says Eastern vice-president Ed Holbert, "We are after the people who go to Las Vegas for the weekend."

Lauro Lines (37,629 tons, 2 ships)

A longstanding veteran among cruise companies, Lauro Lines is dominant in the African, Mediterranean and Aegean markets. The two ships, *Achille Lauro* (23,629 tons) and *Oceanus* (14,000 tons) regularly call at Casablanca, Piraeus and Port Said, among other ports.

Royal Cruise Line (35,800 tons, 2 ships)

With the purchase of *Doric* from Home Lines in 1981, Royal Cruise Line is moving into the front ranks of the industry. The 25,300-ton ship has been extensively remodelled before sailing as *Royal Odyssey*. She has joined the small, sporty, first-class *Golden Odyssey,* the 10,500-ton ship that launched the company in 1974.

From the start, *Golden Odyssey* has been the finest ship regularly serving the Aegean and Mediterranean areas. As evidence of the partnership growing between aviation and shipping companies, *Golden Odyssey* was designed to accommodate precisely the number of passengers carried by a charter Boeing 747. All Royal Cruise Line tickets are sold in the United States, and all include airfares; there are no exceptions made.

According to Duncan Beardsley, a P&O veteran who has been a senior executive of Royal since its earliest days, "*Golden Odyssey* is the only ship you board at the Los Angeles airport."

Owned by Greek businessman P.A. Panagopoulos, the company operates from headquarters in San Francisco.

Commodore Cruise Line Limited (34,000 tons, 2 ships)

One of the best known Caribbean lines for 17 years, Commodore has recently acquired and rebuilt a 30-year-old ship and resailed her as *Caribe I.* She has joined the well known 11,000-ton *Boheme* for regular cruises out of Miami.

Hapag-Lloyd of Germany (33,819 tons, 1 ship)

A major German cargo company with some involvement in cruising, Hapag-Lloyd, in recent years, has operated the 1953 *Europa* (21,514 tons) and the 1938 *Bremen* (32,000). Both ships, now retired, have been replaced by a gleaming new *Europa* (33,819 tons). The ship operates exclusively in Europe and predominantly in the German market.

'K' Lines-Hellenic Cruises (32,200 tons, 5 ships)

One of the companies operating exclusively in the Greek islands and Aegean area, 'K' Lines has been in business for more than 70 years. Most of the company ships are small, though the new *Constellation,* which has won rave reviews for luxury and comfort, is 12,500 tons.

Sun Line Cruises (28,000 tons, 3 ships)

Sun Line ships *Stella Maris* (4,000 tons), *Stella Oceanus* (6.000 tons) and *Stella Solaris* (18,000 tons), have been well accepted for many years in the Aegean and Mediterranean. The company, which was established in 1961, has recently made a move into the Caribbean. The ownership and the crews are Greek.

Pearl Cruises of Scandinavia (20,340 tons, 2 ships)

This relatively new company has carved out a unique market in the far east and the Orient, with regular visits to the Peoples' Republic of China. Owned by J. Laurhzen of Copenhagen, the company operates like a veritable United Nations, with registry in The Bahamas, Scandinavian officers, Asian crew and an American marketing organization.

The company's first ship, *Pearl of Scandinavia* (actually the 15-year-old renovated and modernized *Finnstar*), quickly established a fine reputation and the company has recently added a second vessel, the new and modern *Princess Mahsuri* (7,940 tons).

American Hawaii Cruises (20,300 tons, 1 ship)

In 1979, President Jimmy Carter signed a bill redocumenting the 20,300-ton ship *S.S. Independence* under the U.S. flag. This was an important moment in cruising. Not since the demise of United States Lines, the Matson Line and American

President Lines (as passenger lines) had a passenger ship sailed under the American flag.

Under U.S. maritime law, no foreign ship—including passenger transport—can conduct trade between two United States ports. Foreign ships are allowed to leave a U.S. port and return the passengers to the same pier; they cannot transport people from one U.S. port to another. Many companies in the industry have lobbied to conduct voyages from Los Angeles or San Francisco to Hawaii for a multi-island cruise, or to offer the reverse trip (in either case, with a one-way flight). The U.S. Jones Act prohibited this sort of commerce, although no U.S. ship existed.

A group of investors in San Francisco purchased *Independence* from the C.Y. Tung group of Hong Kong. (In the shipping world, Tung periodically shows up with interesting schemes; Tung tried to convert *Queen Elizabeth* into *Seawise University* before the disastrous fire destroyed her.)

No luxury had been spared in 1951 when *Independence* was built in the United States for the unheard of sum (for such a small ship) of $50 million. After buying the vessel and establishing American Hawaii Cruises, the owners spent years, until mid-1980, completing the refit and renovations.

Independence regularly cruises the Hawaiian Islands, with assorted fly cruise packages from the mainland. The company is largely financed by Hong Kong money, most likely C.Y. Tung himself.

Fred. Olsen Lines (22,800 tons, 2 ships)

A Norwegian company that operates principally in the Canary Islands, Fred. Olsen Lines has two vessels *Black Watch* (9,000 tons) and *Blenheim* (13,800 tons).

Astor United Cruises (18,800 tons, 1 ship)

A new firm in the cruise industry, Astor United's modern ship *Astor* spent its first spring and summer in northern Europe and Scandinavia, before sailing to the Caribbean in late 1982 for a season out of San Juan, Puerto Rico, and Port Everglades, Florida. This ship's hospital may be the best equipped of any at sea, boasting complete X-ray and water therapy equipment, and seven dialysis machines.

World Explorer Cruises (18,100 tons, 1 ship)

Part of the C.Y. Tung group of Hong Kong, *S.S. Universe* is a floating university. Students book aboard for credit courses, in various disciplines, endorsed and regulated by the University of Pittsburgh and the University of California (Irvine). Constructed in 1952 *Universe* was refurbished in 1976. Two educational semesters are offered each year, with conventional cruises booked in between.

Polish Ocean Lines (15,024 tons, 1 ship)

Formerly the Dutch liner *Maasdam,* the Polish ship *T.S.S. Stefan Batory* makes regular North Atlantic crossings between Montreal and Gydnia, Poland, and other European ports. Public rooms are tasteful. There are very few first-class cabins, and 60 per cent of lower cabins are inside (some have no facilities). But the fares are remarkably low and tipping is not expected.

Since the outbreak of the conflict in Poland, *Stefan Batory* has had a precarious life. Schedules have been erratic, some seamen have jumped ship in western ports and she has been greeted with protest rallies.

Lindblad Travel Inc. (14,450 tons, 3 ships)

Adventurer Lars-Eric Lindblad, until recently at least, stood totally alone in the cruise ship industry. His renowned 2,300-ton *Lindblad Explorer* eschews the calm seas of its more timid competitors and sails, for example, over mountainous waves and into the gales of Antarctica. Other, similar trips are offered, all designed only for the hearty. People have waited years to pay premium fares for one of *Explorer's* 92 berths.

Lindblad also features several smaller vessels for cruises through African waterways and assorted other adventures. More conventional cruising is marketed for the 10,000 ton former Portugese ship *Funchal* and the most recent acquisition, the 2,150-ton *Lindblad Polaris*.

The Hellenic Mediterranean Lines Co. Ltd. (13,800 tons, 2 ships)

A company with 50 years of service to the Greek islands and Turkey, Hellenic Mediterranean operates the modern *Castalia* (9,000 tons) and *Acquarius* (4,800 tons.)

Bahama Cruise Line, Inc. (10,595 tons, 1 ship)

In the 1970s, Bahama Cruise Line's *Freeport* established its reputation in the economy Caribbean market. Renamed *Veracruz,* she was chartered to the now bankrupt Canadian firm Strand Holidays. Bahama Cruise Line took her back after the demise of Strand in 1981. She now sails from Montreal and Halifax — and from New York — to the Caribbean.

Sun World Cruises (5,813 tons, 1 ship)

This company's ship, *Regina Maris,* commissioned during the 1960s, has bounced through a series of German owners. Currently registered in Singapore, with West German officers and a Filipino crew, she has most recently cruised out of Santo Domingo to various Caribbean islands. *Regina Maris* is marketed by American Lloyd Lines out of St. Louis.

3

The Floating Palace

SHIPS OF THE EIGHTIES

There are those who still cherish visions of lost elegance on the seas. The memories of velvet splendor tend to negate the steerage compartments where the multitudes — the overwhelming majority of those who travelled by sea — were packed below decks. As many as a dozen people would share a cabin and a single wash basin. Food was minimal, entertainment nonexistent.

Cunard's chief wine steward, Harry Little, remembers with fondness his 20 years on *Queen Mary*. First class was gracious and opulent living, but dull by today's standards of entertainment and recreation. "It was a roaring night when they had bingo," Little remembers. One of his colleagues recalls that on *Acquitania*, 35 crew members shared one cabin and usually had to eat while standing up. Harry Little currently serves wine in the *Queen's Grill* of *Queen Elizabeth 2*.

Unlike the multi-class panoceanic liners of the past, today's ships advertise one class. Cabin size and degree of luxury vary tremendously, but food, entertainment and amenities are the same for all. Every cabin has private facilities, usually a sink, toilet and shower stall. Tub baths are offered in the deluxe staterooms.

The ships are rarely engaged in transport. Mostly they are hotel resorts that float to several destinations within the period of one week. With levels of passenger-pampering that would put any hotel to shame, the better vessels shine in the spheres of food, entertainment and recreation. They are, in fact, floating palaces.

30,000 JOYFUL TONS

In 1975, the ideal cruise ship weighed 20,000 tons — large enough to offer the required comforts, small enough to flit from island to island. But staggering increases to the costs of construction, fuel, food and salaries have forced the industry to seek economies of scale. With larger ships, companies have found that they can double capacity while increasing costs by only 40 to 50 per cent. Technology has improved, and the 30,000-tonners can sail as artfully as their smaller sisters. And the market has been so buoyant that the sales people are confident they can fill the larger capacities.

The typical 30,000-ton ship is greater than 700 feet in length and measures about 100 feet across the beam. She has 11 or 12 decks, at least two dining rooms, two swimming pools (possibly one indoors), numerous lounges, one major showroom, a full-scale casino, a movie theatre and meeting rooms. A crew of 500 serves 1,100 passengers. The major cabaret room seats an audience of at least 600, and there are two other rooms each capable of handling 300 at a sitting. There is deck space for quoits, shuffleboard, badminton, golf nets, table tennis and skeet shooting. The ship offers a sauna, gymnasium and massage room. Cocktail service is easily available on all open deck areas. The recreation space is convertible for open-air dances, moonlight barbecues or a daily poolside smorgasbord for passengers who prefer not to dress up for lunch.

Passenger cabins in the modern ships are delightful. Every inch of space is utilized. A standard double cabin is about twelve feet by eight feet with two single beds or perhaps one double. There is a built-in desk, a desk chair and at least one small sofa or lounge chair. Standard cabins are small compared with hotel rooms, but few passengers spend much time in quarters. Deluxe cabins, always with bath, are half again the size of standards; suites, with two rooms and bath, are double that. All but a few staterooms are on the outside.

The most splendid bar on a ship is generally a plush observation lounge high above the bridge. The music heard in this room is always subdued, touching on the classical. The most informal watering hole is near the pool and sports deck. Lounges may range from 30 seats to several hundred and include a small late-night disco.

There are several shops aboard, usually offering artifacts of the cruising area. The shops boast duty-free prices, but the bargains are minimal at best. The ship has photographic studios, a hairdressing salon, a barber shop, card rooms (usually with a resident bridge instructor), a library and several areas for quiet contemplation. An amazing aspect of every cruise is that, with 1,100 passengers on board, no area appears crowded. People are dispersed throughout the ship, involved in a breathtaking array of activities. If a cruise is only three-quarters sold, the ship may seem totally deserted.

All ships this size feature a pleasant 300-seat cinema below decks. First-run movies are shown throughout each cruise, and a number of fine films from the past are often screened as well. Each film is shown at least twice during the cruise; if there is high demand for a certain movie, passenger requests for additional screenings will be accommodated. The cinema is also used for port lectures and special meetings.

Promenade deck was the celebrated walkway of the passenger steamers of the past. In vintage photos and paintings, nattily dressed squires and opulently begowned matrons are seen strolling casually in both directions on a vast boardwalk. That scene exists no more, but today's cruise vessels honor the tradition in their own fashion. Most feature a promenade of the circumference, usually with lifeboats overhead, but the walkway is only slightly wider than the chaises longues that line the bulkhead.

Crew facilities are far better than what is generally thought. The senior officers are quartered in splendid fashion just behind the bridge, with their own mess and lounge areas. Entertainers and other important civilian staff are housed in lower deck passenger cabins. The rest of the company is quartered throughout the bottom two decks. Junior officers and more important civilians have private rooms. Most other crew members share a cabin with one other person. Only rarely are crew quarters more crowded than two to a cabin.

Sharing the bottom decks with the crew are the engine room, laundry, quartermaster stores, print shop, crew mess, lounges and a small health club. The atmosphere below decks is quite different from that of the passenger areas. There are no expensive works of art, no wood panelling, no carpeting; just basic steel. It is noisier, especially near the engine room at the stern. That being said, the accommodations are excellent. Crew members decorate their cabins with souvenirs of ports of call, stereo equipment, carpeting, art works and pinups.

To senior officers on inspection, finding photographs of naked bodies is preferable to finding the real thing. But even when that happens, a tolerant eye is generally cast.

A CITY GOES TO SEA

A ship embarking on a voyage is as self-sufficient as a small city. She carries all necessities: food, fuel, a communications centre, spare parts and the people necessary for operations and maintenance. As last week's passengers tearfully go ashore, trucks are waiting at the pier to stock provisions for this week's vacationers. It is a harrowing day for the crew members in charge; turnarounds are completed in twelve hours, sometimes even in eight.

A ship preparing for a seven-day cruise will take on sufficient supplies for eleven days, strictly as an emergency precaution. There is little dependence on ports en route, except under special circumstances. Tropical ports generally have less stringent standards of hygiene and quality control than travellers expect. It is generally wisest to deal with dependable ports of origin, although there are notable exceptions. For example, ships visiting Central American and Caribbean ports during times of peak sugar prices are able to purchase the refined product at one-third the supplier's price. Quartermasters are always quick to seize bargains that come available.

A one-week cruise will consume over 500 tons of bunker or diesel fuel (in excess of 115,000 Imperial gallons). More than double that amount will be taken on board as a precautionary measure. Fuel consumption varies greatly with operating speed, time in port and weather encountered along the way. A usual stock of food will exceed 180,000 pounds — 90 tons — half of it beef, lamb, fish and poultry. Up to 2,000 cases of spirits will be loaded aboard: 24,000 bottles of ale, wine and liquor. Back-up stocks in ship's stores ashore can be in the tens of thousands of cases.

A day at sea means the consumption of 3,600 pounds of meat, 8,500 assorted pastries, 475 quarts of ice cream, 220 pounds of

Behind the scenes the crew eats excellent food in simpler surroundings.

A captain in his quarters. Shown is the office and sitting room.
A bedroom and full bath lead off this room.

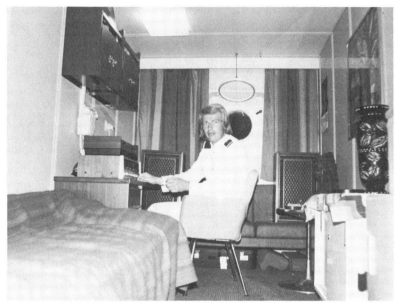

A junior officer's quarters (top), on the lower decks of the ship.

Crowded and cluttered crews' quarters provide comfortable, basic accommodation.

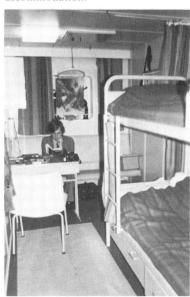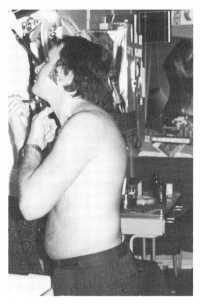

butter, 800 pounds of fruit, 140 pounds of shrimp, 20 gallons of mayonnaise, 470 pounds of pasta, 1,200 pounds of potatoes, 1,000 pounds of other vegetables, 200 gallons of coffee, 28 gallons of cream and 600 pounds of sugar. In one day, 27,000 dishes and 11,00 glasses are washed and sterilized, requiring 80 gallons of detergent. These figures relate to a 30,000-ton ship. On the giants, the figures numb the mind. *Norway* carries 125,000 pieces of china and glassware, 21,000 sheets and 32,000 towels and wash cloths. On *Queen Elizabeth 2*, which carries 2,000 bottles of pickles and sauces, 15,000 eggs are consumed daily. Passengers are overwhelmed by the quality and quantity of food, and there is no scrimping on crew meals either.

Regulations vary from ship to ship, but there are always rules governing the consumption of spirits by crew members, and no alcohol may be consumed within eight hours of a duty call. Where an officer's or a crew member's work involves public safety, regulations on alcoholic consumption are most stringently enforced. There is often a quota for per capita consumption in crew quarters, but violations are not uncommon. On occasion, officers will pull blitz inspections of crew quarters in search of contraband.

To get around such inspections, ingenious schemes known only to the crew are devised. On one Christmas voyage aboard a Norwegian ship, a number of seamen smuggled in a respectable quantity of hard liquor from a Caribbean freeport. Crew speculation was that a cabin search was forthcoming. The goods had to be stashed. Late at night, in an open area on a passenger deck, metal acoustic tiles on the deckhead (ceiling) were discreetly lowered and dozens of bottles were snugly fitted into the rafters. The acoustic tiles were snapped back into place.

The next afternoon the ship's entertainment staff were holding a Christmas party for the children aboard — immediately underneath the bottles. Sometime during the noisy party, the ship lurched heavily in a sudden sea swell. Bottles clanked overhead and a few broke. The rum and whiskey started to seep from the ceiling, dripping very gently over the children.

There were some startled looks toward the roof when the drips hit a few foreheads, but condensation is not unusual. More disturbing was the sweet odor that started to permeate the area. At first everyone shrugged and took no notice. As the problem increased, a hostess climbed onto a chair and pulled down some tiles. Two bottles shattered to the floor. The children had a splendid time. When they finally returned to their cabins, carrying with them the cloud of fumes, many parental questions followed. The cruise staff energetically explained the precise nature of the children's get-together.

THE MARKET

Before the industry was rejuvenated through short-holiday cruises, ship's patrons were largely middle-aged-plus individuals who had grown to love the sea during the era of glory. The demographics today indicate that the average age of passengers is rapidly coming down. Generally speaking, the longer the cruise, the older the clientele. Also, people shop for cruises on the basis of a package price, not according to the cost per day. Many holidayers will book onto a three-, four- or seven-day trip, even though another line offers a much better per diem value for a longer cruise.

There has been a significant increase in the number of short cruises and a decline in the 14-day-and-longer market. A full 82 per cent of passengers are in the one-week (or under) cruise market. Packages of 18 days or longer, including all the celebrated world cruises, represent less than 2 per cent of the annual passenger volume.

The shipping companies have been perplexed by the reluctance of active business executives and professionals to select cruising as a holiday, though when these travellers do choose cruising, they come back. (The cruise business has the highest repeat factor of any vacation alternative.) The competition for the professionals is with first-class resorts. At a resort, as on a ship, a vacationer must unpack only once. However, his scenery never really changes.

The cruise industry has formed an organization to assemble data, to train travel agents and to publish various guides to ships and their companies. With a mandate to promote the industry in general, the Cruise Lines International Association has compiled some fascinating statistics.

CLIA has calculated that only 5 per cent of the vacationing public has ever taken a cruise. Eighty per cent of passengers on a given ship are cruise repeaters. The entire industry grew in revenue from $1.5 billion in 1978 to $2.8 billion in 1980; total passengers soared from 895,000 to 1.3 million. More sobering figures show that operating costs have jumped by 25 per cent per year during this period. In 1979 alone, there was a 78 per cent hike in fuel costs.

The most important cruising areas are the Caribbean, the Mediterranean/Aegean, Mexico/trans-canal, Alaska, Australia/South Pacific and, to a lesser extent, North Cape (Norwegian fjords). Cruises to the sun have a younger clientele than those headed to colder climes.

Passenger preferences often move in unpredictable directions, and the corporate forecasters and ship designers have made their mistakes in planning for public taste. When the modern fleet of sleek 20,000-ton cruisers started entering service in the late 1960s, it was thought that little need existed for luxury suites and deluxe cabins. A ship would offer no more than four suites, which were actually two small rooms or, in many cases, one large chamber with curtains to separate the beds. In efforts to create one-class ships, standard-class doubles dominated; of 300 cabins on board, most ships had perhaps 20 deluxe cabins.

Passenger demand for the deluxe accommodation has baffled the designers. The grand penthouses, verandah suites and large apartments on the older tonnage (above 35,000), regularly sell out. On all ships, the most expensive cabins sell first. The newest ships are offering much more deluxe space, and older vessels are undergoing conversions to meet the demand.

A 30,000-ton luxury cruise ship costs a minimum of $110 million to build, almost double what it would have cost a decade ago. Over the same period, the average price per passenger per day for a cruise has jumped to $160 from $60.

The best cruise buys are in the Miami market, with an average per diem of about $145, plus assorted subsidies tossed in for return air fare to the passenger's home. On the U.S. west coast to Mexico, and from Vancouver to Alaska, the average ticket is $175 per day. For the luxury leaders, most of them in the 14-day-and-longer market, the average per diem is $230 but the price buys more square footage of cabin space. *Queen Elizabeth 2* is $350 per day on her most expensive trips (trans-Atlantic).

CLIA conducts travel agency seminars, collects data and

promotes cruising, but the most powerful organization of the companies is the International Committee of Passenger Lines, based in New York. ICPL fights the major battles, and there is a tough one in progress at the moment.

The American government in recent years has decided not to allow cruise ship conferences and conventions as tax deductible items. The Internal Revenue Service regards cruises as "frivolous."

For the ships, these meetings represent a major source of revenue. On rare occasions a large convention would charter an entire vessel. Generally, groups of two dozen to 50 would book passage for a meeting. For a cost less than the equivalent in a shore-based hotel (when food and beverage were added), a group could enjoy a new and interesting venue. The ship's public rooms provide every need for a conference, including extraordinary levels of service.

There were many abuses. For example, a few doctors might travel together, deducting the cost with a claim that they talked about surgery over their meals and drinks. But the cruise industry argues that just as many abuses occur at shore-based resorts, which still enjoy tax deductibility for meetings. The feeling in the industry is that it is being deliberately discriminated against because of the foreign ownership of the vessels — a victim of the American hotel lobby — despite the hundreds of millions of dollars that the ships pump directly into the U.S. economy.

Costa Line chief Dr. Piergeorgio Costa says the IRS decision is "the one negative effect 'The Love Boat' has had on cruising." Apparently, during hearings in Washington, one congressman remarked that he knew meetings could not take place on a ship because of what he saw on television.

4

Captains
and Lesser Nobility

THE CAPTAIN

If there is a position of authority, legal power, responsibility or even social grace to match that invested in the master of a passenger vessel, it truly must be a challenge to Divine Providence. Maritime law, an inheritance from the ancients, gives the captain total dictatorial rights over his ship and all who sail with him — passengers, officers and crew.

The power is absolute. Once at sea, no passenger, no officer or crew member — no one, not even the owner of the vessel or the entire ship's company acting in concert — can appeal the master's judgment. At sea, a strike or even individual action against a captain can be considered mutiny, an offense for which the punishment ranges all the way to death.

Masters' provisions of maritime law, with the awesome authority attached, would provide a veritable Shangri-La for those of fragile ego who quest a throne, were it not for the flip side of the coin: responsibility. A captain's position is not for the weak. Every captain lives with the nightmare of maritime court, a hearing where one is guilty until proven innocent. Every decision at sea must stand up to scrutiny back in port. Every incident, especially if a tragedy is involved, makes a captain vulnerable to charges of negligence and possibly jail. Every decision is measured by the owner's ruler at the home office, where the captain is a mere employee. And in maritime court, acquittal is not enough: the blot of mere suspicion is a permanent blemish on the cherished master's papers. In the other court of judgment — the corporate world — to be relieved of a command is tantamount to professional bankruptcy.

The law is the same for masters of all ships, both passenger and cargo vessels. But for each kind of captain, the workload and responsibility are demonstrably different. A cargo captain manages only money and the lives of two dozen seamen. His cruise ship colleague sits on a corporate investment of $100 million or more. His staff numbers 500, and his cargo consists of 1,100 hungry, thirsty, playful and pampered human lives. As one captain crudely puts it: "$100 million worth of insurance policies."

If the cruise ship never even left port, the master's duties would equal those of a hotel manager. At sea, with 1,600 souls under his absolute command, he must be everything from navigational wizard to charming dinner companion, from fire chief to master of ceremonies, from bank manager to public relations director. Cargo ships visit only sophisticated ports with tugboats and expert pilots; the cruisers frequently face the delicate navigation of tropical reefs and sandbars.

During a cruise, passengers devote a great deal of time discussing every detail of the ship and the industry in general. As a general rule, the more they talk the less they know. Those passengers who understand the business always find eavesdropping an amusing pastime. ("What time is the midnight buffet?" "How far above sea level are we?") Invariably, there is the passenger who explains the pecking order among the officers, revealing that the captain is "just a figurehead," hired for his wit and manners, not his seamanship.

In fact, the captain is a seaman first. The prime consideration of a cruise company is finding an individual who can babysit an investment portfolio more precious than that in the hands of most bank managers. The insurance brokers, generally Lloyds of London, consider simultaneously the structure of the ship and the credentials of the captain. It is immaterial to the insurers whether the skipper mixes martinis for his passengers or tosses drinks into their faces. It is the seamanship, the experience and the track record of the captain that must pass the insurance broker's scrutiny. The master's credentials will dictate the insurance premium. If he is also a gracious host, that is merely a bonus.

Rising through the ranks in the shipping business can be a frustrating affair. It has become increasingly difficult to obtain master's papers, the certification necessary to command a great ship. Standards of education have risen dramatically, and it is no longer possible to apprentice and work one's way up the ladder to the top. Classroom instruction at a maritime academy and written examinations are required at various stages of the certification process. A talented and determined young officer can obtain the papers by the time he is 30. He will likely wait at least 20 years for his first command.

A newly qualified master will likely hold a position no higher than first officer (fourth in the chain of authority), and on the bridge of a cruise ship there may be as many as four fully qualified masters. Companies prefer to develop their own people, and officers tend to be confined to their country's own ships. The retirement of a captain in any cruise company is a momentous event, sparking a chain of promotions.

A captain's paperwork alone would be sufficient to drive an ordinary mortal over the brink. Everything, by law, must be filed and recorded. The ship's log includes reports from every major department head aboard ship, including a daily statement from the medical doctor regarding drugs issued and passengers treated and their progress. The captain, except in the event of illness or absence when the staff captain assumes command, is the only officer entitled to touch the log. He must file endless details of weather, navigational factors, distance travelled and fuel consumed, and engineering reports and schedules. If a ship goes down, it is the log that contains every relevant piece of information related to the crew, the passengers and the functioning of the ship.

Many captains feel ignored by the corporate office. Policies, schedules and operating procedures that the captains view as unworkable are often foisted upon them without consultation. At sea, the master is a god. At home, he may be just a number in the personnel department's computer. The more advanced firms in the business rely upon their captains' advice. Ron Zeller, president of Norwegian Caribbean Lines, says his captains enjoy the status of vice-presidents in the company.

The command of a passenger ship was once the most glamorous, most admired job in the world, but much of the glitter has vanished. Airline pilots today capture the glory. The captains of aircraft can earn $150,000 or more yearly. The captains of ships work for a third of that salary. But the aircraft pilot's workload and responsibilities pale to insignificance when compared with those of his equal on the water.

All passenger liner captains — at least those who survive their first cruise — have exceptional management and seafaring abilities. There can be no more impressive display of talent than a master on a flying bridge, without a pilot, gently sliding his huge ship against a rubber-lined pier. The vessel moors like a feather landing on the grass — every time.

Well, almost every time.

It was always a great occasion in Suva, the capital of Fiji, when *Iberia* sailed into the harbor. One balmy afternoon, thousands of citizens in their native finery lined the dock. A brass band heralded the ship's arrival with a musical tribute. Formally attired local dignitaries stood proudly in front of the band, waiting to conduct the ceremonies.

As the white hull inched toward the pier, a sudden wind caught the stern. The vessel lurched. The stern jumped to life, pushing toward the crowds on the dock. For a second, the spectators froze. Music jarred to a halt. And then the rush. The crowd, followed by dignitaries holding their top hats, scattered among the equally panic-stricken bandsmen in the rush from the pier.

Iberia, all 30,000 tons, came chasing after. The ship smashed into the wharf among the scattered and abandoned musical instruments, splintering the port facility and jarring loose just about everything inside.

Another P&O captain, John Crichton, startled the crowds one day in Vancouver when he brought *Sun Princess* bow-first toward the shoreline and the pier. He suddenly turned the ship on the spot, and the onlookers were abruptly faced with her stern. The local papers gave great play to the theatrics, but the truth was not told. *Sun Princess* had been caught by a sudden gust of wind. The manoeuvre was made to avoid a crash into the pier. John Crichton, who died in 1982, was one of the most flamboyant captains in the business.

It was another British captain who struck his ship on a Mexican reef. The vessel sat idle for two days. Consoled by a friend, the master wryly admitted, "That sort of thing can spoil your whole day."

THE CAPTAIN'S NOBILITY

In the resort atmosphere of a typical cruise, it is often difficult for passengers to realize that they are on a ship and that seamen are in charge. Passengers are for the most part exposed to the cruise director, a civilian who carries significant responsibility, and his social and entertainment staff. The setting suggests a playful hotel with lots of uniformed "bellmen." When officers are present in the dining room or lounge, they behave exactly as the passengers do, enjoying the merriment. Occasionally the captain is seen grilling hamburgers for a moonlit party on the open deck topside, or the chief engineer is spotted piloting his substantial midsection under a limbo bar. But that is likely the extent of passenger contact with the officers.

Only in the rare instance of an emergency do the true functions of the officers become apparent. At that point, the cruise director and his staff may be given a morale-boosting assignment, but their insignificance in the scheme of things quickly becomes visible. The hotel becomes a ship, and the people in uniform, sporting various stripes and decorations, are the ones who count the most.

The captain's responsibility is shared by the staff captain. The chain of command proceeds through the "deck officers": chief officer, first, second and third (and sometimes more). The chief engineer, whose officers and crew toil belowdecks astern, is not part of the chain of command, but on the ship he is second in importance only to the captain. Peripherally assigned to the deck staff are the chief radio officer and his three assistants, who handle all forms of communication. (It should be noted that certain titles as well as overall staff structure vary from line to line.)

The hotel manager (some lines use "purser," the traditional title) is responsible for all areas related to passenger and crew service. His principal aides are the chief steward (responsible for bars, dining room, galley and cabins), the chief purser (accounting, purchasing and officer services) and the cruise director (entertainment and recreation). The maître d'hôtel and chef report to the chief steward.

The passenger service officers, including the medical doctors, enjoy considerable status on a ship but are strictly out of the action in matters relating to seamanship.

Gold braid and stripes on the epaulets are signs of true sea power. There are many variations within the industry, but always the captain's decorations are obvious. A captain boasts a full five stripes while a staff captain has four and a half. The chief engineer, the medical doctor, the chief officer and the hotel manager wear four stripes.

Sporting three stripes are the first officer, the first engineer, the chief steward, the radio officer and the chief purser.

Officers also wear colors or insignia, to denote their shipboard departments. Bridge officers wear either a diamond insignia or blue colors between their stripes. Engineers display a propeller or purple colors. Radio officers have their insignia, but most frequently they wear a green color between their stripes. The hotel staff of a ship have white between the gold braid; the medical staff, for reasons best left to the imagination, wear red between their stripes.

A ship is a highly structured class society with every member of the company fitting into a rigidly policed slot. Seamen, general maintenance staff and galley hands, receiving only a basic salary and no other amenities, are at the bottom of the ladder. Food, lounge and cabin stewards, with the basic pay generously supplemented by gratuities, are one rung higher. Junior civilians, who enjoy a better salary but are not permitted to fraternize with passengers, are a class by themselves. These civilians include the nonmanagement staff of shipboard concessions, clerks, resident musicians and specialists such as the printer. The cruise director, his senior staff and the featured entertainers have a status similar to that of the officers.

The officers are at the top of the pecking order. They subdivide into two groups: three or more stripes, and one- and two-stripers. All officers receive entertainment allowances and have comfortable quarters plus access to all passenger amenities. The only residents who don't wear a label, are the passengers. They are, for want of a better description, without class.

Officers with three or more stripes live well — very well. Their salaries, at the lower end, may be the same as the total income of a well-tipped steward, but the net effect of their career package puts them substantially above. Salaries are comfortable, benefits excellent, and the long-term outlook is generally optimistic. The minute he takes the first step, a career officer knows the number of rungs there will be on the ladder. Success will be a combination of experience, education and credentials.

Junior officers in the engine room and on the bridge face a series of shoreside marine college programs, examinations and a seniority system at sea. Radio officers require education at the most sophisticated communications centres. Increasingly, in the hotel departments of the ships, officers are required to have formal education in hotel administration.

Most of the ship's crew is hired as casual labor. Senior civilians are on personal contracts. But the officers, members of guilds and unions, and long-term company employees are all career people. They are guaranteed long annual vacations at home, with travel expenses to and from the ship paid by the company. Often the travel is first class. They benefit from special tax advantages. All personal living expenses at sea, with only minor exceptions, are provided by the cruise line. Their salaries collect in bank accounts or, in the case of family men, are sent directly home.

The Staff Captain

Second in command is the most frustrating position on the ship and one role that defies definition. The staff captain is a fully qualified master in his own right, and he draws a salary not far behind that of the skipper. When the captain enjoys his annual leave, it is the staff captain who assumes command.

It is the captain who determines how his alter ego is employed. The two men generally divide duties according to individual interests. For example, if the captain is happiest with his charts and seafaring duties, much of the entertainment obligation may be passed on to the staff captain. Most often, the number two is the man in charge of personnel matters, including crew discipline. He supervises the arrival of crew members after shore leave and the drinking regulations in quarters. When there are searches of crew decks for contraband, it is the staff captain who leads the party belowdecks. It is his duty to be the bad guy of the ship.

One of the two must be on call at all times and, in most cruise companies, either the captain or the staff captain must be aboard in port. The staff captain tends to be the captain's only true friend and confidant aboard ship. They share decisions. But the frustration faced by the second in command is that serious problems in any of the ship's departments go straight to the top. There can be no legal delegation of ultimate authority.

Behind the staff captain on the bridge come the other deck officers, the links in the chain of command. They all have watches and special areas of responsibility. One is the principal navigational officer, scanning the charts for reefs, markers, sunken vessels, sandbars and potential anchoring positions at the harbors on the schedule. Another officer is assigned to organizing deck labor, and docking and embarkation teams. Ship safety and emergency drills are looked after principally by one officer; another officer might be assigned the difficult task of organizing launches to take passengers to and from the ship at a port where no pier facilities exist. Through it all, it is the staff captain, with the assistance of the chief officer, who ensures that the captain's wishes are carried out.

For a dozen different reasons, it is a painfully thankless job. But the position of staff captain is the final step toward the crowning achievement of a career at sea.

The "Chief"

Engineers may be the strangest lot aboard ship. They surface from their noisy caverns only to eat and be merry. The responsibilities of a chief engineer are endless: engines, ventilation, refrigeration, air conditioning, the electrical system and the plumbing. A chief may worship his engines, but every nut, bolt and door handle also falls under his domain.

Chief engineers are extremely possessive. When they walk the deck they tend to consider everyone, from the captain to the youngest passenger, a trespasser in their mechanical realm. Ask a chief who runs the ship; he will proudly give you the answer.

The chief's office is a computer centre just over the engines. Its control panel is a duplicate of the one on the bridge, and there is a bank of thousands of dials that monitor every pulsebeat of the diesels and check water pressure and the

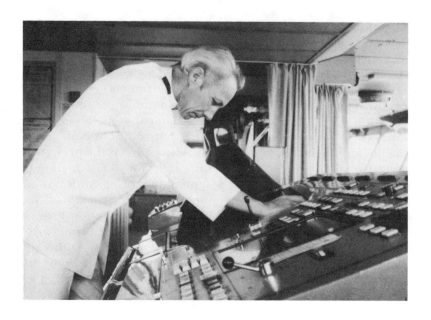

The Staff Captain on the bridge. Modern instruments provide
information about the ship and its location, but ultimate responsibility
still rests with the Captain.

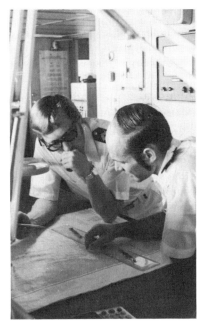

Monitoring the ship's complex control systems.

Plotting the ship's position on the charts.

The engine room.

machines that convert seawater to drinking water. The engineers are able to record every time a passenger flushes his cabin toilet.

A robust Norwegian chief engineer, taking a tour group through his control room, explained that the main device was identical to the equipment on the ship's bridge, complete with throttles. Asked if the throttles were run from the bridge or the engine room, the chief grinned and replied, "No, no. We let them do that — they like to play with the controls."

An engineer's sense of proprietorship is entirely justified. The electrical wiring, the piping, and the heat and air conditioning conduits on one ship run to the millions of miles. The spare-parts inventory is a warehouse of thousands of fixtures used to repair anything that could possibly go wrong at sea. Constant contact with the home office is kept to control the perpetual inventory of spare parts and tools; when a spare is used, its replacement can be waiting at the next port.

It's impossible to have a comfortable conversation with an engineer — the chief, his senior officers or his principal staff. To them, all aboard are intruders. When a stateroom tap ceases to pour water, the engineer grudgingly arrives to make repairs, convinced that his tap is perfect. It must be the passenger who has problems.

Actually, the engineers are among the most charming and interesting people aboard the ship — oil and grease mixed with spit and polish. But since no one expects much in the way of smooth manners from them, they enjoy a far freer lifestyle than do their fellow officers. They will put on the starched dress whites to lure a lady to bed. When the lady opens her eyelids in the morning, however, her prince has vanished. Standing before her in greasy coveralls, the engineer is off again in search of his one true love.

Retired ship's engineers are in great demand as maintenance supervisors for major buildings. They are self-sufficient, not prone to call outside contractors. They are trained to understand the interrelationship of a multiplicity of systems: heat, air conditioning, ventilation, lighting and so on.

When you see an engineer anywhere on a ship, forgive him if he appears to be squirrelly. His ear is tuned to the piping behind the plush panelling, to the faint rumble of his cherished diesels down below. He's sniffing for the slightest malodor seeping through the air conditioning, listening for the tiniest missed beat of a motor, straining his eyes for the flicker of a light bulb.

Through many years at college and at sea, the chief engineer has reached the pinnacle of his profession. He is the only person aboard who can talk to the captain with a measure of equality.

The Officers of the Radio Room

The author of the phrase, "nothing is so insular as an island," had obviously never been on a ship. On the seas, a ship's hierarchy is the only government that exists, and no group of people are so consistently out of touch with the rest of the world as a ship's crew. The ship is capable of maintaining its own survival, with an engine room to keep it afloat and moving, a clinic and galley for the population and a communications centre to pay grudging homage to land.

In the same sense that a ship's bridge resembles a control panel at Cape Canaveral, the radio room may be likened to a sophisticated broadcast facility. The communications equipment is the umbilical cord tying the ship to land at all times. From a ship-to-shore call to impress Aunt Mabel at home, to the computer facilities that plug in the ship's spare-parts inventory to the home-office ledger, the radio room's uses are infinite.

The radio officer and his three subordinates form a satellite department, just off the bridge. At least one officer is on duty at any time. Through the facilities of tape recorders, Morse code messages and radio telephone, the ship and its people listen to and talk to the rest of the world. Every message is manually decoded and typed by the officers.

Passengers sitting comfortably in their staterooms can phone home thousands of miles away. The quality of the communication ranges from excellent to terrible. When a call doesn't go through, there is no charge and it's just a matter of trying again. There are dozens of marine radio centres throughout the world. Contact is maintained with the centre nearest the ship, and through this facility all traffic passes. Radio operators at sea and ashore regularly scan their frequency dials to monitor incoming messages. (There is often a teletype machine in the radio room, a speedy but expensive form of communication, for long or complicated incoming or outgoing messages.) Ship-to-shore phone calls and telegrams are profitable for the cruise line. Revenues from these sources on an 1,100-passenger vessel total at least $15,000 per month. The per-minute cost of a call ranges from three to fifteen dollars, depending on distance.

While a cruise is in progress, passengers receive daily summaries of world news. Highlights of the news are sent from a nearby marine radio centre in Morse code to all ships in the neighborhood. Radio officers transcribe the Morse into English.

The brief reports are just enough to limit the feeling of isolation at sea without placing a mariner back into the troubled world. Radio officers tend to be rather dull technical chaps, but they can display a sense of humor. For example, when world news is slack they've been known to help out. Once, as a ship embarked on a cruise, a radio officer invented a minor war in the Outer Hebrides. Every day of the cruise, he updated the reports, creating a considerable amount of conversation aboard ship. As the trip sailed to a conclusion, he neatly ended the war with a declaration of peace.

Because of a cruise vessel's medical capability, national coast guard services and marine radio stations ashore closely chart its movements. The system works both ways. If a passenger ship has an extremely ill crew member or passenger, beyond the capability of the ship's doctor and infirmary, the coast guard will instantly dispatch a helicopter for a dramatic air-ambulance pick up. More common, however, is the need of cargo ships and small craft for the service of cruise ship physicians; when an urgent message is received, the two ships steam toward each other and the ailing seaman is transferred by launch to the floating resort.

Emergency calls carry urgency and involve special procedures. Such calls include serious news from home for a passenger or a conversation between a ship's physician and a family doctor regarding a patient's medical history. Sometimes, supplies must be urgently requisitioned in order to be delivered to the next port of call. The radio room also provides a steady flow of weather reports and navigational information for the bridge officers. Weather maps arrive through telephoto facilities.

The duties of a radio officer are not restricted to the radio room. Although the chief engineer's staff includes electricians to handle most assignments, jobs that fall into the category of electronics are often looked after by radio room officers. Among these jobs are repairs to closed-circuit radio and television features within the cabins, microphones and amplifiers in the lounges, and the projection booth of the cinema.

One radio officer on a British ship, in a manner and tone achieved only by the English, was proudly displaying his room to a group of passengers. He stressed the urgency of the work and the sophistication of the equipment. As his speech rose to a fitting climax, the teletype started clacking. He paused. "There's something coming in now. Let's take a look."

In ticked the soccer scores from the old country . . . news that would make one seaman appreciably more affluent.

The Doctors

A 30,000-ton ship carries two medical doctors and three nurses. There is a fully equipped hospital, a pharmacy and an operating room. The largest ships in the industry often have a dentist aboard.

There is a myth surviving that physicians at sea are young and inexperienced or old and senile — or that they have been drummed out of their base of practice because of some sinister error. The tale further continues that they are hiding in perpetuity on the sea. Perhaps there is some historic basis to that myth; today, there is not an ounce of truth in it.

A cruise line cannot afford the risk of hiring an incompetent doctor. The ship is legally responsible for whatever transpires at sea. Malpractice suits could run into the millions; it would be illogical for a company to seek any but the best doctors available. Nor is there a shortage of highly qualified medics around. Physicians who desire a career at sea may be rare, but cruise companies are besieged with applications from top-rated practitioners who wish short-term adventure and escape.

The work is not difficult. There will be an occasional heart attack. Arteries that have been lethargic for decades are suddenly thrust into action, as passengers bob and weave on the dance floor. Sometimes, sadly, there is death.

Minor surgery can be performed, but every effort is made to stabilize the patient until a shore-based hospital is reached. When serious incidents occur, coast guard helicopters land on the sports decks of ships to evacuate the patient. When surgery is performed in the ship's hospital, the doctors make incisions slightly larger than normal. The medics claim that the movement of a ship makes it more difficult than usual to perform the delicate procedures; more room to work is required.

Each new load of passengers brings new ailments. Passengers often arrive with precise instructions from their personal physicians for treatment and medication. There are always hypochondriacs.

A typical ship's surgery is compact but well equipped. There are two small five-bed wards, an examination room and an operating room. The hospital is capable of complete anesthesiology. Most lab tests can be performed on the ship. There is x-ray equipment, an electrocardiograph, and equipment to monitor a patient's vital functions.

Appendectomies are the most frequent operations performed on a ship, but even they are rare. If surgery is necessary on a ship where there is only one doctor, a call is placed to doctors among the passengers to scrub and assist.

The most persistent problem at sea is not much of a problem at all — seasickness. It is the source of unending controversy. Today's ships invariably cruise in the smoothest waters. They all have large stabilizers — retractable winglike fins that project from the sides of the vessel. The pitch into the waves can be altered to suit the sea conditions. But people still get sick, and doctors still distribute barrels of pills.

The medical controversy focuses on the origin of the illness. There is a large body of evidence that says seasickness is psychosomatic. There is an equally large body of evidence — the victims — the argues to the contrary. Supporters of the psychosomatic school have a difficult time explaining why tiny babies sometimes come down with *mal de mer.*

As a ship is about to embark on a cruise, the doctor invariably is besieged by passengers in search of seasick drugs — "just in case." These passengers are always the first to be stricken. The slightest ship's movement will produce illness in

BEAUFORT SCALE

Beaufort number	Wind speed		Weather chart symbol	Descriptive term	Sea criterion	Wave height in feet
	Knots	Km/hour				
0	0	0		Calm	Mirror like	–
1				Light air	Ripples	$\frac{1}{4}$
2		10		Light breeze	Small wavelets	$\frac{1}{2}$
3	10	20		Gentle breeze	Large wavelets, scattered white horses	2
4		30		Moderate breeze	Small waves, frequent white horses	$3\frac{1}{2}$
5	20	40		Fresh breeze	Moderate waves, many white horses	6
6		50		Strong breeze	Large waves, extensive white crests	$9\frac{1}{2}$
7	30	60		Near gale	Sea heaps up, foam blown in streaks	$13\frac{1}{2}$
8	40	70		Gale	Waves of greater length, foam blown up	18
9		80		Strong gale	High waves, spray affects visibility	23
10	50	90 / 100		Storm	Very high waves, overhanging crests, sea surface has white appearance	29
11	60	110		Violent storm	Exceptionally high waves hiding ships, visibility affected	37
12		120		Hurricane	Air filled with foam and spray, visibility seriously affected	45

some passengers. There have been many reported cases of seasickness while a ship was still docked at a pier.

When a ship hits rough seas, the parade to the infirmary begins. The medical staff, at the first sign of rough seas, pile small envelopes of pills on a table under a sign, "Seasick Pills — Help Yourself." Then they stand back and watch the legions come pouring through the door.

The roughest seas of a cruise, usually when the ship turns into open water (more often going north than going south), are predictable. They normally occur at precisely the same place, varying only in intensity, on every cruise along a previously travelled route.

The Beaufort wind-force scale measures sea conditions from zero for speeds below one mile an hour (calm) to 12 or higher for speeds above 72 m.p.h. (hurricane). Every crew member has his own theories about seasickness, but a common estimate is that 40 per cent of passengers will become ill in a sea of four to five. Four represents long, even waves; five is the point at which the waves start breaking into whitecaps. In a condition of six or seven, when the sea grows high with many whitecaps and a heavy spray over the ship, about half the passengers will become ill.

Conditions of four rarely exist for more than a day or so on most of today's cruises, and conditions of seven are rarely encountered at all. The stabilizers are used nearly all the time at night, eliminating up to 90 per cent of the motion and helping the passengers sleep. But they cost about two knots in speed, meaning additional fuel consumption. Whenever possible in the daytime they are retracted.

Ship's crew rarely experience seasickness. When it does occur, it is most often among the galley hands, entertainers and other nonseamen of the contingent. A study of the faces of officers and crew during an uncomfortable sea, when the dining room is half full at mealtime, leaves suspicion that they take a secret delight in the passenger misery.

Bad teeth is the most common medical problem of the crew, occurring principally among natives of countries where dentistry is not very advanced. Venereal disease, a prize brought back from shoreside conquests, is not uncommon.

For passengers, each cruising area presents its own special brands of illness. Mexico is the land of Montezuma: diarrhea and occasionally dysentery from infected foods. Some passengers always insist on drinking the water, either straight or in ice cube form. Invariably, they visit the doctor back on the ship. Trips to Alaska produce the expected colds and respiratory ailments. In warmer climates, doctors watch for heat prostration and any virus indigenous to an area.

Elderly people often arrive for cruises the victims of upset dietary habits, long waits at airports and jarring bus rides. While a voyage is in progress, many drink and play too hard. On shore excursions, older passengers suffer from trying to keep pace with young guides and more vigorous companions.

Many babies have been delivered on ships, though expectant mothers rarely book passage close to the due date. One current crew member of *Queen Elizabeth 2* was born on *Queen Mary.*

After seasickness, bruised or broken limbs is the most common medical complaint. Victims of strenuous activity on the sports deck regularly arrive at the hospital for treatment.

When death occurs at sea, usually because of a heart attack or cerebral hemorrhage, there is a cold-storage morgue to keep the body until the cruise is completed. In the case of cruises to distant oceans, bureaucratic red tape can make it impossible to send a body back home by air. It is at the discretion of the captain to bury the victim at sea. The service is short and simple. The ship briefly comes to a stop as the body is cast into the deep. When a crew member dies, the ship's mood remains sombre for days afterward.

In one case, a ship cruising in the South Pacific had a sudden deluge of deaths. Between the time the vessel started a four-day journey through small tropical islands and the time it again emerged into international waters, eight elderly passengers had died. The ship's morgue held six, and two extra bodies were stored in one of the empty refrigerated food lockers until a mass burial could take place outside territorial waters.

A modest fee is charged for medical services and pharmaceuticals aboard ship. Seasickness pills are free. On some ships, the doctors and nurses are on straight salary, with the revenue going to the cruise line. On others, the physicians are on small salaries but really live off their fees.

Officers' Salaries and Other Benefits

"There is nothing more fractured in the world than the

salaries in this industry," a cruise executive once explained. Rates of pay vary from country to country, from company to company and, in some cases, from ship to ship within the same cruise line. The Norwegians and Dutch pay the highest salaries, the Greeks and British the lowest. The Italians are somewhere in between.

It is believed that Captain Torbjorn Hauge of *S.S. Norway* is the highest paid officer in the cruise business. For 1981, his income was reported to be in the $70,000 per annum range. Other Norwegian and Dutch captains trail him by $5,000 to $10,000. Most cruise captains are in the $50,000-a-year bracket, but the British and Greeks may earn as little as $38,000. It is reported that the captains of *Queen Elizabeth 2* are paid not much more than $40,000.

Chief engineers are paid about 5 per cent less than captains. Staff captains are about 10 per cent behind the masters. With each level down, the wage falls between 5 and 10 per cent. The most junior cadet officer earns between $10,000 and $12,000 yearly.

Senior officers are camped in spacious quarters just behind the bridge. The captain, the staff captain and the chief engineer, and possibly the hotel manager and the doctor, reside in two- or even three-room suites. All the senior officers reside in cabins overlooking the sea; they enjoy steward services at all times. On some ships, the cruise director is housed on the officers' deck; on others, he will likely occupy a passenger cabin.

Junior officers, who may be accommodated in crew quarters belowdecks, have private cabins. All commissioned officers enjoy the privileges of the officers' mess, which is always near the bridge. The mess serves breakfast and other meals to officers who do not wish to join the dining room during breakfast and lunch. Coffee and pastries are available in the mess at all times, and there is always a serve-yourself bar.

On some ships, the captains and senior officers receive as cash bonuses a percentage of revenues collected in various activities. The duty-free liquor merchants at St. Thomas are generous to the captains who deliver their customers. All captains receive cases of liquor when they visit the Virgin Islands. There was a story about a Norwegian captain who, upon retirement, was found to have a warehouse full of spirits.

One ship gave its captain a share of the bingo profits. The cruise line had a policy of starting a bingo game every time there was rain. Rather than have the passengers evacuate the pool deck and retire for naps in the cabin, the thinking was that bingo would keep them spending money in the public rooms. This captain was disciplined when it was discovered that he deliberately followed the rainstorms around the Caribbean. Some bingo games lasted 12 hours.

The Norwegians may enjoy the top salaries, but their taxes at home are the highest. The British, by a long measure, have the best leave provisions in the business; senior officers enjoy five months leave each year, divided into several visits home. Most cruise lines offer their top at-sea staff three or four months leave. The vacation provisions may seem magnanimous, but it must be remembered that top officers are on duty 24 hours a day and rarely work fewer than 80 hours in a week. Pension benefits are excellent. Retirement is customary at age 60.

It is remarkable how solid the marriages of seamen tend to be. Captain Bob Arnott of *Queen Elizabeth 2* says he can think of no cases of divorce among his many colleagues over the years. Senior officers are permitted to bring their wives aboard the ship for extended cruises during the year. In some companies, this is complimentary; in others, there is a charge.

Uniforms can be expensive, blacks for winter and whites for summer. The policy for outfitting the officers varies within the industry. Some companies pick up the entire tab, but most often such expenses are shared. The uniforms are tailored and replaced on a regular basis, for which a set fee is deducted from the officers' salaries.

The simplest way to describe a senior officer's expenses is to say that there aren't any. Everything, with the exception of shoreside purchases, is covered by the company. The senior officers have an allowance for wine and liquor in the dining room, for cocktails in the public rooms. At the officers' mess, drinks are available for pennies. One officer goes on the wagon during his annual leave, in the hope of avoiding alcoholism.

In the dining room, where the senior officers each host a table of passengers, proper etiquette is for each party at the table to buy the wine on successive evenings. This can sometimes be awkward. The officer is the first to buy. On the next night, if none of the passengers makes a move, the table will be dry for dinner. Occasionally, a couple will buy a bottle and drink it themselves. Wine stewards try to assist; once they sense a proper rotation at a table, they will place the wine list at the appropriate setting each evening. Officers generally purchase more for the passengers than they receive in return, and they frequently suffer through some ghastly choices from the wine list.

It is rare to see an officer in the dining room on the first night out. The second night of a cruise is the captian's welcome-aboard party. Just before dinner, the main lounge opens for complimentary cocktails, and passengers line up to shake the captain's hand. After the procession passes, the master welcomes everyone aboard and introduced his principal officers. It's on "captain's night," the second evening of a cruise, when the officers generally make their first entrance to the dining room.

In terms of comforts and rewards, officers do not lack, yet they tend to crave the more subtle pleasures of life. After a few months at sea, most of the ship's company would yearn for a day of driving in the country. They miss their families. Living with one's work is convenient, but there is no escape, and there is no detachment. Comments one senior officer, "We have everything, but it's all rather artificial."

Officers' Lifestyle

As the white-uniformed officers collect along the bar, just after dinner each evening, the nature of their pursuits soon becomes obvious. The French and the Italians are great mixers, off on a new conquest each evening. Scandinavians tend to be more rigid and remote. The Latins sweep their ladies off the floor. The English approach is with a certain stuffy elegance. Whatever the style, it works.

It surprises no one to learn that seamen away from home for eight months at a stretch are known to be adulterous. What is more remarkable is that despite the constant availability of fresh faces, a substantial number of officers have the reputation of being uninterested, preferring instead to retire to their cabins to write home.

A learned eye quickly notes the ladies in search of an officer.

(Officers shy away from the staff beauties; romances with junior crew members lead to awkward entanglements.) For the curious observer, the bar scene is interesting. A dozen officers cluster early in the evening to scout the room. Gradually, they dissipate, moving through the ballroom and appearing at the tables. Because they seem to retire early, it must be assumed the sales pitch is quick and effective.

Stories are endless about women who try to set records for themselves. One woman, determined to spend a night with every officer on a particular ship, had missed the chief purser. One night in the cocktail lounge, she successfully manoeuvred him onto the dance floor. While they were waltzing, she whispered in his ear that they might retire to his cabin for a drink. The purser laughed it off, continuing to guide his partner around the dance floor. The young woman finally protested, "I'm the best lay on this ship!" The purser chuckled, asking her how she knew that. "Ask the doctor," she replied nonchalantly.

There are almost no secrets among the officers who live so closely to one another. The corridor between the cabins and suites is narrow, visitors are easily spotted, usually prompting an exchange of winks between passing officers. Less discreet officers compare notes; within a few days, the easy marks are well catalogued.

Some captains are dynamite among the women, dashing from exploit to exploit and never losing their authority. On a few ships, the officers have a seniority system, with the captain allowed first pick. Most captains, however, live rather lonely lives. They have numerous social obligations to look after, most of them tedious, and while the officers are free for as many flings as they wish, the captain's behavior is expected to be exemplary. There is no way he can smuggle a friend into and out of his cabin without it being ship's gossip the next day. In fact, the crew grapevine begins each time the master dances with a lady passenger.

THE SHIP'S COMPANY
Usual hierarchy for an 1,100-passenger, 30,000-ton modern cruise ship

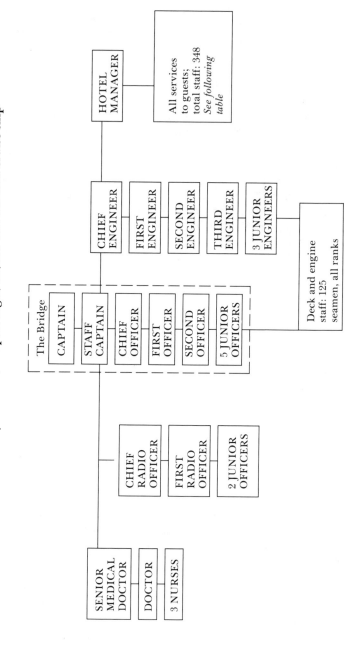

TOTAL SHIP'S COMPANY: 500

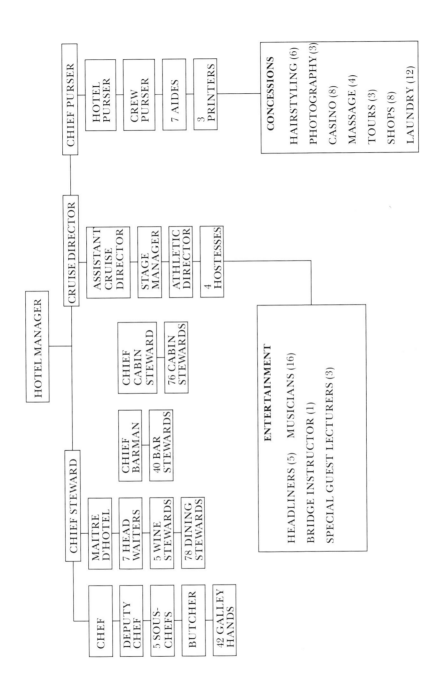

HOTEL MANAGER

CHIEF STEWARD

CHIEF PURSER
- HOTEL PURSER
- CREW PURSER
- 7 AIDES
- 3 PRINTERS

CONCESSIONS
- HAIRSTYLING (6)
- PHOTOGRAPHY (3)
- CASINO (8)
- MASSAGE (4)
- TOURS (3)
- SHOPS (8)
- LAUNDRY (12)

CRUISE DIRECTOR
- ASSISTANT CRUISE DIRECTOR
- STAGE MANAGER
- ATHLETIC DIRECTOR
- 4 HOSTESSES

ENTERTAINMENT
- HEADLINERS (5)
- MUSICIANS (16)
- BRIDGE INSTRUCTOR (1)
- SPECIAL GUEST LECTURERS (3)

CHIEF CABIN STEWARD
- 76 CABIN STEWARDS

CHIEF BARMAN
- 40 BAR STEWARDS

- MAITRE D'HOTEL
- 7 HEAD WAITERS
- 5 WINE STEWARDS
- 78 DINING STEWARDS

- CHEF
- DEPUTY CHEF
- 5 SOUS-CHEFS
- BUTCHER
- 42 GALLEY HANDS

5

The Nobles of fhe Floating Palace

In the old days of passenger shipping, all matters of accounting and guest services came under the umbrella of an officer so powerful his staff would quake with trepidation when he entered a room. They couldn't determine whether to bow, salute or play dead. The officer held the unassuming title, "purser." Not "chief purser," just, simply, "the purser."

In modern times, with so much emphasis given to food, recreation and entertainment, most companies have adopted the more descriptive title, "hotel manager." Of a crew of 500, it takes 150 to run and maintain the ship. The other 350 crew members work for the hotel manager. He is responsible for all galleys, dining rooms and cocktail lounges; for all entertainment and recreation functions; for cabin services; for accounting and business; and for the operation of the printing presses and all independent concessions aboard (photographic services, hair salons, laundry, casino, shore-excursion services, massage parlor and retail shops).

The title "hotel manager," while gaining wide acceptance, still generates controversy. There are some companies (P&O Cruises and its Princess subsidiary, for example) that continue to use the traditional "purser." In the past, a purser was a seaman first; passenger service was a second priority.

Since the cruise ship is a floating resort hotel, most companies look for qualifications suited to shore-based facilities. The university credentials and actual experience that would impress hotel chains looking for executives, would win favor with a cruise line in search of a hotel manager.

Many of the leading cruise companies have diversified into the broad travel field and own hotel resorts and/or tour companies. Cunard, a subsidiary of British hotel giant Trafalgar House, is the outstanding example. Not only is there a chain of

Trafalgar hotels bearing the Cunard name, Cunard's ship passengers are offered discounts and even free rooms at the company's hotels, and discounts on rooms in any Interconti-nental Hotel. The Cunard Line operates two major resorts in the Caribbean. Norwegian Caribbean Line has recently bought a resort at Port Antonio, Jamaica. Princess Cruises' subsidiary, Princess Tours, conducts shore excursions for the company ships and also offers packages that have nothing to do with the sea. Princess Cruises recently purchased the Casa Sirena Mari-na Hotel in Oxnard, California, just south of Santa Barbara. It is a major resort acquisition, and the company plans to actively seek out other properties.

The companies expanding into wider travel activities plan to integrate the new products with the ships. Marketing depart-ments will offer combined cruise-and-land packages. The com-panies also plan to develop personnel for the ships through their hotels division, in a program involving a combination of training on land and at sea.

The hotel manager on a ship has three principal officers under his command: chief purser, chief steward and cruise director.

The Chief Purser

The purser's office is the business heart of a ship. It is always centrally located, usually in the main lobby and near the shopping arcade. Although in a hotel manager system the purser's status has been reduced, "chief" has been added to the title. His remains an important function. The chief purser is the business manager, responsible for crew and passenger accounts, payroll, information services, the telephone switch-board, the printer's shop, purchase requisitions, shipboard concessions, relations with customs and immigration officers in all the ports — and all complaints.

A chief purser has two principal assistants: hotel purser and crew purser. The senior of the two, in charge of passenger business, is the hotel purser. The crew purser handles payroll, personnel contracts, benefits and the business matters related to the concessionaires on the ship. There is a support staff of about ten, manning the information desk and the switchboard, and performing clerical tasks. The purser's office also serves as the ship's bank, taking deposits from the ship's bars and retail outlets, exchanging currency for passengers and guarding the vault.

The ship's daily newspaper is an adjunct to the office. The editor assembles the next day's schedule of activities, informative stories about the ship and upcoming ports, and a round-up of world news. The finished copy is taken to the printer for publication. It will then be distributed to every cabin on the vessel, while the passengers are at dinner or during the night.

On a typical ship, there are about 44 people who work in concessions. Their employers are companies that signed a contract with the cruise line to render a specific service. The concessions are managed through the purser's office.

The purser's office endures its worst moments when a ship is in port; passenger demands for information, currency exchange and assistance arrive in a flood. Customs and immigration officers are a constant nuisance. They come aboard at every port. After the passenger list is checked and approved, passengers may proceed ashore. The customs and immigration people can exercise the right to search all cabins, although they rarely bother. In some of the banana republics and some of the South Seas Islands, it is not uncommon for customs officials to arrive early in the morning and stay all day. They expect to be wined and dined and, occasionally, they ask for gifts of liquor or more expensive items. Only a foolish purser would turn down the requests. The customs people have the power to delay a ship's departure for several hours and, with the approval of higher authority, for a day or more — and the cruise ship must keep on schedule. It is not unknown in the United States and other major countries for customs officers to expect special favors and gifts.

An experience in Haiti illustrates the kind of aggravation a purser must learn to endure. A ship steamed into the harbor at Port-au-Prince one morning, where several of the passengers were to terminate their cruise and fly home. Those departing were told to clear customs in the morning, but one bumptious and scatterbrained lady from New England chose to ignore this message. Since her plane was not leaving until evening, she marched ashore for a day in Haiti, leaving her luggage in her cabin and not clearing customs. Six customs agents, all wearing mirrored sunglasses, went to work in an antichamber off the purser's office. When the departing passengers had been cleared, there was one still missing. Urgent pages rang through the ship. A steward found the lady's bags in her room and realized what had happened.

The Haitian officials settled back to enjoy a day on the ship. They spent the morning sipping cocktails by the pool, which were followed by a lavish lunch. The chief purser watched them nervously all day. If at any moment, out of curiosity or provocation, the customs officials decided to, they could have investigated any of a number of things on the vessel.

Late in the afternoon the woman strolled up the gangway and to her cabin for the luggage. She was instantly and rudely hauled to the purser's office. The inebriated customs officers, sunglasses slightly askew, were retrieved from the bar.

"Were you looking for me?" she queried.

The Chief Steward

The hotel manager's most important assistant is the chief steward. He manages an army of 270 people who look after every aspect of food, beverage and lodging for the passengers, the crew and the officers. His principal officers are the chef and maître d'hôtel and, on a slightly lower plane, the chief barman and chief cabin steward.

The chef and maître d' usually make more money than their boss. Most ships' chefs command $40,000 a year. The maître d' has a much lower base salary, but through tips can become the richest staff member aboard ship.

Both chef and maître d' consider themselves artists. Often, the chief steward's major worry is to keep his sensitive department heads from physically assaulting each other. The maître d' has unchallenged power in the dining room, but it ends abruptly at the swinging doors of the galley.

Embarkation is the most miserable day of a cruise for any maître d'. A new contingent of passengers must be sifted into place. To conserve space, most ships have a two-sitting arrangement for the dining room. Breakfast and lunch present no problems for the staff. In the morning, many people eat in their cabin, and at lunch, a deck smorgasbord eases the pressure. Dinner is another matter. The evening meal is a major function of life aboard a ship. Early sitting tends to run from 6:30 until 8 p.m., followed by the second contingent.

Cruise lines make every effort to have passengers indicate their sitting preference long before the cruise embarks, but there are always many who neglect the detail. Elderly people and parents with young children tend to prefer the earlier meal hour. Young couples most frequently choose late sitting. On cruises to southern waters, where the average passenger age is the lowest, two-thirds of the guests will request late sitting. This creates a modest recurring nightmare for the maître d'. Passengers who had submitted their preference on the return card that came with the ticket, don't face a difficulty. People who have a problem no doubt failed to make the advance arrangement. On northern cruises, around-the-world excursions or the 30- 45-day junkets, where the average age is high, the maître d' faces the problem in the reverse; everyone seems to want early sitting.

Most passengers want tables for two by the window, which rarely exist. There are a few small tables scattered throughout the dining room, but the majority of diners sit at tables of six or eight. All but a few guests blend in well, enjoying for the balance of the cruise the company of the new friends made at the dinner table. A good maître d' tries to size up his passengers in an effort to create amiable dinner seatings.

The Captain's Table is at the head of the room, most often with honored guests of the cruise line seated around the master.

Everyone is settled to some degree by the first evening of the cruise. The second day brings a rash of requests for transfers: by people who don't like their sitting or their table mates, or have encountered a long-lost friend aboard ship. The maître d' makes his final seating arrangements on day two.

A day in the dining room begins 30 minutes before breakfast, when the maître d' and at least two of his headwaiters hold a meeting of stewards to discuss the day's shifts and activities. Some stewards, particularly those who worked at the previous midnight buffet, are not present; they have been given permission to sleep in. Certain stewards are assigned to the noontime deck smorgasbord, others to the dining room luncheon. Before every meal and, particularly prior to the evening session, table stewards are instructed about the menu selections. They are advised what to recommend, told how the specials are created, and given any unique serving instructions. The chef often participates in these sessions.

Groups of passengers travelling together pose special problems. A group of a hundred may all want to eat together at the same sitting in the same section of the dining room. Even parties of six can pose difficulty if advance arrangements have not been made.

Maître d's want all passengers to leave the dining room happy. Since the food itself is a major contentment factor, there is a natural tendency to blame the chef for every failure. The chief steward hears complaints that the galley was slow serving up the dishes, and therefore the meals were late getting to the passengers. The maître d' protests that this hurts the tips his stewards will receive at the end of the cruise. A bad-food complaint goes first to the service staff and then to a headwaiter. The headwaiter brings it to the attention of the maître d', who then deals with the chef. The chef flies into a rage. The chief steward tugs them apart.

Passengers develop a warm relationship with their stewards. The waiters learn, for example, that Mrs. Peabody doesn't like garlic. They tell the cooks. When garlic slips by, the chef is again the target of service staff venom.

If the dining room crew is sensitive about the food quality, the chef is obsessed with the quality of service. He is convinced that the maître d' and his entire staff should be behind a hamburger stand. He has no respect for their comprehension of the food arts: how to serve a dish and particularly the urgency of getting it to the table hot. On the menu each night, there are one or two selections of which the chef is very proud. There are also one or two items which are less successful. The chef blames the service staff when the features are not pushed.

With rough guidelines from headquarters, the chef prepares the menu. Plans for three- or four-dozen dinner menus can be made well in advance, but there are always specials and alternative selections. Menus are printed daily on the ship's press. Breakfast is a standard affair, with a menu featuring anything a passenger might possibly wish: juice, cereal, fresh fruit, sausages, pancakes, ham, steak, bread, rolls, croissants, Danish pastries, and every kind of egg imaginable, including fancy omelets. The food is served in whatever quantity the passenger desires. The chef plans for early morning pastries and coffee (served in the bar before the dining room opens), breakfast, a midmorning tea, a multicourse lunch, a deck smorgasbord at noon, high tea in the afternoon, dinner and a midnight buffet. The chef's 50-member galley team may begin working as early as 2 a.m. The bakers are the first to arrive and begin preparing the thousands of breads, rolls and pastries that will be consumed during the day. The first food service is at 6:30 a.m., with continental breakfast offered in the sunrise cocktail bar.

One chef said the English, away from home, will eat just about anything. If a passenger contingent is composed predominantly of Australians, New Zealanders and British, lamb will represent about half the meat served. Scandinavians demand fish in large quantities, the French seek adventure in their cuisine and the Germans are not terribly fussy so long as the food is German. Americans and Canadians prefer beef. The chef said the menu is always a risk, but competent planning and a careful study of passenger eating habits are the keys. Food preferences of passengers are scrutinized on the first few nights of a cruise and specials for later nights are then planned, based on those tastes.

The galley at meal time is the most exciting place on the ship. Dining room stewards charge in and out, shouting their orders. The chef and his sous-chefs stand watch throughout the area, occasionally stopping to try a particular dish, then passing comments to the cooks. Cooks at the grills prepare and adapt throughout the meal. An early rush for one selection may mean a brief panic and a fast change in quantities of dishes under preparation. The chef stands at the order counter, appearing to have a computer memory of the special quirks of the passengers on each steward's roster. He knows, for example, that Fernando is serving the lady who is allergic to garlic, or that Karl is handling the chap with the diabetic diet.

The bar manager and his 40 assistants serve up to 20,000 bottles of ales, wines and spirits every week. As in any hotel or restaurant, firm controls must be established to avoid staff pilferage in the bars. There have been a number of chief barmen of ships who have retired wealthy, not entirely because of wages and tips.

One chief barman liked to play pranks on his colleagues. When the ship's crew and junior officers would sign chits in the public rooms or their own mess, the barman would store them in a box. Rather than submit them to the purser's office, he would hold some back until he had amassed a substantial pile for each crew name. He would then advise a crew member that a backlog of several hundreds of dollars worth of chits had been "found." The ashen-faced seaman would beg the barman not to send them all to the purser at once. So the chits were phased through over a period of months, and the chief barman would exact favors from his victim.

An important but not so aggravating an area of the chief steward's world is cabin service. He has a head cabin steward plus at least 70 attendants who do the legwork. Each steward has a dozen passenger and officer cabins to clean, twice each day. The staterooms are made up each morning with a change of towels and linen, and the beds are turned down at night. The stewards, and in many cases stewardesses, are required to do everything — within the bounds of decency — that a passenger may ask for: laundry collection, room service, taking liquor orders and running special errands. They cook and deliver room service breakfasts.

The Cruise Director

The cruise director, from a passenger point of view, is the most prominent character aboard. Once the ship is sailing safely on course, and after the guests have been fed and comfortably housed, it then falls on this man's shoulders to make the vacation a truly memorable event. He is responsible for all entertainment and recreation. The cruise director is the master of ceremonies at all shipboard functions. At his command, entertainers are hired, fired or promoted.

When a director prepares a cruise, his charts resemble a plan for the invasion of Normandy. Listed are the dozen movies that will be offered in the cinema, the port lectures, and the addresses to be given by special guest speakers who may be along. With his hostess, the cruise director plans library hours, and bingo, bridge and other games. His athletic director helps to pencil in on the charts quoits, shuffleboard, golf lessons at the net, exercise classes, table tennis competitions, games in the swimming pool and trap shooting off the stern of the vessel.

The cruise director, his assistant and the stage manager plan the lounge entertainment. The ship has a resident band of 16 accomplished musicians. The full group performs nightly for major dances in the main lounge, and backs up the headlined show of the day. The musicians split into smaller groups for the late-night cabaret or private parties. There are featured male and female vocalists, a dance team and perhaps a magician, puppeteers, country-and-western singers or any of a wide variety of acts. On every ship, from cruise to cruise, the format is constantly changing.

As a cruise comes to an end, the cruise director and his principal assistants are found huddled in their office planning for the next trip. They know what will be available for entertainment, and from that base, they put together a cruise agenda. They plan activities for every minute of every day, they arrange a different featured show for every evening. The shows vary with the cruising area; on occasion, native bands are brought aboard at the ports for special evening performances: marimbas in Mexico, steel bands in the Caribbean, banjos in Alaska.

In the planning of cruise entertainment, careful note is made of upcoming holidays and special locales. Christmas brings a special show, New Year's Eve matches any celebration on land, and Easter brings gaily colored bonnets and songs of the season. When a ship crosses the equator, King Neptune makes a grand appearance. In waters where fish are plentiful, enterprising cruise directors pull out the fishing rods and hold a competition. Lines drop from the deck to the water, 75 feet below. Meanwhile, a ship's launch is waiting below to unhook the fish and rebait the line.

Every cruise has its theme dinners. Captain's Night starts with the welcome-aboard cocktail party and concludes with a formal session in the dining room. On Ladies' Night, the women order the wine, hold the chairs and select the dancing partners. On Fiesta Night, everyone dresses in tropical attire. On Pirates' Night, the ship is overrun by buccaneers. The evenings tend to be childish affairs, but the passengers seem to crave the fun — and cruise lines fill the demand. Some of the best shipboard entertainment events are put on by the crew, an anything-goes-Showboat-style performance in the Music Hall tradition. If the ship's company has representation from many cultures, ethnic music and dancing presentations may be offered.

There was an entertainment explosion in the cruise industry during the seventies. Instead of small combos and cruise staff presenting the nightly fare, numerous headline acts began to rotate through the ships of a given fleet. Today, many companies offer special cruises starring some of the biggest names in show business. Others promote theme cruises, featuring jazz, classical, country-and-western and other specialities, all headlined by highly talented performers. There is a small orchestra plus several smaller bands on every ship.

Princess Cruises has gained great public support for its full-scale musical productions, miniversions of some of Broadway's greatest musicals. The entire cruise staff of the company must display minimum standards of vocal, musical and dance abilities, and all headline performers, when they join the ship, know that they must also work in the feature productions. "Fiddler on the Roof" and a tribute to Cole Porter have been among the most acclaimed shows.

The Miami-based cruise lines often have several ships of one fleet cruising the Caribbean in close proximity to one another. This makes it possible to fly star entertainers from ship to ship, thereby maintaining variety. Royal Caribbean Cruise Line makes extensive use of helicopters to transport the entertainers.

Norwegian Caribbean Lines has a standard policy of name entertainers aboard the flagship *Norway*. Jack Jones, Phyllis Diller, Nipsey Russell, Pat Boone, Norm Crosby, Martin Mull, Charlie Callas and Rita Moreno are just a few of the celebrities who have appeared on the ship.

Royal Caribbean executive Rod McLeod says that the ships must cater to young and old, to just about every taste in every show — a strange combination of "Don't Sit under the Apple Tree" and disco. As the night wears on, the younger passengers predominate and the disco gradually takes over.

Norwegian American Cruises presented a "Whodunnit" special on a 1981 trans-Atlantic sailing of *Vistafjord*. Passengers were joined by a paroled bank robber, a police detective, a judge, a woman of mystery and an incorrigible crook. They all played parts in an audience participation crime re-enactment. Passengers heard lectures on law and order and even learned how to rob a bank.

The cruise lines' headquarters all have a large entertainment department. Policies and ideas are established as each company tries to get the edge on the competition. On the ship, the cruise director manages all events and performers.

The personality of the cruise director soon affects just about everyone on a ship. Most are entertaining masters of ceremonies, lively wits and personable companions, always quick to ask a lonely widow for a dance. They act as if powered by radar, detecting passengers who are not enjoying themselves. Most cruise directors are pleasant playboys. Their enthusiasm is usually infectious. After two days at sea, a good cruise director will own his passengers. A wink will bring a laugh, a suggestion will bring a song.

On one cruise, a director spotted an elderly lady sitting by herself outside the card room. He discovered that she was embarrassed by her bridge playing. The director chatted with her, learning that poker was her best game but that she had not been able to play since the death of her husband.

The cruise director then sought out the editor of the newspaper and they prepared an announcement for the next day. The paper asked poker players to report to the hostess at a set time. It was carefully stated that contestants would play for chips, with prizes to be awarded to the winners. The marathon lasted ten days. The widow in whose benefit the event was staged had the time of her life. There were four men and one other woman in the competition. And the poker-shy lady walked away with the top prize, valued at a hundred dollars.

Cruise directors are not always so capable. On one of the more prominent ships a few years ago, the director was so poor that passengers were embarrassed to attend a show. His jokes were stolen from books and were poorly told. His efforts at starting singalongs were so feeble that they would generate only a half-hearted response. But he was not fired for incompetence. It was discovered that he was a raving homosexual who, garbed in women's clothing, would intimidate junior crew members. When complaints finally reached the captain, the cruise director was immediately dropped at the next port. Homosexuality at sea is both commonplace and tolerated. As with all sexual activity among the crew, the ship demands only discretion.

The quality of entertainment has come a long way. John Martin, in recent years an assistant cruise director with Princess Cruises, remembers his late 1960s experience as cruise director of the Chandris liner *Australis* (now *Italis*). With a total staff of two hostesses and one three-man combo, Martin, himself a musician and entertainer, attempted to satisfy 2,500 passengers.

Things have changed.

6

The Palace Guards

The elite corps of a 30,000-ton modern cruise vessel is remarkably small. Those who wield any degree of influence, from casino manager to entertainment headliner, and from sous-chef to captain, number no more than 60. The remaining 440 are the workers who make everything happen. They can be separated into two groups: the seamen who work the ship, and the passenger service personnel.

Seamen and Other Laborers

Seamen handle the labor and trade specialties of the engine room and look after maintenance, safety, storerooms and general repairs. In most cases, they are career sailors and certified members of seafarers' unions in their home countries. Their foremen are the $20,000-a-year petty officers, the whip-crackers who usually have their own private mess. (Numerous nonseamen, but career-veteran personnel — sous-chefs, wine stewards and headwaiters — also enjoy the status of petty officers and all mess privileges.)

A major ship cruises fifty weeks of the year and spends two weeks in drydock for annual refit. Major work is done during this hiatus, but it actually represents only a small percentage of the annual maintenance workload. Maintenance is a continuous process, conducted according to a strict agenda every day of the year. In port, passengers will see seamen suspended over the side of the ship on ropes and platforms, retouching the whitewash. Railings are revarnished at sea, and occasionally open decks are sandblasted in preparation for a new coat of lacquer. A carpet crew come aboard at one port, recarpet an entire deck at sea, and get off at the next harbor. Norwegian Caribbean Lines boss Ron Zeller recalls the time he visited the dining area lavatory prior to dinner. Then he returned after the meal. "The washroom tiles had been replaced while I was eating."

The sailors tend to make a slightly higher base salary than do the rest of the crew, and their fringe benefits are decidedly more comfortable. But when it comes to living conditions, they are the bottom class aboard. Seamen are expected to be hardy. Instead of two-to-a-cabin comfort enjoyed by most of the crew, there may be three, four and even more sharing a cabin. They are, by virtue of their merchant marine status, subject to stricter discipline then are civilian crew.

Many countries (including Norway, Greece and Italy) have strict crew quotas as a condition of national registry. A company must employ a set percentage of nationals, and crew members are protected by the seafaring unions of their home country. It is for this reason that many cruise lines register their ships in Panama, Liberia and other less-then-fussy countries. There were howls of protest in England when Cunard registered its *Countess* and *Princess* in Nassau and a bitter debate when it was proposed that the same would be done with *Queen Elizabeth 2*. The change permits a firm to hire a lower salaried crew, but, to this date, the protest continues against Cunard, and *QE2* still retains her British registry.

Seamen's unions around the world protest what they view as the exploitation of Third World citizens. There are companies that are notorious for such exploitative practices, and no firm has an entirely clean record here. People from Indonesia, Central America, Mexico, India, and the Cayman Islands and other poor Caribbean communities will work for a fraction of what the international seafaring unions demand. One company paid its Central American crew base wages in 1981 of as low as $110 per month, although the firm argued that with overtime the average salary was $400 a month, plus all living expenses paid for.

Holland America carries on a century-old tradition of employing natives of Indonesia. P&O continues with its generations-old practice of employing Goanese, from the tiny former district in Portuguese India, on the Arabian Sea. The motivation of the shipping companies was, and to some extent remains, to cut crew costs. Meanwhile, it has become a high honor among the people of these countries to be selected to work on the ships. There are many hundreds of people waiting for each job opening. When the seamen from Indonesia or from Goa retire to their native societies after a career at sea, they are considered wealthy citizens. P&O in 1982 is at a crossroads. In the company's Princess fleet the dining rooms of two of the ships have been staffed by Italians. On *Sun Princess*, Goanese served the passengers. The Goanese are friendly, cheerful and more dedicated than most stewards, but they are not as much fun and not as professional as the Italians. Passenger comparisons forced P&O to change. In late 1981, *Sun Princess* welcomed a dining room team of Italians into its crew. The Goanese were absorbed into other jobs with the cruise line, unhappily losing the prosperity of gratuities. P&O's principal cruise executive, Len Scott, genuinely fond of the Goanese tradition, says it was a sad decision. In 1982, the P&O Cruises fleet (apart from the Princess subsidiary) retain the Goanese, but increasing sophistication will likely demand changes as the years go by.

Other labor on a cruise ship, aside from the 125 seamen and civilians who work in the storerooms, is composed principally of those who toil in the ship's galleys: dishwashers, cooks, deck-swabbers and general laborers. Most of these people are pursuing a cooking career, hoping to rise to higher paying positions in the future. There are ships on which dining room staff share some of their tips with the galley hands, but they are rare. On one vessel, the dining room and cabin attendants put 25 cents per passenger per day into a general fund administered by the maître d' and the chief cabin steward. The contribution is made whether the passengers tip or not. The kitty is subdivided according to a point system, with senior galley staff earning more than their juniors; for the average junior, it can generate more than $200 a month in extra income.

The average total income enjoyed throughout the industry in 1981 by seamen and nontipped labor was about $700 to $800 per month. This included the base pay for a 70-hour work week (seven ten-hour days) plus overtime. All living expenses are paid. There is a lengthy annual leave (up to two months), with air fares paid by the companies. Although the total income is taxed, by the home country, true tax advantages are enjoyed. All personal living expenses, a good portion of clothing costs, and home travel expenses are tax free.

Stewards and Stewardesses

The people who make or break a cruise, from a passenger point of view, are those up front delivering the service in the dining room, the lounges and the cabins. They are often the wealthiest people aboard. Except on rare occasions, the stewards or stewardesses are unmarried and free of financial commitments. They are in pursuit of short-term and highly profitable adventure, not a career.

The cabin and dining room stewards are subdivided into about 35 two-member teams. Each cabin pair caters to about 15 staterooms, and the dining room pairs each serve 30 passengers, in two separate sittings. A portion of the service contingent is assigned to the crew's, petty officers' and officers' messes, usually on a rotating basis. The steward exclusively assigned to the captain enjoys the highest status among the service personnel. Captains are pampered with valet, food and catering services almost beyond imagination.

The stewards are usually effervescent personalities who labor diligently on behalf of their wards, always with the tip at the end of the cruise in mind. A move away from the traditional steward-busboy teams in the dining room is gaining popularity in the industry. The more modern approach is to have two stewards of equal stature and uniform, at least in the passengers' eyes, although one will be the senior ultimately responsible for the table. It gives the maître d's more flexibility assigning staff. They place an extrovert with an introvert, one with an excellent command of English with one less able to converse, or one with a high level of food knowledge with one who has a flair for service and presentation. In the steward-busboy situation, the steward takes about two-thirds of the tips paid by the passengers; in the equality approach, the split is equal.

Lounge stewards, whose gratuities come drink by drink and chit by chit, are solo performers. There are about forty on a ship divided among eight bars and several shifts. A watering hole is open on most ships for all but two or three hours of a 24-hour day. Lounge stewards are called upon to serve at cocktail parties — both official ship functions and private affairs held by passengers — in addition to their regular duties. On major occasions, such as the captain's welcome party, most of the ship's stewards are assembled in the main lounge.

Increasingly, young women are being hired as lounge and cabin stewardesses, but they rarely appear in the dining room. Maître d's are of the opinion that women lack the necessary authority, the polish or the calm professionalism they seek. Asked about the discrimination, one maître d' snapped, "Women are too noisy. They clank things around and gossip to each other rather than doing their jobs."

Dining room stewards who intend to stay in the cruise business aspire to become headwaiters or wine stewards. Food and cabin stewards can expect to earn $20,000 or more yearly, mostly from gratuities. Wine stewards can earn $25,000. Headwaiters, with much higher base salaries, each captain a dining room section. They handle complaints and special food requests, and often prepare flambés at table side, or desserts such as crêpes suzette. Most headwaiters earn about $30,000 yearly. A good maître d', enjoying senior officer status and salary, as well as tips, earns in excess of $40,000 annually. Lounge stewards and bartenders earn about the same as their dining room and cabin colleagues. Often, they develop tip-pooling arrangements. All personnel who enjoy cash tips declare this income for tax purposes . . . according to conscience.

The service staff of a ship is hired through European personnel agencies or catering companies. Applicants have a variety of reasons for signing on, usually just a desire to travel. Service employees are signed to contracts ranging from six to eight months, with the provision that the company will pay the air fare back home at the conclusion of the term. If an employee signs off before the contract period has terminated, the company is under no obligation to cover travel expenses and, in some instances, the cruise line is in a position to deduct the cost of transportation to the ship from the final paycheck.

Service staff and others on the ship covered by contract have no vacation provisions. They can negotiate separate deals for themselves if they wish to sign a second agreement at the termination of the first one. It is common for a steward, at the end of his first term, to sign a new contract. A deal may be struck that a paid vacation home will be offered after the second term, with air fare back to the ship if there is to be a third term. At sea, service staff work seven-day weeks, occasionally enjoying a free morning or other period. When the ship is in port, they are given shore time only after various tasks have been performed.

Employees who choose not to renew a contract are normally removed from the roster. If they wish to return to sea at a later date, they will likely have to return to the original hiring agency and proceed from scratch.

The Working Vacationers

The lure of adventure attracts large numbers of civilian employees to the sea. Aside from the department managers, the majority of purser's clerks, hostesses, entertainers and concession workers are in the business only for short-terms experience. Many of them enjoy a lifestyle similar to that of the passengers. They work exceptionally hard and long hours, but the experience and the exotic destinations make it all worthwhile. Contracts are for six months or longer, and are renewable.

The ship's resident musicians are hired under contracts similar to those for other civilian employees. They are paid salaries of $800 to $1,000 monthly — about the same as hostesses and clerical people make. Bandleaders earn more. All the resident civilians live in crew quarters and dine in the crew mess.

The visiting entertainers — the showtime headliners — fare much better. There was a time when the industry could attract superbly talented people for a modest rate. Even stars could be lured to sea with the offer of a free cruise. But the cruise market is so competitive today that entertainers can command fees resembling what they would be paid ashore. The stars are housed in passenger cabins and they are fed in the main dining room. They are expected to buy their own wine and drinks in the public rooms, but passengers invariably look after most of this expense.

The clerical personnel in the purser's office, the editor of the ship's newspaper and the printer are also aboard more for the fun of it than for a career.

The editor is often a young student with an eye toward a journalistic career. It is a busy job. Funnelled to him through the purser's office come all announcements that must be brought to the attention of the passengers. The job involves a daily trip to the radio office to obtain world news highlights, and then the editing of the material to fit space available. There is also a daily meeting with the cruise director, when the editor receives the next day's agenda. Prior to each cruise season, the editor researches historical and geographical features of upcoming ports of call.

Most of the modern cruise lines have sophisticated offset printing equipment on their ships for the publication of the newspaper and the preparation of daily menus. The newspaper is a high-class job, eagerly sought by passengers each day.

One young editor, while his ship docked at Leningrad, added a brief editorial to the front page of his newspaper: "We are proud, today, to be publishing the only free newspaper for thousands of miles in many directions through the Communist world."

The Subterranean World

Every ship has two worlds. Passengers see just one.

From the cocktail lounge over the bridge, to the sports decks, promenade deck, public rooms and four decks of passenger accommodation through the vessel, the ship is a floating gallery of art, expensively furnished, panelled and carpeted. For the passenger, that is the ship.

Behind an array of "No Admittance" signs, from the top of the ship to the bottom, private companionways permit crew members to roam the many decks without ever encountering a passenger. Off the lobbies of the lowest passenger deck are doors marked "Crew Only." They lead to the subterranean world.

Through these doors and one flight down, the carpeting disappears. The lowest two decks house all but a handful of the ship's company. The walls of the hallways and the cabins are painted marine steel, sometimes decorated by crew members to improve their own environment. The cabins surround other belowdecks facilities: the laundry, the print shop, the quartermaster's stores, the crew's mess, gym and bar, and the engine room at the stern.

A descending passenger finds the change in atmosphere

dramatic. Noise levels are higher. At first glance, the setting appears squalid. At a second glance it is not squalid — clean but spartan. Crew members in various states of dress or undress are dashing about in all directions. Dozens of languages are heard reverberating off the steel walls and creating an echo-chamber effect. The same staff who are so immaculate and polite in passenger areas, are zipping around in T-shirts or stripped to the waist, laughing, joking and going about their business. It is their home.

A typical crew cabin is not much more than two bunks (upper and lower) against the wall, a tiny couch, a table and a wash basin. In some otherwise identical cabins, a third bunk has been added. Older ships have cabins for eight or twelve, and the seamen's home is a bunk and a locker. In all crew quarters, communal toilets and showers are scattered throughout.

Men and women live in the same area. Romance between crew members is actively discouraged, but when it happens . . . it happens. Regulations vary within the industry, but most companies are rather tolerant. In rare cases a man and woman are permitted to share a cabin. Washroom facilities are segregated by sex. On ships with very few women in the crew, romance regulations are the strictest and the women often enjoy private cabins.

Quality of facilities varies according to a person's rank and stature. Junior officers living in crew quarters have private cabins. An assistant cruise director enjoys the same treatment. Cabin accommodation is based on a combination of seniority, crew preference and ship contingencies. Individuals who have been with the ship the longest have the best chances for quieter bunks. Those who have just joined on may be perched on top of the engines. Camaraderie among employees of a department is encouraged by cabin pairing, and an effort is made to pair dining room steward teams. However, in order to keep the peace, it is also desirable to accommodate cabin partnership wishes when possible.

The decor of individual cabins ranges from exceptionally pleasant to positively horrid, depending on the taste and efforts of its occupants. The cruise lines attempt to make the cabins as cheerful as possible, with drapes and carpeting, but the residents are the real decorators. Some cabins have beautiful hooked rugs on the floors, others a week's dirty laundry.

Crew members are required to keep their quarters tidy and to follow regulations for laundry calls, but enforcement is rather informal.

Generally, crew quarters leave the impression of being the world's largest novelty shops, with trinkets and tokens of ports of call adorning every corner. There is no shortage of stereophonic equipment, all bargains purchased at various free ports. At night, the cross fire of loud music and vocal arrangements in many languages can be truly bewildering.

Increasingly, husband-and-wife teams are found working on a ship. Usually, such a team is the result of a shipboard romance, but occasionally couples do apply and are hired as a team. Among these was a young couple in Finland who had itchy feet. The husband, an airline steward, led an interesting life, but his wife was bored with her secretarial duties. Day after day, as she drove to work, she passed a huge cruise ship under construction. By the time the name *Royal Viking Sea* was painted on the ship's stern, husband and wife were excitedly talking about a career on a cruise ship. They wrote an application to Royal Viking Line and were hired; she became a cabin stewardess, he went to work in a lounge. For months at at time they rarely saw each other — she worked days and he worked nights. They were housed in a tiny two-bunk cabin. The top bunk was for storage.

Many Cultures

A cruise vessel is a cosmopolitan world. The ethnic mix of the crew incorporates diverse cultures; in one extreme case, 28 nationalities were represented by the dining room staff alone. Officers and seamen tend to be from the country in which the ship is registered, service staff from one or two ethnic groupings. The recreational and entertainment staffs vary according to the nature and locales of the cruise.

Life belowdecks is a reflection of the cultures aboard. The different groupings stick together and their social activities centre around the music and the humor and the nostalgia of the home country. Food served in the crew mess caters to many nationalities, with a strong leaning toward the tastes of the largest contingent aboard.

108

The laundry concession is almost universally manned by Chinese employees of a large company based in Hong Kong. It is rare for any of the dozen launderers, except the foreman, to speak a word of a language other than the native tongue. These men live together in a special section of the ship and cook their own favorite meals.

Goanese on P&O vessels enjoy total cultural autonomy. The majority of them are Roman Catholic, and their quarters feature a small shrine. They also have a private galley, where the scent of curry emanates at all times to engulf most of the ship's lower decks. The top Goanese on board holds the position of *Serang*. There is one *Serang* for the deck crew and another for the service staff; through these representatives, the officers instruct, control and discipline the Goanese society aboard.

When a ship is in port it is not uncommon for the Chinese and Goanese, among other crewmen, to barter for livestock ashore. Rookie crew members get quite a shock when they casually stroll down a corridor to be greeted by a stray chicken, sheep or pig. The animals are slaughtered for food and, with some religious groups, for ceremonial purposes.

Men (of both sexes) and Women

The vast majority of crew members are young, virile and active. Sex is not only a focal point of shipboard conversation, it can be something of an obsession. Ship regulations, varying from company to company, attempt to discourage romance among crew members for the most basic of reasons: entanglements cause trouble. The task isn't as difficult as one might expect; many crew members, after all, are at sea to escape various forms of involvement.

Residents of passenger vessels are rather liberated individuals. The close quarters of accommodation produce a family-like atmosphere, enhanced by the communal washroom facilities. There is an air of detachment from the world, which reduces levels of inhibition. Nude beach parties in tropical zones are always on the agenda, and only a few individuals decline an invitation.

A persistent problem is the communal cabin accommodation. When one resident has some action going, the roommate must go elsewhere. Various systems of codes are employed. On some occasions, a crew member will rent his room to another for money or other favors.

It's difficult to keep anything secret on a ship. One chap who had been asked by his roommate to vacate at a certain hour, did so without question — after he had planted a tape recorder under the bottom bunk. The roomie soon arrived with a young beauty parlor attendant.

Later, at the crew bar and before assorted colleagues, the tape recorder dutifully repeated the full event, delighting the audience with the final few comments.

"Boy — that was quick," the girl muttered.

He sighed. "Yeah . . . well you really turned me on."

"I didn't have time to do a damn thing!"

Homosexuality is not so much a problem as it is a fact of life in the cruise industry. Some ships rigidly try to control it, but when large numbers of service staff are hired sight unseen, the situation is unavoidable. The percentage of gays in a staff can be extremely high among the men.

One gay steward explained it this way:

"The cruise ship is one area where we can be ourselves, and not feel threatened. It is an escape from the street, in many ways comfortable where the world is hostile and uncomfortable. It is as basic as feeling accepted where you are."

Ships with small homosexual populations can't really credit the situation to good management. The gays of the business have little interest in ships where they will be considered oddities. Once a ship reaches a point where a large portion of the men are homosexuals, it can be assured that the percentage will rise dramatically as time goes on. Friends lobby on behalf of friends, stories circulate throughout the world, and the personnel companies become unknowing agents.

It is really of little consequence. Crew members don't pass moral judgment on one another. The sight of two men dancing at a party or embracing on a couch or holding hands in a corridor doesn't shock too many employees. There are many gay partnerships sharing cabins. The only disturbing aspect of the situation is that the more effeminate homosexuals may be extremely bitchy, jealous of their mates and demanding. Arguments and fights are disruptive to every member of the crew.

The straights of the crew, particularly the Goanese and Chinese, are God's gift to the whorehouses of the port towns. One seaman boasts regularly that he plans to title his biography, "Cathouses from Singapore to Santiago." He will list prices and compare food service, drinks and girls, using a ratings system similar to the famed Michelin restaurant guide.

Possibly the favorite port in the world for ships' crews is Acapulco, where a cavalcade of taxis waits at the ready to transport seafarers to the pleasure palaces. The most luxurious bawdy house is *Quinta Rebecca*, a mansion high on a hill. But *La Huerta*, a large motel enclosing a central courtyard and restaurant, is a veritable industry. Customers can go to these facilities simply to drink or to purchase the various pleasures. Those short of cash but high on courage can journey to what the Mexicans call their Red Light District. On both sides of a bumpy dirt road, lines of females, from young children to senior citizens, stand in front of shacks, waiting to give pleasure for negotiable fees. The price can be very reasonable.

About three-quarters of a ship's company are restricted to the two-deck living area for their entire free time. Only the top entertainers, the officers, the cruise director's key people and a few concession employees can drink in the public areas and attend passenger functions.

Night time is always lively. The crew get around their restrictions with enthusiasm. Everyone manages to smuggle some booze on board from the free ports, and more bottles are obtained through nefarious means from the bar staff. The crew bar has a supply of alcohol, but it is controlled by the officers. There are drinking restrictions on most ships, and the bar is one area where they can be enforced.

Private parties are in progress in various cabins, with stereos blasting and participants crammed into the tiny rooms like college students hitting a phone booth in the heyday of that craze. On most evenings, some kind of party is going in the crew bar. At least once a week, a spontaneous gathering erupts, eventually involving just about every member of the crew.

Things get going about 10 p.m., when the dining room staff is finally through for the day. From that time on, constant reinforcements arrive as different groups come off shift. As the bars close, from 11 p.m. until 3 a.m., the stragglers pick up the momentum. The parties feature dancing and singing in many languages. Often musicians from the ship's band and featured entertainers come down to join the revelry when their duties are completed in the passenger areas. The "Queen Bees," the more notorious of the gay fraternity, are prominent at the parties, dressed in drag and often with their "children" in tow.

If the social life lacks anything on a ship, it is variety. Parties are always going, with singsongs and assorted merriments, but one night runs into the next and the hangovers seem to be very much the same as the days go by. The one challenge to break the monotony is the chase of female passengers, a sport ardently pursued by many crew members, particularly those in contact with passengers in their daily work. It can bring fine adventure, as numerous ship regulations have to be overcome to bring it off successfully.

Discipline

All crew members are expected to be fully aware of the ship's rules and regulations. These cover everything from the clothing to be worn in public areas to the booze that can be consumed in the course of a day. The officers are usually tolerant in the administering of most rules, and turn a blind eye to others, but a few regulations are rigidly enforced. An employee who insults a passenger will be immediately dismissed, in most cases, unless the explanation is satisfactory. If a cabin steward makes advances to a female passenger in her cabin, and it is reported, the steward will be out of a job. Unreported — most of the time — such advances have led to extracurricular income. In port, crew members who go ashore have a definite curfew hour, and an officer is at the gangway to log the time of arrival back. Late arrival brings punishment of one kind or another, and if a sailor misses the ship he may find himself out of a job and faced with the expense of travelling on elsewhere. At the very best, travel to meet the ship at the next port will be at his own expense.

Punishment can take many forms: extra tours of duty, cancelled shore leave at an upcoming port (a tragedy at Acapulco), additional lifeboat drills and, often, fines collected through payroll deduction.

112

7

The Resident Merchants

Cruise companies are unsurpassed in their particular fields of expertise: ship design, passenger service, food, recreation and entertainment. There are, however, a few peripheral areas where it makes more business sense to farm out the work to companies equally professional in their own areas. On most ships, there are several concession operations, which rent space from the cruise line and kick back a percentage of their gross sales.

In most specialty areas, a relative handful of large corporations dominate the concessions in the cruise industry. When a cruise company requires a concessionaire for a specific service, advertisements are run in trade publications, and several firms bid for the work. The contract is awarded to the company that offers the best combination of financial rewards and quality workmanship. The cruise line usually owns all of the equipment involved, and its use is part of the rental package, along with expenses for the care and feeding of the concessionaires' employees.

The concession holders hire and train their own staff for the seafaring life. In some instances, the managers have a full run of the ship, eating with passengers and enjoying the entertainment. More frequently, however, the concession employees enjoy the same status and live with the same restrictions as ordinary ship's crew.

There is a trend in the industry for the cruise lines to take ownership of and direct charge over the concessions. Carnival Cruises owns and operates every service on the ship. The company says that this is a more profitable route, that there is a greater degree of control over the revenue-producing facilities and staff. Yet having totally abandoned concessions, Carnival is now considering bringing back the Chinese launderers; company management of the washers and dryers has proven to be more expensive and less efficient. Many of the cruise companies with shipboard slot machines now own and operate their own; the cost, from the Bally corporation and other manufacturers, ranges from $3,000 to $6,000 per unit.

P&O's Len Scott resolutely defends the use of concessionaires. "We are experts in passenger shipping and we must therefore presume that other companies are more professional in their area of operation, whether it be beauty parlors or retail shops," Scott says. P&O's Princess subsidiary even uses a private Italian catering firm, based in Genoa, for its galley and dining room operations. The Cunard Line also remains enthusiastic about its concessionaires. Among concessions on *Queen Elizabeth 2* are a flower shop and a branch of Barclay's Bank, offering the best shipboard currency exchange rates and financial services in the industry.

The Casino

Gambling casinos from Las Vegas to London are generally controlled by a government-appointed commission, to ensure that the games are honest. But shipboard casinos are entirely uncontrolled, a situation that could raise some concern were it not for the fact that complaints are extremely rare. Carnival Cruises president Mickey Arison explains that a company would be extremely foolish to tamper with the games. "It pays you to run a fair game, because you are going to win anyway."

Most of the ships at sea have banks of slot machines. Full-scale casinos, with blackjack, roulette and other games, are less common. Ships of Norwegian registry are by law not permitted to offer any gambling beyond slot machines. And the Norwegian Royal Viking Line refuses to have anything to do with any form of gambling. Says its president, Warren Titus, "Slot machines are not the kind of image we try to project."

Where casinos are operated by concessionaires, the ships sign a contract with the London sporting clubs or other shore-based gambling centres. The casino staff are on the home payroll of the concessionaire. A small bank of 40 slot machines generates action of up to $750,000 per month and a gross profit, before staff costs, approaching $100,000. This is split between the cruise line and the concession.

The Photographers

Ship's photographers are a unique species, dedicated to upholding a longstanding tradition of being as weird as possible. Three or four companies throughout the world have the industry's photo concessions virtually in their grips. The photographers' talents range from adequate to good.

When a passenger walks up the gangway at the start of a cruise, the welcome aboard comes in the form of a flash in the face. The next night, as every passenger queues up to shake the captain's hand, the photographers are clicking away at machine-gun speed. The same kind of scene recurs numerous times during a trip. A passenger on a shore excursion may be climbing a national monument in a foreign land, then turns around to find the same smiling photographer. He snaps once again, and then scurries off to catch another passenger in a proper pose. Late some night, a passenger dressed like Captain Hook and staggering, will be greeted by a photographer who gives permanence to the questionable moment.

It takes only a day or so for the passengers to get the idea. Two days into the cruise, along a public corridor, several hundred identical color photographs are posted — gangway scenes with only the faces changing from picture to picture. They are for sale. From that point on, a different picture selection is posted daily.

There are two and sometimes three photographers on each ship. They share a cabin in crew quarters but tend to be a social unit entirely unto themselves. Public areas of the ship are off limits to them from the point of view of personal socializing, but their lucrative work keeps them visible most of the time. Passenger quarters are also off limits, but the photographers' pursuit of women passengers finds them there most of the time.

Cruise passengers inevitably carry their own cameras, but it's difficult to get someone to snap husband and wife posing with the captain. The ship's photography team operates under the proven principle that everyone wants a shot of the romantic gangway moment, of themselves with the captain and of themselves winning a spot dance prize or caught during some other memorable occasion.

The photographers, employees of large firms such as Trans-Oceanic Photos of New York, work at a frenetic pace, shooting and processing up to 5,000 photos weekly. The pictures are sold to passengers for about four dollars each. Based on an industry average, about 40 per cent of photos taken are sold during a cruise, but on successful voyages the figure can be as high as 70 per cent. The photographers work on a straight commission of 20 per cent of the gross revenue and can earn a handsome annual income. The shipboard photolabs have sophisticated equipment, designed for speed if not top quality.

Passengers experience tremendous difficulties with their own cameras. Ship's photographers are greeted by daily parades of Instamatic owners. One lady, after a shore excursion, brought her camera to the photo shop. It was hopelessly jammed with sand and beyond repair. The lady left it with the photographer, who placed it on a back shelf. The next day, another woman came in with an identical Instamatic camera, but the problem was quite minor. The photographer retired to the back of the shop, returning with the sand-clogged instrument.

Before the woman's startled eyes, he picked up a hammer and savagely pounded the camera. It was shattered beyond recognition. He gathered the pieces and offered them to the customer.

"There. That should fix it," he said deadpan. The woman rushed from the shop in horror. The little joke took a great deal of explaining.

The most common question fielded by the resident professionals is, "Where do *you* send your film for processing?"

"The lost city of Atlantis, Ma'am," is the common reply.

One ship's photographer said his strangest request came from a man who offered him $100 for a special assignment. The passenger had been married, for the third time, just that day. The ship was about to embark on the couple's honeymoon cruise, and the groom asked the photographer to cover the first marital roll in the sack — a request gleefully accommodated.

A group of photographers on a ship regularly cruising out of New York to the Caribbean invented a speed test game. The race was to see who could make the first conquest among each new crop of female passengers. At first, it was considered to be a feat if the act could take place by the time the ship reached Bermuda. With each new sailing, however, new records were set. Eventually, a proud seaman was to emerge from a lady's cabin four hours after embarkation, to win the awe and

116

admiration of his colleagues. (By this time, the game had been enthusiastically taken up by other quarters of the ship.)

A crew member remarked one day that the ultimate achievement would be to seduce and physically entertain a passenger between the time the ship left dock at New York and the moment it passed under the Verrazano Narrows Bridge, with the Statue of Liberty in the background. And who, but a photographer, could perform such a remarkable feat?

One day, as a smart looking passenger came up the gangway, the photographer snapped her picture. He offered to help her with her hand luggage and to escort her to the cabin. She graciously accepted. Inside, he took her photo again while he continued the conversation. He suggested a splendid way to launch the cruise. After a few jokes, she agreed. She was more than startled when he jumped off the bed at the conclusion of the act, shot a quick picture, pulled on his clothes and madly dashed out of the cabin. As he emerged on deck, witnessed by several crew members, the Verrazano Narrows Bridge was about to pass over the bow.

The Ship's Shops

The number of retail shops on a ship varies from one small boutique to a full array of elaborate stores. A range of duty-free items is offered to passengers, from the inevitable heaps of souvenirs to fine crystal and china. Large quantities of clothing are sold. The use of the words "duty free" is rather liberal. While an item is duty free to the retailer, the price indicates that the entire saving is not passed on to the customer. Usually operated by large shoreside concessionaires, the shops offer a selection of artifacts and handicrafts from the cruising area; for example: seal fur and hematite jewellery (Alaska), wood carvings (Central America) and silverware, woollen ponchos and print shirts (Mexico).

The shops stock all expected sundries: sunglasses, suntan lotion, shaving gear, cosmetics, and so on. There are bathing suits in a limited size range and selection, expensive watches and jewellery. One shop manager said the most expensive item he ever sold was a lady's diamond-studded watch, priced at $4,800.

Women are by far the biggest buyers. The first few days are busy, with small items such as suntan lotion being sold, plus a great deal of browsing going on. The middle of the cruise, when passengers do most of their shopping ashore, is very quiet. Business perks up near the end of the trip, with a high percentage of total gross sales being rung up during the final two days.

One store manager had a rather embarrassing moment one afternoon early in a cruise when his store was packed with customers. A gentleman asked if there were any more bathing suits, other than those on display. The manager recalled that his new order had contained a box of suits. His assistant was dispatched to retrieve the box from the storage area. When the box arrived, it was dropped in the middle of the crowded shop. The top was clearly stamped: "Bathing Suits — Men." He tore it open, and a number of people looked in at the same time. The box contained the flimsiest of female lingerie — dozens of sexy mini-bras and panties in various enticing designs.

"That isn't quite what I'm looking for," the customer advised the embarrassed manager, as the audience collapsed in laughter.

Store hours aboard ship are irregular. While in port, the shop is closed, completely, because of its duty-free status. If goods were sold, sales duty would have to be paid to the country in which the ship is docked.

The younger the passenger contingent, the better the store sales will be. A successful ship's shop grosses about $10,000 weekly.

Hairdressing and Beauty Salon

The women who run the ship's beauty salon are often great sailors who spend years at sea. There are a number of beauty firms that cater to the shipping industry, many of them extensions of large beauty parlor chains in Britain, the United States or the ship's country of registry. The staff, generally made up of a manager and five assistants, are fully qualified hairdressers who are also trained to cut men's hair. A ship's beauty shop has numerous chairs and dryers for women, and one barber's chair discreetly tucked into another section, away from the odors of the various hair chemicals.

118

Staff normally sign on with a one-year contract, after which their employer flies them home for a holiday. If they wish to remain — and most of them do — they are flown back after their vacation. The beauty staff members are among the most lively individuals aboard, participating in crew shows for the passengers and in nearly every belowdecks activity. They seem to enjoy the close-knit family atmosphere of the ship, the travel and the adventure.

A problem in the beauty concession is that all the women passengers converge at once. The ship's newspaper advises that a special formal function will be on a certain night, and all the ladies will attempt to get fixed-up for the occasion. It's impossible to accommodate all; the best advice is to inquire about important shipboard events at the start of the cruise (the beauty parlor staff will know), and to advance book on day one all the appointments desired. An appointment can be cancelled later, with no bad conscience on the eve of important functions, because the waiting list is substantial.

Sauna, Massage and Health Club

Most ships today feature a sauna and massage facility, frequently contracted to a private operator. The turnover of masseuses tends to be rapid, with shoreside firms offering the job to staff members as something of a reward. There are separate facilities for male and female passengers.

It's always a popular facility. The two women who do the massages are thoroughly professional, and the fees charged are modest. Many people just take advantage of the saunas, which are free on most ships, without enjoying a massage.

There was a scandal on one shipping line not many years ago. A clergyman decided to go for a massage. After his rubdown, clad only in a towel, he entered the sauna. A few minutes later his masseuse, now totally nude, followed him inside, suggesting that for an extra fee her service could be more thorough. The clergyman quickly departed and dressed, immediately complaining to the purser. The two women in the sauna were dismissed and sent from the ship at the next port. Their company faced the responsibility of getting them back home, and the firm later lost the contract to serve the cruise line.

The captain of the ship ordered a thorough investigation into how long the small-scale whorehouse had been operating. Through a series of interviews with crew members and some passengers (well known to the company) who had signed massage charges on their bills, it was determined that the business had boomed for several weeks.

The clergyman's was the first complaint.

The Laundry

The most fascinating society on a ship is formed by the group who toil in its bowels, washing thousands of articles of clothing, bedding and linen each week. Most of the cruisers are serviced by a Hong Kong-based firm. A normal ship contingent numbers about 12, only one of whom need have the ability to converse in broken English.

It is always a hot, uncomfortable, steamy environment. Once the hotel manager and the laundry manager agree to terms of service, no member of the ship's personnel interferes in its operations. The laundry handles more than 20 tons of washing and dry cleaning in a week. Towels and sheets are replaced on a regular basis in the 550 cabins. Linen is changed constantly in the dining room and lounges. The wash flows in from galley staff, officers, crew and passengers. It is efficiently laundered, dry cleaned and pressed, before being packaged and returned back up to daylight.

A visitor to this world within a world, through the steam and sweat of the environment, will see a half-dozen smiling Chinese workers bowing a greeting and then continuing with their work. When they are off duty, they live apart, entertaining one another and preparing their own food.

Through the laundry go jewels, silverware and money. The staff is scrupulously honest. Passengers often find their wash returned with money pinned to the back — bills that had been left in the pockets. When something valuable is missing and a suggestion is made that it might be in the laundry, the machines all stop and the launderers search every item in their massive inventory.

They work on short-term contracts, as long as one year at a stretch before being flown back to Hong Kong by their employer. After a brief vacation, they are reassigned to another ship or, if a vacancy exists, back to the original. Frequently, the Hong Kong managers use a platoon approach. A team of 12 will work one ship for a year, then take a one-month vacation. They are relieved by another platoon starting a one-year assignment. When the holiday is over, the original group is assigned to relieve another team on a new ship.

Shore Excursions

In recent years, fewer and fewer companies have been bringing aboard outside travel consultants to run the tour packages ashore — either the day trips offered when a ship is in port, or the multi-day overland journeys built in to a cruise package. It once was common for land-based travel experts to work the ships. Today, however, the purser's office generally acts as a commissioned sales agent for different tour operators in various ports of call. And, for more sophisticated multi-night shore packages, many cruise companies have their own travel subsidiaries.

Shore trips can be harrowing experiences. Mexican air-conditioned buses are remarkably similar to non-air-conditioned vehicles operating elsewhere. The roads, like the one ascending from Acapulco toward the interior, can be frightening. There are always bumps and jolts, plus occasional mechanical breakdowns. Tropical climates can bring monsoons and, with the rain, mud to mire the buses. Passengers are always warned what to expect and advised to wear sturdy walking shoes. Women persist in stepping off the ship in heels.

One recent and eventful cruise trip offered exciting shore packages to South American destinations that involved bus and air travel. The plane trips were from spartan strips in the port towns to bumpy dirt runways in the mountains — or in the middle of jungles. The two aircraft were DC-3s: freighters with seats hastily snapped inside. Primitive is an overstatement for the accommodation offered. When the ship's passengers arrived for their flight, they saw a youngster on the wing of the aircraft measuring the fuel contents with a dip stick. Coca-Cola was served by the co-pilots during the flight. At the destination, the pilots and co-pilots of the two DC-3s caused further concern when they started dismantling an engine on one of the aircraft.

A typical chef's buffet — something delicious for everyone.

Enormous quantities of food are consumed on each trip. The vast amount of frozen meat shown here won't even cover a single lunch on the QE2 where this photo was taken.

One place where too many cooks *don't* spoil the broth! Gleaming modern galleys and huge staffs are required to cope with dozens of choices offered each day. A typical 14 day cruise can consume 50 tons of food!

Getting the food to hungry passengers and serving it with style
keeps the waiters busy and the passengers happy.

Whether eating formally in the dining room or casually at a poolside buffet, good food and good companions to share your table are a big part of everyone's happy cruise memories.

8

The Cargo:
80 Tons of People

A veteran captain once described his difficulties this way:

"The problem with a passenger ship is that your cargo is walking around all the time."

It was an understated way of describing the behavior of the passenger population. Although every customer is unique, there is a common factor: all have paid $150 per day or more for the privilege of being aboard a cruise ship. By the time liquor and sundries purchases — and tips — are added to the bill, a couple will spend $2,700 for a week. The price commands a high level of service.

Most passengers are a pleasure to serve. They are eager, happy and undemanding. Every ship's steward will confirm that those who are the most pleasant are also the most generous with their gratuities. The complainers, who demand so much, are rarely willing to give anything of themselves. Few people are disappointed by what they receive. Before making the substantial investment they did some investigating. They knew what to expect, and what they find on the ship usually exceeds the promises made by the promotional brochures.

Friendships develop between the passengers and their dining room stewards. Long conversations are held daily with a favorite bartender. The social hostess becomes a foster parent to a good many children. Long after the cruise has ended, post cards and letters are exchanged between crew and passengers. Crew members have friends in just about every port of the globe, and they regularly visit the homes of former clientele.

THE CAPTAIN'S TABLE

The greatest honor a ship can bestow on a passenger, at least in terms of high-seas tradition, is an invitation to dine with the captain. Procedures for seatings at the captain's table differ widely. On some ships, the master hosts a new group every night. On others, the captain and senior officers dine together. The latter arrangement may occur if the captain has difficulties with the majority of languages spoken, or it may be because the cruise line believes that no passenger will be offended if none is honored.

The usual policy at sea is for the captain to select a group of eight to twelve passengers who will be at his table throughout the cruise. Although the choice of companions is exclusively that of the master, he selects his table from a "commend list" prepared at the corporate headquarters. The company determines who the VIPs aboard will be: wealthy businessmen, show business celebrities, major travel agents, prominent journalists or passengers who have done substantial business with the line. As the master studies the list, he may spot the name of an old friend and invite that person to join the table. If a single woman is invited, an effort is made to find a single man, for balance. When the table choices are not obvious, invitations are often extended to the passengers occupying the ship's deluxe suites. The invitation is not a command request. There are many celebrities who want peace and seclusion on a cruise. If the captain's invitation is turned down, no offense is taken. To be on the "commend list" does more than assist the captain in choosing his table. The list is posted in every bar and public room, and cabin stewards are advised to give a little extra to those named on it. Passengers on the list who don't make the captain's table dine with a "four-striper" — staff captain, chief engineer, hotel manager or doctor. The VIPs are invited to a series of private parties in the captain's and senior officers' quarters during the cruise.

The captain's table does not always make for the most enjoyable dining experience. Guests tend to be overly formal, and the service staff can be too nervous and anxious to be at their best. One purser, overlooking the elaborately dressed assembly at the nearby captain's table, commented, "The very, very dull, very, very rich. The captain does well to stay awake."

PASSENGER GROUPINGS

Although every passenger has his/her own delightful traits, we have created nine categories, each covering a particular group that transcends age or nationality.

Lemmings

There is always a substantial group that simply does what it is told. If the cruise director suddenly marched toward the stern and dropped into the wake, these legions would come splashing after. It is doubtful that they ever sleep. Their ears are constantly tuned to the public address system, as they may be asked to participate in some event. They form conga lines when they're suggested, burst gleefully into song when the MC clears his throat and laugh vigorously when the hint of a joke lingers in the air.

Tigers

These brave souls are masters of their own health, bouncing briskly out of bed with the sun's first wink over the horizon. It's onto the promenade deck for a few laps. Tigers possess sweatsuits, swimwear and athletic apparel of various shapes and colors. After their morning laps, they drop the sweatsuit onto the deck, and the swimsuit is once again baptized in the pool. It was a tiger on a South Seas cruise who received quite a shock during his morning dip. The evening before, a group of crew members had been off in a launch, snorkelling. To impress the gals back in the boat, three of the guys landed a small octopus. Not to be outdone, the women challenged the men to bring the creature back to the ship. After dark, it was hoisted aboard by a rope and lowered into the saltwater swimming pool. When the first pool customer arrived the next morning, his escape was more vigorous than his entry.

Tigers conclude early morning exercise with a sauna and a massage. They are sometimes disgusted to find that the sauna doesn't open until 9 a.m. Their breakfast consists of prune juice and healthfood cereal. Narcissists all, they spend much of the day on the deck, tanning in the sun and participating in deck sports. They eat exotic dinners, but always in moderation. Their day ends with a brandy, watching the main show of the evening and a stroll on the deck. They retire early.

Fish

The tigers are greeted in the early morning by another breed of passenger. The fish pop aspirin at 7 a.m. as they stagger into the elevator, roll down a corridor and then lift themselves onto a bar stool.

"Bloody Mary, please Fred," they groan to the bartender.

Sometimes, for variety, they round off breakfast with a Danish pastry and a coffee. Several drinks later and they evaporate, reappearing on the deck later in the day sipping a martini. Their recovery by nightfall is remarkable. In the swing of things, holding court in the midnight cocktail lounge, they toss back double scotches. They fall off the stool at 3 a.m., crawling back to their cabins to prepare for the early morning bar opening, just a few hours ahead.

Hippos

These people cannot get enough to eat. They gobble from early morning until bedtime, pausing in their chomping only long enough to nurse heartburn. Breakfast is cereal, mounds of pancakes, ham, eggs, sausages and bread. They complete that endurance test just in time to catch bouillon and pastries mid-morning in the lounge. At lunch they seriously sample the poolside smorgasbord, trying a number of delicacies before going down to the dining room for a five course affair.

"After all, Horace, we paid for all of this. We might as well eat it."

Mercifully, they pass out early in the afternoon, requesting a wake-up call at four o'clock, which, by coincidence, is high tea — offering an assortment of delightful pastries. It nicely carries them through until the cocktail hour, when they chew peanuts and pretzels in the bar. Dinner consists of bread, turtle soup, avocado salad, chicken kiev, duchess potatoes, baked alaska and coffee. At midnight — three hours, six bromos and two beers later — it's time for the midnight buffet.

"I know, Alice, I know. We paid for it."

Road Runners

You can always tell the road runners by the pained twist to the face and the darting, glassy eyes. Their day starts twelve hours ahead of everyone else's, actually the night before. They plan their attack on the hundreds of conflicting activities. In their cabin notebook on the bed, they chart and scheme like Patton preparing to cross the Rhine. Breakfast in their cabin, 9 a.m. exercise period, port lecture at 9 o'clock . . . a conflict! Solved. There will be five minutes of exercise followed by the last half of the lecture. Table tennis at 9:30, part of the golf lesson at 9:45. And so it goes all day. They see half of the afternoon movie, which disgustingly coincided with bingo, then it's a quick hand of bridge and a fleeting glance at the engine room in the last moments of a tour. After all, they paid for everything.

Foxes

Each cruise brings its contingent of determined ladies in search of crew conquests. The matronly often reward their suitors with handsome tips. The young and aggressive give away their charms to eager participants. Foxes can be spotted most of the day in bikinis, sunning by the pool and inventing reasons for conversation with every passing uniform. They talk to the chap painting the railing and the steward serving drinks. Officers are the best target. A fox will subtly trip over a radio officer's toe as the band is bursting into song.

Wolves

A ship is a very sad place for passenger wolves. The foxes are not interested; they are after starched whites. And there are too many wolves in the crew. All of them have their sea legs, a confident air of nonchalance and a direct hit-or-miss approach that succeeds as often as it fails. That means two tries in ten minutes and one will be a direct hit. Passenger wolves invariably leave the ship, confidence shaken, wobbling down the gangway. With luck, a crew member will whisk them off to Acapulco's *La Huerta,* or some equally distinguished institution.

Possums

These people sleep all the time. Their cabin number is "Do Not Disturb." Sometimes they make it to a deck chair, where they would quite like to have a drink if it was not such an effort lifting an arm to signal a steward. They tend to make it through dinner, after which they spring to life like a thunderbolt, belt back a series of shots at the bar, and then pass out once again.

Hyenas

This group is always having a smashing time, sailing through the day slapping people on the back, pouring drinks, hosting parties and displaying the best golf swing, shuffleboard serve and dives into the pool. Husband and wife appear in matched outfits. They tell the kind of jokes that require expansive theatrics, laughing so hard at the end they seem to fall into seizure.

THE "UGLIEST" PASSENGERS

On every cruise, one or two passengers cause so much disruption on a ship that they immediately become known to the entire crew. There used to be a term on British ships to describe these people: "Godzillas." Although the term seems to be disappearing in modern shipboard jargon, it remains rather descriptive.

There was the lady who complained every night about the food, while her table mates were delighted with the fare. After a typically embarrassing scene one night, she rose from the table and smashed her plate to the floor. While her steward cleaned up the mess, an unidentified crew member quietly dropped two sleeping pills into her tea. She passed out at the table. When she awoke the next day, no one would tell her who had stripped off her clothes and put her to bed. The lady spent the rest of the cruise, much humbled, trying to explain that she was not a drunk.

Another chronic dining room complainer was particularly vehement one morning when her steward brought her two strips of Canadian bacon, rather than the one strip she had distinctly ordered. She raised similar issues throughout the cruise. One evening, after she had been particularly obstreperous, her two stewards bowed gracefully at her every complaint. They were in a playful mood that evening. She issued a complicated dessert order, and the waiters retired to the galley. Soon they returned, presenting a lettuce salad topped by a scoop of ice cream. The stewards dashed off to avoid her inevitable howl, leaving the rest of her table holding their sides with laughter. She was no more popular among her mates than she was with the crew.

And there was the chap on an Alaska cruise who demanded a total refund when the ship hit rough waters off Sitka. He grumbled that he had paid for a cruise on "the Inside Passage," not the outside waters. The crew explained that 90 per cent of the trip was "inside," but the ship had to turn around at some point. He was not appeased.

Godzillas take everything seriously. They constantly compare the cruise to others they have taken. When they read the dinner menu, they are quick to advise that on their favorite cruise line there is always a more generous selection. They can be found many times a day at the purser's office, registering a complaint or attempting to render incomprehensible some minor matter listed in the day's agenda.

These people are notorious for poor tipping. One steward who had given a couple excellent service for two and a half weeks was rewarded at the end with a two-dollar gratuity. The sensitive steward, when he returned to the galley and saw the amount, was extremely upset. He was convinced that his service must have displeased the passengers. He marched back to the table and returned the tip with apologies to the guests. The customer was offended. When he complained to the purser about the "rude insult," the steward was dismissed on the spot.

Another incident brought a fairer measure of justice. One

132

steward on a large liner had but one group of passengers to serve during a six-week voyage. His sole responsibility was a raucous group of ten unmannerly passengers. After serving as many as 1,200 meals to this horde, he was rewarded with five one-cent coins. The passengers laughed with gusto at the steward's reaction. Much later, when the ten pranksters walked down the gangway, a shower of garbage rained on their heads. The dining room steward was standing above them, along the rail.

SEX: THE CREW AND THE PASSENGERS

Strict rules govern relations between crew and passengers — except in cases where no one is caught. The tough rules mean little more than asking a colleague to stand watch as his friend sneaks down a passenger corridor in the dead of night. Those who are successful (Italians are particular masters of the sport) use the most direct approaches.

Dining room stewards case the room on the first evening of the cruise, with an eye out for attractive, unattached women. Spotting a target, a steward will get a closer look by taking roundabout routes between his tables and the galley. Satisfied, seating charts are then checked for names and room numbers. After dinner, the enterprising steward will phone a woman's cabin to suggest, "I have a lovely bottle of cold champagne. I don't want to drink it alone. May I come to your cabin and share it with you?" If rejected, he simply moves on to the next name on the list.

Champagne is expensive, but the stewards consider it a good investment. Middle-aged women can be extremely generous to their young suitors. If a ship cruises out of a major port on a regular basis, it is a common sight to see expensive cars waiting for the vessel to dock. The more active sailors have rich ladies waiting in several ports.

It is difficult for a dining room steward to wend his way to a passenger cabin. A cabin steward, who is perfectly in place delivering champagne to a cabin, will frequently assist his friend. As the delivery is made, the dining room chap will stealthily creep along behind. Passenger corridors can be quite amusing in the early hours of the morning, especially if there is a large contingent of Italians on the staff.

Some women receive many calls during a trip, all unidentified. Those who decline the offer won't ever learn who was calling. Occasionally, a complaint will reach the purser's office. Less frequently, a crew member will be caught and disciplined. If the passenger makes a serious charge, the employee will be dismissed.

The best targets are women travelling alone or in groups of three or more. Two women produce poor odds. They share a cabin and usually end up defending each other's virtue. Groups of three are seeking adventure.

The question most often asked by a woman after a sexual event with a crew member: "Do you do this all the time?" The predictable reply: "Only when I'm in love, my dear."

There are two categories of aggressive women among cruise passengers. There are those who are after the medals and those who are just after the men. The former aim at officers. The latter like nothing better than to disappear into crew quarters and spend the rest of the voyage in a variety of arms. This is not an uncommon occurrence. On an English ship just outside Fiji a few years ago, a rookie crew member was whistling his way toward the men's shower early one morning. He entered the room, flung his towel on a hook and sauntered nude into the shower area. He was startled to find a naked young woman soaping herself under the shower. He recovered his composure and the episode ended happily. When a woman ventures belowdecks, where she will often stay for the duration of the cruise, it becomes a noteworthy item in ship's gossip.

Occasionally, wealthy and lonely male homosexuals appear on a cruise, attempting to buy the favors of crew members. It is an easy task. A generous tip to a steward will carry the request to a willing crew member. Sometime later, the cabin phone rings and a deal is struck.

Company executives and ship's officers downplay crew-passenger sex as much as they can, implying that very little takes place. The more extravagant boasts of some crew members can be written off, but the Cadillacs parked at the wharf to pick up junior members of the crew, and the cars purchased for the occasional seaman, stand as a testament to some kind of activity.

What is amazing, if it is assumed that a vibrant sex world lies hidden within the bulkheads of the ship, is how quiet it tends to be. After midnight, with the exception of the one raging cabaret, the ship is as calm and sedate as a cathedral on Monday.

9

Anatomy of a Cruise Ship:
One Vessel on One Day

As a compact floating palace steams from port on a new adventure, with a fresh payload of vacationers, another story is about to unroll. Let's look through the portholes, from top to bottom, on a day in December. The following story is mostly fiction, but the episodes were drawn from notes gathered on a cruise from New Orleans, down the Mississippi, and across the Caribbean to Central America. The ship was the 22,000-ton *Royal Viking Sea*, one of the most luxurious in the world. She has a capacity of 500 passengers, a crew of 320. This cruise was 75 per cent full.

THE TIME: 0300 Hours

The elderly cleaner, his vacuum strapped like jets on his back, saunters along the corridor. Most of the ship is in darkness. Laughter and conversation rumble down the hall from the Emerald Club, the ship's late night cabaret.

They'll tame down after a few days, the cleaner mumbles to himself.

The bar manager at the Emerald Club smiles patiently at the woman and the two men sitting on the stools in front of him. The rest of the club is vacant. The band packed it in 30 minutes ago, and most of the customers wandered or staggered out behind them.

A portly chap stammers, "I'll have another double ... and another for my friends." The bartender nods. Ship policy is to keep the place open until the last passenger decides to leave — within all due reason. This will be the last, the steward decides as he serves the drinks.

"There you are," he says.

He turns to balance his books — and lock away the inventory.

Even with all the luxury and activities aboard ship, visiting foreign ports is always a highlight of any cruise. Venice above, Curacao below.

Not all ships cruise only in warm waters — this one makes its way
through floating ice off the coast of Alaska.
Picturesque Puerto Vallarta on the Mexican Riviera.

The last day of a cruise is like death and rejuvenation. One cargo of passengers is set ashore with all the hassles of customs, immigration and the stevedores. The ship is refuelled and restocked. And then, midday, the new contingent of guests arrives, fresh and excited, with friends and relatives along for bon voyage parties.

For the crew, the process is as painful as childbirth. They load the provisions and educate a new group of clients. There is an endless series of obstacles: carrying on the luggage, collecting passports, printing passenger lists, dealing with a host of complaints and requests as the new group gets settled, arranging the dining room seating, catering to the bon voyage parties, launching the cruise and, finally, holding the emergency drill.

The passengers play and drink hard that first night. They will tire and relax later.

The hotel manager, finishing a brandy in his suite, looks at his watch: 3 a.m. He climbs into bed. If embarkation is like childbirth, day two, with the final problems to sort out, will be like puberty. He sets his alarm for 7.

The young officer on the vacant bridge stares down at the bow, which rises and falls in perfect rhythm, slicing the black sea. He walks past the automatic pilot and glances at the radar scope. He notes on his charts the position of nearby ships.

A passenger stands alone on the dark and silent promenade deck, his jacket billowing and his hair tossing in the breeze. He looks down over the railing at the symmetrical shapes of foam shooting from the hull into the blackness. The stars, crisp and clear, beckon into oblivion.

A seaman emerges from the depths into the control centre of the engine room. His duty officer, puffing on a cigarette, is scanning the dials — speed, fuel, water pressure, air conditioning . . . He adjusts the pitch of the stabilizing fins to suit the changing sea conditions.

Without looking up from his controls, the officer speaks in Norwegian:

"It's still down there, I assume?"

The seaman chuckles.

"A little noisier than usual I think, sir."

The officer nods. "The chief doesn't like the fuel he gets in New Orleans."

The nurse is reading her files. Among the new load of passengers there are four diabetics, one paraplegic, a variety of cardiac cases and an assortment of people requiring medication for one ailment or another. A number of special diets are requested, but only one will require consultation with the chef later in the morning.

She would have been in bed, sleeping off her shift, but one passenger is in the infirmary. The excitement and refreshments of embarkation have taken their toll on one of the heart patients. It's nothing serious, she thinks, but the doctor doesn't like to take chances.

The nurse glances at the electronic dials that instantly transmit the vital body functions of the patient, who is resting comfortably in the infirmary next door. Everything is normal. He'll be out in the morning.

She is relieved that the Caribbean/Gulf of Mexico season brings little in the way of rough seas. Seasickness produces panic rushes to the hospital. During this season, there have been only a few minor requests for pills each time the ship cleared the Mississippi into the incoming flow of the Gulf.

The phone interrupts. The nurse lifts the receiver.

"Hello? . . . No, I'm sorry, the doctor is not in. This is the nurse . . . Well, I'll come down and take a look . . . If we need him, we'll wake him up . . . Okay, right away."

Vomiting. Probably just an Emerald Club client, the nurse thinks as she takes one last look at her patient's readings. She pokes her head into the infirmary and, satisfied, flips a switch on the electronic equipment. If there is any change in the status of the heart patient, an alarm will sound automatically in the doctor's cabin.

She leaves to see the new case.

Holding a tray of sandwiches and coffee in one hand, the night stewardess raps on the cabin door with the other. It was a long trip to the galley, just part of the worst shift of her job. It will last two weeks and then be over for another few months. Hired as a cabin stewardess, it was her turn in the rotation to man the overnight phone. Her job is to help passengers with instant clean-ups in the case of accidents, or to handle food requests such as this one.

She is greeted by a buxom middle-aged woman dressed in a bathrobe. The husband, fully clothed but dishevelled, is stretched out on a bed. The woman is apologetic.

"I'm so sorry to bother you, miss, but we partied a little too much in the afternoon."

Her husband interrupts: "Then we slept right through dinner."

The stewardess, placing the tray on the table, smiles. "That's okay. I'm here all night. But did you know that there is a big buffet every night at midnight in the Windjammer Room?"

The passengers hadn't known.

The attractive young woman slips from the room. In an hour she will be collecting room service breakfast orders from the cabin door handles and taking them to the galley.

The bakers in the galley are placing their first tray of Danish pastries and croissants into the oven. They will be served fresh with tea, coffee or Bloody Mary when the Dolphin Bar opens at 6:30 a.m., then again at breakfast in the dining room. While the breakfast rolls are baking, the men will start kneading dough for the endless loaves of bread and the buns that will be consumed at breakfast and lunch. Then will follow the fancy pastries for lunch, before the shift concludes at 10 a.m.

The bakers live strange days — 2 a.m. until 10 a.m. At that time, the bakery shuts down for a few hours, reopening in the early afternoon with another shift to prepare breads, pastries and desserts for dinner.

Two Chinese launderers, without speaking, jam the over-night collection — mostly dining room linen — into the huge, powerful washing machines. Their job, in the dead of night, is to clear away the surplus before the bulk of the daily workload — and the rest of the workers — arrive in the morning.

The officers' mess on bridge deck is just about empty. Two officers, sipping cocktails, had completed their shift in time for a drink and a dance in the Emerald Club. They are winding down in the mess.

"Not much this time around," one of them comments.

"Oh — I think I spotted a few possibilities. Did you see the one in the red dress?"

A cheerful receptionist at the purser's counter is joking with the Emerald Club bar manager. It is 3:30 a.m. now. The steward has just dropped off his night's bar receipts.

"We're having a beach party at Playa del Carmen. Are you coming?" the steward asks the cute receptionist.

"With or without clothes?"

"Both," he replies.

She muses for a moment. "I'll just be finishing my shift when we anchor."

The steward persists.

"No you won't. You quit at eight. That's when we drop the shore-excursion passengers at Cozumel. By the time we sail over to Playa and anchor, it'll be noon. You've got to come."

She laughs. "I'll wear a bikini."

He groans. "What a disappointment."

She answers the telephone, chats for a moment and then returns the receiver to its cradle. She makes a note on a chart.

"A wake-up call?" the steward inquires.

"Cabin 226. One of your customers, I assume?"

"That's right — my last. A big guy. What time is he getting up?"

She glances at her pad.

"He said something about sunrise — 6:30."

He gives her a knowing nod.

"One of those — a Bloody Mary rise at the Dolphin."

The cleaner, the heavy canisters on his back, aims his vacuum at the peanut and pretzel remnants on the Windjammer Room floor. He jumps with a start as a sailor slaps his metallic back.

"How are you, pop?" the seaman asks.

"Always good, son. You gave me a shock. Looks like a quiet trip, not many aboard."

The seaman shrugs as he punches his time clock. He turns to continue his perpetual rounds, commenting to the old man, "Makes no difference to me."

THE TIME: 0500 Hours

At 5 o'clock in the morning you could shoot a cannon down any corridor of the vessel. Even the cleaner has stopped for coffee. The silent watch continues on the bridge, in the engine room and in the hospital. The launderers are shifting their load into the dryers and the bakers are well into their morning baking assignment. The stewardess is collecting breakfast orders from the cabin doors and the purser's receptionist is handling a few overnight duties. But the cavernous public rooms of the vessel are silent, as *Royal Viking Sea* plods patiently toward Cozumel. The seaman on the watch, punching his clock at every station, may meet an insomniac or two, but the peace is rarely disturbed.

The most junior of the ship's three radio officers is sitting in the complicated communications centre, feet on a desk, reading a novel. It has been a long, busy night.

There had been late night cables dispatched by passengers to announce their departure to the folks back home. These were taken over the phone from the cabins, typed, read back and then transmitted by Morse code. The radio officer has been screening the frequency channels constantly for incoming calls. There had been several ship-to-shore phone calls, including one by the doctor to a physician in Texas, concerning a patient who suffered a mild heart problem the previous evening. There had been two incoming cables for passengers, decoded, typed and slipped under the cabin doors. If they had sounded urgent, the guests would have been wakened.

Just a routine night. Before the end of the shift, the weather charts will be received by telephoto and delivered to the bridge. Detailed reports of messages received and sent, and passenger account billings, will be prepared for the boss. The officer will also have to decode and type out the overnight news synopsis, recorded earlier in Morse on the tape, in preparation for the early morning broadcast.

There is only slight activity on the lowest two decks of the ship. A few showers are going, and a few more crewmen are lathering up in their cabins. The early morning maintenance staff is preparing for its six o'clock assignment on the deck, taking down the safety net from the swimming pool, filling the pool with fresh seawater and neatly arranging the deck chairs through all the public areas.

The two short-order cooks who prepare the crew breakfast are pulling on clean whites. Then they'll ignite the gas burners in the crew mess. A more senior colleague is off to the galley to collect provisions for the officers' mess.

Whistling in the shower at the other end of the ship is the morning bartender at the Dolphin. He will be wielding the gin, juice and tabasco sauce in 90 minutes.

"Hi, sweetheart."

A crusty old baker calls out to the night stewardess as she sails into the galley, her bright orange Royal Viking pinafore swinging with her movement.

"Good morning. I've got all the breakfast orders," she announces.

The baker pushes the rolled dough on the table.

"The sous-chef is not here yet. How many today?"

The stewardess looks at the pile of door cards in her hand.

"I don't know. About 60, I guess."

The baker nods.

"That means a busy day in the dining room. They all like to try the menu on the first morning."

THE TIME: 0700 Hours

There is but one word to describe the scene: pandemonium. People are rushing in all directions, some in pajamas, some in underwear, some nude, some in towels and a few in uniform. The stewards, seamen, stewardesses and most of the rest of the crew are readying for their morning duty. There is pushing and shoving for the showers, and many say to hell with it and just wash and shave in the cabin.

The headwaiter who is running breakfast service has called a meeting for the dining room at 7:30, just 30 minutes before the passengers arrive to gorge themselves. A few groggy victims of last night's crew party are resisting the best efforts of their roommates to bring them to consciousness. One solves the problem quite nicely: he rolls his pal onto the floor.

Those who had been able to beat the breakfast rush at the crew mess watch the huge line-up form at the door and dig into their eggs and sausages. Between bites, a dining room steward laments to his companion on the other side of the table, "I've got to go to the bridge today. Late back in New Orleans."

New Orleans, with a 36-hour stop, is the highlight of each cruise for the crew. Many of them don't make it back on time.

The friend nods. "I was late last time."

"What happened?"

"Extra boat drill — in Jamaica."

The steward looks relieved. "That's not too bad. As long as I'm not cancelled in New Orleans next time — for a lousy 20 minutes late."

His friend sighs in sympathy. "How many got it this time?"

The guilty crewman swallows a mouthful of sausage. "Not sure. I hear about 50."

They will be paraded before a deck officer during the day.

In the theatre, the stage manager, roughly dressed and unshaven, sits alone before the electronic console. He gulps two aspirins and a mouthful of water. He cues the two tapes before him, and two of the three radio channels on the ship boom into music.

144

There will be the usual first-morning complaints, he says to himself. Passengers who neglected to turn off their cabin radios overnight will be awakened by the music. They'll learn.

There had been a few drinks after the show with the cruise director and the entertainers. The stage manager clears his throat, opening the microphone on the third radio channel.

"A good morning to you on behalf of the captain, the officers and the crew of *Royal Viking Sea*."

Good, he thinks. The voice works.

"And now," he announces, "a summary of the overnight news. There was increased tension last night in the Middle East . . . ."

Two stewards roll the breakfast trolley along the corridor, popping into one cabin after another. It's a rotten assignment for a dining room steward, but the fascinating sights you sometimes see in the cabins make it almost tolerable. The stewards handle the assignment on a rotating basis.

A middle-aged passenger dressed in a sweatsuit is trotting along promenade deck. It had been brilliant sunrise, and the day promises an excellent start on a suntan. As he rounds the narrow deck corridor at the bow, he runs into a 40-year-old woman, trotting from the other direction.

After apologies both ways, she asks, "Which one of us is to change directions?"

"Allow me," he says. They trot off together.

"Look at those nuts," one passenger says to another.

The pair, outside the Dolphin Bar, gaze down over the railing into the pool. Three passengers are splashing around, enjoying a refreshing start to the day.

The other replies, "Tarzan will feel threatened. Can I buy you a refill?"

They turn their backs to the gushing wake, the clear waters and the blue skies off the stern.

The Dolphin has been pushing spirits for half an hour. A handful of determined passengers have congregated on the stools along the semicircular bar, sipping their Bloody Marys, Bloody Caesars and other favorite morning remedies.

A more sensible group, lounging at the tables, are drinking coffee and munching breakfast pastries.

The clerk at the information desk, weary at the end of her shift, is telephoning one cabin after another, waking up passengers who had requested the service. The people who wish to have a morning chat are trying her patience. It is difficult enough to make ten calls at the stroke of each quarter-hour.

A colleague, sitting beside her, is handling the incoming calls. Most are information requests.

A dozen officers have gathered in their mess. Most eat light breakfasts.

The captain makes his entry. All the officers rise, variously offering good mornings to the master.

"Good morning. Be seated please," the captain says as he heads toward the coffee percolator.

A junior officer continues his conversation with the staff captain.

"I've got over 40 to discipline today," he explains. All late in New Orleans — from five minutes to three hours."

The staff captain smiles. "Three hours!"

"That's right — ran from the taxi to the ship as we were pulling up the gangway."

This brings a chuckle from the senior officer. "He must have had quite a time."

The young officer explains that the problem was getting worse instead of better every time the ship visited New Orleans, despite punishment on every occasion. After he tells the staff captain of the extra lifeboat drill at Montego Bay last time around, he asks for advice.

The staff captain thinks for a moment. "I think you should do the same thing. Let's not be too harsh. New Orleans is the only good port for them this time. Maybe those who were more than an hour late should have Fort Lauderdale leave cancelled — but boat drill for the others. We can be more rigid on the world cruise."

Everyone aboard was eagerly awaiting a 96-day global excursion scheduled to start in January.

THE TIME: 0900 Hours

The mood of the dining room is effervescent. The passengers are starting the first full day of their cruise, chatting to one another and digging into a variety of breakfast concoctions.

For the stewards, breakfast is at once more casual and more difficult than the other meals. Passengers arrive in waves from 8 a.m. until 10, always enough to keep the staff occupied but never enough at any one time to keep them busy. The slow pace always frees a few stewards, on a rotating basis, to sleep in and relax.

At the morning meeting, the headwaiter had handed out the day's assignments. Those who were given the morning off would handle lunch, dinner and the midnight buffet. Others were assigned to the deck smorgasbord for the noon hour, and a few were designated for private cocktail sessions. The lunch menu had been explained prior to breakfast service. Announced now is a 2 p.m. meeting of all dining room staff: the maître d', headwaiters, wine stewards and table stewards.

Breakfast, flawless and casual as usual, brings only one minor incident. One passenger, who insisted upon having his eggs fried for only a minute, sent them back three times. When the final effort arrives, meeting his approval, the steward says, "Now I know, sir. They'll be like that for the rest of the cruise."

In a corner of the dining room — actually an extra wing closed off because of the smaller passenger population — the maître d' browses over his seating charts. The usual battery of requests for changes in table assignments had followed the first night's dinner. He is trying to accommodate.

An equally difficult task is staff employment. With only two-thirds of the dining room full, he'll have a difficult time motivating the stewards. With fewer passengers, service should be better, but it doesn't work that way. The small crowd means less challenge, less drive and, more important, fewer tips. Perhaps a pep talk at the afternoon meeting will help, the maître d' considers. As an incentive, he will offer more free mornings and lunch hours, and longer shore leaves.

On the other side of the bulkhead, the chef looks through the glass walls of his tiny office at the busy breakfast preparations. On the grill a hundred eggs are frying to different specified consistencies. The rotating toaster churns out crisp brown slices by the dozen, and a dining room steward sails by with a stack of pancakes.

The chef returns to his deliberations. The printer has been pestering him for the evening menu. A mere technician, the chef thinks. It will be captain's night, but the set menu provided on previous cruises won't work. The veal offered by the suppliers in Fort Lauderdale had been totally unacceptable. Duckling, obtained at the last minute in New Orleans, brought the opportunity to try a new specialty: duckling à l'orange. The menu will feature all the usual alternatives.

The chef pencils the changes on the menu, then lifts the telephone to call the printer.

A sous-chef enters the small office.

"Yes?" the chef inquires, his fingers poised on the telephone dial.

"I don't think the bread is very good this morning," the subordinate says, dropping several slices of bread on the desk.

The chef surveys the texture, then chews a sample.

"Better than they'd get at home. But you're right, I'll speak to the baker."

Ten women — in everything from sweatsuits to bikinis — and two men stand in formation on the small sports deck between the Windjammer Room and the smokestack, under the Gulf of Mexico skies.

"Now," the svelte instructress orders, "the bicycle — everyone down on your back."

She demonstrates the manoeuvre, lying on her back: legs high in the air, buttocks supported with hands on the waist, legs pumping vigorously. As the unlikely athletic contingent attempts the exercise, the leader bounces to her feet chanting a rhythm.

"Pump, pump, pump," the instructress shouts.

She moves among the throng, correcting the more obvious flaws. Then she shouts again, "Okay — up on your feet. Running on the spot!"

She bursts into a high step. "Go, go, go! Faster, faster, faster."

A deck officer, in a crew meeting room belowdecks, sits facing a dozen seamen. He explains that the wooden handrails of the vessel will all be revarnished while this cruise is in progress. He advises the contingent to be generous in the placing of "wet paint" signs and to be cautious in areas where passengers may be present. The officer also advises that the staff captain has expressed displeasure at a few sea stains that were visible on the hull while the ship was docked at New Orleans.

The seamen moan.

The photographers face a rugged day ahead. As they settle into the long routine of plugging roll after roll of film through the seven-minute color processing machine (passenger embarkation shots snapped the day before), they also must prepare for the second major photographic task of the cruise: the captain's receiving line tonight.

The embarkation prints — 400 of them — will be up on the board tomorrow; the shots to be taken tonight will be ready the day after.

The doctor shakes the elderly man's hand.

With his wife at his side, the man who had endured the heart worry the night before is being discharged from the infirmary.

Just take the pills as I directed and you will have no trouble," the doctor advises. "I talked to your doctor at home last night, and he told me that you could whip me in a fight if I give you a hard time."

Both the man and his wife laugh.

"Well, I'm sorry to have caused you so much trouble for nothing," the patient says.

The doctor nods. "I'm just pleased that you are well."

The woman looks at the physician.

"I'm going to take him for breakfast and we are just going to lie in the sun all day. You've been so wonderful."

"You can thank the nurse for that," the doctor smiles.

"Oh, yes. Where is the young lady?" the patient asks.

"She's gone to bed. She was up all night ... with you," the doctor replies.

The more energetic among the passenger population are scattered over the stern sports area, either splashing in the pool or challenging one another to games of shuffleboard, quoits or table tennis. There are some taking mad swings at golf balls, aiming at a target in the net.

Engineers huddle in a conference about an overnight problem: a few toilets in passenger cabins had backed up and serious water damage occurred. The purser's office is moving the passengers to other quarters, a blessing made possible by the vacant cabins available. The cause of the problem has been diagnosed and repairmen are on the scene.

The printer puts down the phone. He directs a pained look toward a friend who popped in to say hello.

"He doesn't understand," the printer says.

"Who?"

"The chef."

The printer explains that the dinner menu has just now been finalized.

"Captain's night, and he delays the menu. I was really going to do a job tonight. Even if I skip lunch, with the passenger list to print, and the menus, and then the newspaper arriving for publication this afternoon, I'll never make it," the printer complains.

The greasy seaman considers the problem and then encourages his friend. "Sure you will. The chef's a bit strange, but he's a great cook. I hear he was offered a job at the best hotel in Haiti."

"They can have him," the printer says, unimpressed.

The cruise director stares glumly at the cablegram. He had asked for newer and better movies for future cruises. The note from head office advises that competition with television and prices in the catalogue were simultaneously growing more fierce. The upcoming selection cheers him but little.

His principal vocalist on this cruise woke up this morning with a sore throat. It's doubtful she'll be able to perform. And the Christmas cruise is coming up. That will take a good week of planning and charting, given the features and entertainment available.

There is a knock at the cabin door. The assistant cruise director enters. He is excited, talking even before his presence is acknowledged.

"Did you hear how well the Homestead Act went down last night?"

The act is a young couple, Elmo and Patsy Shropshire, who with a guitar and banjo present country-and-western music in such a charmingly innocent style that passengers always fall in love.

The director comments, "Imagine farm music a hit on a cruise ship."

"I think we should bill them more often," the assistant suggests.

"Let's try it. But two weeks is a long time with the same audience. Let's see how the passengers continue to react."

Huddled over coffee in the captain's cabin is the ship's cabinet: master, staff captain, chief engineer and hotel manager. The three officers have just presented detailed reports to the captain. The hotel manager complains about the plumbing problems and the difficulty in moving passengers.

The chief interjects. "I said many weeks ago that we needed new equipment. If they can't get the spare parts to me, there's nothing I can do. All I can do now is patch the dike."

The captain agrees. He advises that the needed parts will be waiting in abundance the next time the ship reaches Fort Lauderdale.

The chief engineer seizes the initiative. "And I told you about the bunker oil from New Orleans. It is no good. Just look at the dirt flying from the stack. Even the passengers are complaining."

The captain is amused, but he says nothing. Chief engineers never care about passengers — except, of course, to score debating points.

But the captain does tell his chief, "I know, but we are stuck with it for one more cruise. It's better than last year during the crisis when we couldn't buy fuel anywhere. We had to hit the black market."

The chief is unimpressed. "Not much better," he says.

In the purser's office, managed by a rarity in the industry —
a female chief — the staff are finalizing the overnight bar
accounts, setting up passenger ledgers for the two-week cruise,
reviewing concession accounts and moving the flooded-out
passengers into new accommodation.

The storeroom staff are going through the usual motions of
shifting around cases of liquor — tossing extras on the service
elevator up to the ship's bars — and sorting out food supplies,
when they hear angry mutterings from just down the hall.

A storeman pokes his head into the butcher shop.

"Something wrong?"

The butcher looks up. "Two hundred damned ducks!"

The storeman is bewildered.

The butcher explains, "The chef has decided to have duck
tonight."

Throughout the passenger areas, adapting their routines to
the sleeping habits of their wards, the stewardesses are discreetly slipping in to change sheets, vacuum, resupply the towels
and fill any specific requests.

In a few days they will be adjusted to their passengers'
waking times, and the workday will proceed much more
smoothly.

In the crew gym, in a corner of the lower deck surrounded by
the engine room, four off-duty seamen are having a weight-
lifting competition. Two others are enjoying a vigorous game
of table tennis.

"I don't know if I can take another captain's party day," the
attractive beautician says to the two girls behind the closed and
curtained doors of the hairdressing salon.

Her assistant gives a knowing look. "There's not much we
can do about it," she says, "Feast or famine."

Nearly every female passenger on the ship, it seems, has
decided to have her hair done. And, although the three put in a

152

nonstop day, there is no way that all the customers can be handled. Usually, appointments made the day before will fill the agenda.

"Tomorrow, we'll be offering specials," the other girl points out wryly.

"Just one thing," the manager warns. "No men's hair today. Put them off until tomorrow."

The women open the gates and let in the tide.

The massage parlor is much more relaxed than the beauty salon. There is a man on the table getting his flesh kneaded, a woman expected in half an hour, and three people in the saunas.

THE TIME: 1100 Hours

As a Sunday morning interdenominational service comes to an end in the Saga Theatre, a distinguished Turkish-born professor prepares to deliver a lecture. Dr. Bulent Atalay, a nuclear physicist at the Institute for Advanced Study at Princeton University and department chairman for physics and astronomy at the University of Virginia's Mary Washington College, is a guest lecturer on the cruise. His presence reflects not his vocation but his avocation — archaeology.

His first of many lectures will be an outline of Mayan civilization, the focal point of shore excursions during the next few days.

Dr. Atalay delights in telling passengers that his office is next to the one once occupied by Albert Einstein.

"When I need inspiration, I just put my hand on the wall," he says.

Poolside, a less weighty exercise is in progress. The cruise director has sprinkled silver spoons across the bottom of the swimming pool. A dozen passengers are eager to compete. The object of the exercise is to dive underwater, grasp as many spoons as possible, and then surface. The winner will be the competitor who collects the most spoons in one dive down. Eager spectators are hanging over the rail, Dolphin Bar drinks firm in their mitts.

Bouillon, tea and coffee, with assorted pastries on the side, are being dished up in the Oslo Lounge. While the passengers enjoy the refreshments, a member of the cruise staff circulates among the crowd trying to drum up interest in his yoga lessons that will follow shortly.

"Is bridge the game where you lay down the pairs on the table?" an elderly woman asks the hostess.

The hostess smiles. "No, but how would you like to work on a crossword puzzle?.

"That would be nice," the woman replies.

She is handed a puzzle selection, and the hostess returns to her bridge players. She gives them a brief book of rules which, she explains, govern shipboard competition — unless the players can agree on their own set of house rules. The bridge players will be at it virtually nonstop until the end of the cruise.

Game activities take place in a series of rooms surrounding the ship's central library. A few readers are browsing over the book selection of the modest but excellent library.

The dishwashing staff are processing thousands of plates, glasses and silverware pieces, collected from the dining room, cabins and lounges. The dishwashing machines rarely stop once the day is in progress. One 45-gallon drum of liquid detergent will be consumed before the day ends.

A perplexed lady stands in the ship's store, sorting through the male bathing suits on display. The attendant asks if he could help.

"Would you have a size 50? My husband forgot to bring his suit," the woman explains.

The manager replies with dismay that he lacks the space to carry such a *wide* selection. He says the place for her husband to make a purchase would be in Montego Bay, about one week away.

She leaves disappointed.

It will be a frustrating day in the shop, the manager decides.

It always is frustrating, at this point in a cruise. The new passengers come the first day just to look, not really to buy, except for those who expect the tiny store to be like Macy's in New York.

He tells himself to be content with the sales of film, hats, glasses and suntan lotions. The last two days of the cruise will make up for the lost time.

The shore-excursions manager is extremely angry. He had been dispatched from the home office to straighten out the concession. The complicated packages in Central America had created difficulties earlier in the season; there were the tragic deaths of a few passengers during a bus-car accident in Guatemala. This is his first cruise.

He sits in his office off the main arcade, listening on the phone to the maître d'.

Meanwhile, the manager's staff are coping with a series of passengers trying to sign themselves on the upcoming tours at this, the last minute. Passengers had been cautioned by the cruise line to book their shore excursions long before the ship sailed, because air charters and other complex arrangements were involved in overcoming the difficulties of visiting Mayan ruins deep in the jungle. As it happens, there are a few seats available, and the last-minute requests pose no difficulty.

An excursion assistant is arguing with a woman passenger. "No ma'am, you can't take both trips the same day."

The woman is determined. "I don't see why not!"

The assistant is exasperated. "They go in different directions and arrive back at the same time. Look ma'am. They are both full-day trips."

The woman finally departs to study the matter further.

The maître d' is explaining that his staff are very annoyed. The three members of the excursion team had eaten in the dining room for eight weeks, without tipping the staff. He advises that he is speaking on behalf of the cabin service also: eight weeks, two cabins.

"They thought it was all included in our deal with Royal Viking," the manager protests.

The maître d' advises curtly that it was not. And he presents a price tag: $480 for the dining room, $250 for the cabins.

War with the crew is the last thing the shore-excursions concession needs. The manager concedes the point. "I'll call the purser's office and fix it up on our account."

THE TIME: 1300 Hours

A passenger, encased in a thick, heavy leather easy chair, sits with his wife in the Windjammer Room, the highest point on the ship. They look down on the Gulf of Mexico through the panoramic wraparound windows of the lounge.

"This is truly magnificent," he says to his wife.

He empties his cocktail glass, placing it on the table. They are about to leave for lunch in the dining room — where they will be among the few in attendance.

You can gauge the weather outside at noon each day by taking a quick glance at the dining room. When the sun beams overhead, most passengers are quick to take advantage of it, and for anyone who doesn't wish to dress for lunch, an immense smorgasbord is set up on the deck.

This day is particularly pleasant, and three-quarters of the passenger population, most gathering near the pool or on the sports decks close to and above the Dolphin Bar, are out on the deck. The stewards dishing out the varieties of meats, breads, salads and pastries, and the chap flipping the hamburgers on the grill, are having a hectic time.

Not even the six-course luncheon offered in the main dining salon could take many of the passengers away from the sun.

The radio officer is forced to call a passenger away from the dining room. Urgent news has just come in by way of cablegram. When the passenger arrives on the bridge at the radio room, he advises the officer, "Business news — not very good. I'll have to make several ship-to-shore calls."

The radio officer interrupts. "They are very expensive. Two dollars a . . ."

The passenger cuts him off. "The price doesn't matter. What do you want me to do?"

The officer instructs him to go to his cabin. He makes a note of the radio room number and gives it to the man.

"Call me at this number. I'll get you top priority with your calls," the radio officer tells him.

"Listen, I've just about had it," one passenger blurts out as he tosses his cards on the table.

Four men have been playing poker since the idea was hatched some 14 hours earlier over after-dinner drinks.

Another chips in, "We're all bushed, but if I was a hundred dollars ahead like you instead of being a hundred and fifty down, I'd be buying drinks for the ship."

The winner relaxes, looking around his smoke-filled suite. The four were among ten contest-winning salesmen travelling without their wives or girl friends. Six had started the poker session so many hours ago.

"Tell you what," the winner suggests. "Why don't we get that cute stewardess to round us up some sandwiches and beer. I'll buy the beer."

Another answers, "I've had enough beer. I think I'll escape the smoke, get a good lunch in the dining room and then hit the sack. And tonight, I'm going to find the other guys and scout the clubs."

The loser looks upset. "When do we play again?" he asks.

One member of the group offers the solution. "Let's just enjoy tonight in the clubs. And unless you have any crazy ideas like fleabag buses and climbing Mexican pyramids, we can spend port day with a deck of cards."

Agreement is unanimous.

THE TIME: 1500 Hours

The captain paces his bridge. Several junior officers scurry around it on their jobs at the complex navigational and directional equipment. The first officer brings a computer printout to his chief executive: the weather.

"It might get a little heavy overnight, sir," he says.

The captain studies the printout for a moment.

"Crank it up two knots. We can cut back overnight if we don't need the time," he advises his mate.

The ship is due at Cozumel the next morning.

The staff captain emerges onto the scene. He teases his superior.

"Have you got your speech written?"

The captain just grunts. His welcome-aboard address to the

passengers is scheduled for that evening. It is always the same speech and always difficult to deliver. He was a seaman, not a comedian. The cruise business paid a little better than a cargo career, but not much better considering the increased responsibility. The lifestyle is much better, but he's never really learned to cope with the social obligations.

"I've got to get on with the log," he tells the staff captain as he retires to his quarters.

The hostess is presiding over one of the most difficult tasks in her repertoire: the singles' get-together. All the adults travelling without wives or husbands — or at least other diversions — are invited to meet on an early day of a cruise. It is always the same. A large group of older women arrive to meet their romantic attachments. The young and attractive have met their companions the night before. Women outnumber men five-to-one here, despite the hostess's best efforts to drag — sometimes physically — every eligible male to her gathering.

The stage manager sits back relaxed in the theatre projection room, picking his fingernails and planning the props for the evening show. The movie, "Nine to Five," is running to a packed house in the cinema. It will be shown throughout the cruise, as often as passenger demand dictates.

Behind the closed doors of the dining room, the meeting of 50 stewards, four headwaiters, three wine stewards, the maître d' and the chef is still in progress. The final lunchtime customers to depart had lingered past closing time, and the chef was last to arrive. The maître d' has completed his pep talk and the chef has stressed the intricacies of serving duckling à l'orange.

He is answering menu questions.

"What's this soup made with?" a steward inquires.

"Peaches," replies the chef.

"We'd better not tell them that or we won't sell much," a voice booms from the back of the crowd.

It brings a burst of laughter from the gathering.

The chef smiles politely. "That will be all," he says.

The maître d' is annoyed. It was his job to dismiss the staff. He calls for their attention, announcing the duty roster for the coming meals and the all-important list of those who will have the morning off at Cozumel.

"Bingo!"
The woman squeals her victory as she jumps from her seat, knocking her drink to the floor.
The 50 other players, after a momentary wince, quietly clear their boards as the assistant cruise director calls out the winning numbers.

The chief engineer, completing a passenger tour of his beloved diesels, escorts the group into the control room. A team of travel agents are along on the cruise on a promotional deal worked out by headquarters. The passengers will be given the opportunity to take a tour later in the cruise.
The chief patiently answers the questions that come his way. He is asked about speed and fuel consumption.
"If we go at our top cruising speed of 20 knots, using all four engines, we will consume 65 tons of fuel in 24 hours — about 17,000 gallons," he explains.
The chief marks the figures on a blackboard that is mounted on the wall next to his main control panel. He writes:
20 knots — four engines — 65 tons of fuel in 24 hours.
18 knots — three engines — 45 tons.
16 knots — two engines — 35 tons.
12 knots — one engine — 15 tons.
"It means if we are cruising at 12 knots, to reach our maximum speed we use 400 per cent more fuel to go 75 per cent faster," he tells the fascinated group.

A female passenger, accompanied by a young officer, enters the steamy den of the Chinese laundry. The officer explains that she left her diamond engagement ring in the pocket of a pair of slacks sent out for washing.
The manager bows. "What room are you in?"
She tells him.

"Just checking. We have it," the manager says. He smiles at the relieved passenger and goes to retrieve the lost article.

The postmaster explains to a passenger why it costs 40 cents to send a letter and why the stamps are Norwegian.

"This is a Norway post office. These are Norway postage rates for airmail letters," he says.

On a Royal Viking ship the postmaster wears the uniform of a junior officer but is actually an employee of the Norwegian postal system.

"I'd better explain that on the card," the man says. "My wife will be rather suspicious to get a Caribbean postcard with a Norwegian postmark."

The bar manager protests vehemently to the chief purser. He doesn't like reporting to a woman. The chief steward sits quietly at the side.

"I don't know where the stuff is, or even if you are right," he says.

The purser is firm. "I've checked your sales figures and the inventory in the storeroom. There are at least five cases missing," she says.

The bar manager looks for help from the chief steward. "That's impossible!" He is adamant.

The chief steward intervenes tactfully. "The chef was short three cases of food in his supply at New Orleans. He lifted everything around — personally — and when he rechecked he found the lost items."

The bar manager says he will check again.

Deadline is approaching.

The young newspaper editor puts his sheet together. This one is rather easy. Filling most of the offset paper is a feature story that runs during every cruise of the series, telling about the Maya, and Chitzen-Itza, Cozumel and Playa del Carmen. It is simply a matter now of listing the day's activities, then sending the paper to the besieged printer. The printer has just advised that the passenger list and that night's dinner menu are ready for distribution.

THE TIME: 1700 Hours

A dashing headwaiter, a charming young lounge stewardess in his cabin bunk with him, is making the most of the adventurous off-duty moment when a jarring knock resounds from the steel door.

They stop, staring into each other's eyes.

The knock sounds again.

The girl whispers, "Just be quiet. They'll go away."

The headwaiter ignores the advice. "Get lost!" he shouts.

A cool breeze floats over the rapidly emptying decks, not quite strong enough to obliterate the scent of suntan lotion that clings to the towels and furniture. A few poeple are ending their day with a dip in the pool, and a few others keep the deck stewards hopping back and forth with drinks from the Dolphin Bar.

A small crowd assembles at the stern; a seaman in uniform is conducting a trap-shooting event. Clay dishes, hurled from a strong but small machine, arch high over the wake. A passenger aims, fires and, nine times out of ten, misses.

The seaman takes the rifle.

Five-for-five.

When he hands the gun back, he earns a round of applause from those assembled.

Elizabeth Cuellar, the folk art curator at a major Mexican museum, is lecturing a group of 60 passengers in the Saga Theatre. Unlike Dr. Atalay, the resident lecturer in civilizations past, Mrs. Cuellar is on the cruise to talk about things present. A charming woman, she is dressed in native Mayan fashions.

In the Oslo Lounge the band is packing up its instruments and the stewards are carrying off the remnants of tea, a great daily occasion accompanied by music. The passengers' attack on the assorted sweets was truly awesome.

The beauty parlor manager closes the salon, advising two women that staff can handle no more customers today. In the eight hours since they opened, the trio, working right through lunch, processed 60 mostly happy customers, most of whom required shampoo-and-set.

The scene has been out of a factory assembly line, with one passenger moving off to a dryer as another sits in her just-vacated chair.

"Now, tomorrow, we will stand around and stare at ourselves," the manager sighs.

"No. Tomorrow we will get a few men," an attendant replies.

The curtains of the Emerald Club are drawn, and a sign leans against the door: "Private Party." Strains of music waft into the corridor.

Inside, two dozen guests of a travel agent are tasting canapes and sipping cocktails. A few are dancing to the quiet music of the small band. A portly travel agent, the host of the session, has cornered the staff captain.

"I just love your ship, captain," the agent says.

"Thank you," the officer replies graciously.

"I tell all my customers to use Royal Viking," the agent continues.

Do you tell all your clients that when two dozen of them travel Royal Viking their travel agent rides free, the captain thinks to himself.

He dismisses his thoughts. "I'm so pleased to hear it," he says.

Attending these exciting affairs is just part of the job.

THE TIME: 1900 Hours

There is no competition for this event. The Dolphin closed for business at the usual hour of 6 p.m., and the Windjammer, normally open until after dinner is well in progress, shut down promptly at 6:30. The officer-of-the watch and a radio officer are on duty but otherwise the bridge is silent. There are no officers in the engine room, the purser's office or anywhere else on the ship.

162

A lengthy queue of passengers stretches upstairs and downstairs from the double-doored entrance of the Oslo Lounge. The passengers file, one couple at a time, into the showroom. The ladies are all dressed in full-length gowns. Most of the gentlemen sport dark suits, about a third are in formal jackets, and several step forward with bold checks and candy-striped trousers. One older gent is wearing tails.

The event is the captain's cocktail reception, which precedes the formal welcome-aboard dinner. The hostess greets each party at the door, obtains their names and escorts them to the captain for a brief introduction. The conversation never varies. Words of greeting, a picture by a ship's photographer, and the welcomed couple is escorted by a more junior officer to a seat in the lounge.

It takes more than 30 minutes to complete the receiving line. Through it all the lounge stewards, assembled from every corner of the vessel, rush frantically with the complimentary cocktails. Six hundred drinks will be served in less than an hour.

In one corner the chief purser stands by, watching the proceedings. The bar manager slips up behind her, whispering that the missing booze problem has been solved. The extra cases had been delivered by mistake with the wine to the dining room.

"Impossible," she whispers back. Then she laughs. The bar manager smiles sheepishly.

It's much less formal, but no less regimented and hectic, in the galley. The chef is charging back and forth in front of the huge ovens, checking his ducks.

"Let's not hurry it," he commands his cooks. "Everyone is always late on captain's night."

A sous-chef advises that all the alternatives are progressing nicely. He tells the chef, "We're covered if they don't go for the duck."

The chef looks at his assistant as if he were an idiot. Of course they will go for the duck. Nothing is stated. The sous-chef gets the message.

The procession line finally completed, the captain marches on stage. He awkwardly welcomes the throng aboard, says a few words of greeting, stresses the ship's sincere desire to fill every passenger wish, and proceeds to introduce all his senior officers.

"And finally," the captain concludes, "a rose among the thorns — our chief purser."

He wasn't hired for his oratory.

The maître d' is calling out instructions to his white-jacketed stewards. Their black bow ties bouncing, they rush through the room distributing menus and making final checks of the table settings and the floral arrangements. The wine stewards, in their red tunics, scan the wine list, assuring themselves of available stocks.

THE TIME: 2100 Hours

Of course they went for the duck.

Two hundred had been prepared and 192 were ordered by the 400 passengers and officers in the dining room. The few remaining will be enjoyed by the chef and his principal lieutenants. Not bad, considering the availability of seven main course selections. Only Beef Wellington would have scored higher.

The dinner is progressing. The stewards are emerging from the galley with a variety of desserts.

The maître d' finds his way in and shouts to the chef, "Nothing but compliments coming back."

The chef nods. "Of course." And then he adds, "You must have served it correctly."

The maître d', smiling, bows. "Of course."

The dining room is alive with the murmur of contented conversation. The wine stewards press their way from table to table, presenting chits to passengers who had ordered the extra trappings.

164

The crew mess is always busy. As one flotilla leaves another arrives. The lounge stewards are catching a quick meal, after their labors at the cocktail party. Most will be back to work within an hour.

One steward, wolfing down his veal cutlets, asks those at the table, "Do you think this is the veal the chef was supposed to have rejected at Fort Lauderdale?"

"Worse," a friend replies.

"Oh?"

"It's really not veal. It's caviar left over from last summer's trip to Russia."

Together with his entertainment staff, the cruise director reviews the program for the upcoming show. First, he will lead off with a few jokes and comments — to put the audience in the mood. The vocalists will follow. The female lead is still having difficulty with her throat, but feels she should be able to suffer through. The puppeteers will follow her, before the eight-piece orchestra is let loose for a lively series of dance numbers. The resident dance team will present a demonstration.

This will lead to a break. The band will play through the break and the cruise director will get the passengers dancing. The country-and-western group is scheduled to follow inter-mission. The show will then conclude with the entire company assembling centre stage to lead a rousing singalong.

The passengers are starting to assemble in the Oslo Lounge, ordering their first round of after-dinner liqueurs.

Cabin stewardesses are just completing their rounds of the staterooms, the second thorough clean-up of the day. This time they turn down the beds and leave the newspaper behind.

In one cabin a young Nordic lass met an awaiting male passenger. He instructed her to go about her job and ignore him, but he chatted incessantly. When she went past him, he grabbed her arm.

"You're not too proud for a little fun with a passenger?" he asked.

It happens occasionally. She remembered her instructions. Never show fear. Smile. Be firm. Say no. If that doesn't work, become progressively more authoritative.

None of it proved successful. The drunken passenger persisted. He tried to force a kiss. She pushed his face away.

She protested. "Sir, I suggest you let go immediately. I will inform the captain and you will be put off the ship."

There was a hint of desperation in her voice.

The chap relaxed his grip without letting go.

"Aw, I'm only trying to have a little fun, miss," he said.

She seized the opportunity, snapping her arm away. He made a futile lunge and missed.

The girl went immediately to her superior, who was relaxing in quarters belowdecks. A "problem" had been discovered; his name would spread quickly throughout the ship. And at the first opportunity the hotel manager would be paying him a discreet visit.

THE TIME: 2300 Hours

In all departments of the vessel, with the exception of the lounge and entertainment areas, the work of the day has been completed. Tonight, the late-duty nurse could sleep through a portion of her shift. On the bridge, when the expected heavier seas did not materialize, the reduce-speed order had been given. The purser's office has just about completed the rash of first requests from the new passengers. The engine room, fresh from a thorough scouring during the day, is a vacant mechanical showcase.

Parties among seamen are in progress on the crew decks. As some participants give way to sleep others will take their places. Soon, parties launched by off-duty dining room and galley hands will be in high gear. As these subside, the lounge and entertainment staffs will pick up the tempo.

Several dozen passengers are emerging from the Saga Theatre where the movie, "Ordinary People," has been showing.

The main show in the lounge has drawn to a close. The cruise director stands before the audience, basking in the afterglow of dinner, liqueurs and excellent entertainment. He introduces his performers for a final round of applause.

He instructs the crowd, "Now get up on the dance floor. Our musicians will keep you going here for an hour or so. And, in 15 minutes, the Emerald Club will feature, once again, the Homestead Act. The very popular Patsy and Elmo will let their hair down and go to it. We're a bit stiff for them down here in the lounge."

Patsy and Elmo laugh at the side of the stage.

The cruise director continues. "And, at the Emerald Club tonight, the Sea Trio will keep you jumping until you go to bed, or pass out, whichever comes first.

The Windjammer Room at the bow is packed with those who enjoy a more sedate after-dinner session, conversing or just staring at the stars overhead.

The same heavenly panorama is enjoyed by couples strolling arm-in-arm on promenade deck. For them, there are three added bonuses: the salty fragrance of the sea, the gentle touch of the breeze, the sound of rushing waves.

THE TIME: 0100 Hours

"Now come on . . . let's clap our hands . . . this is the way we do it in Tennessee," the sweet and enthusiastic Patsy is telling her appreciative Emerald Club audience.

And she attacks her banjo. Elmo follows on the guitar. They hit the lyrics, with the passengers singing along. Some become so excited they forget to order another round of drinks.

"Hi pop," the seaman says as he passes the elderly cleaner in the dining room.

"Hi son. Still punching the clock?"

"Yeah. Kind of quiet tonight," the sailor says.

"Pretty noisy upstairs. I'm staying away from the Emerald for a while."

Royal Viking Sea sails into the night.

Passengers enjoying skeet shooting.

A relaxing moment in the bar.

Music on deck is often featured during the cruise.

Professional fitness instructors help passengers shed extra pounds
and keep fit at sea.

Whether you want company and music on a crowded dance floor or
a quiet moment around an almost deserted pool — a cruise offers
something for every mood.

10

The Love Boat:
The Show and the Ships

It was not a great day for the Hollywood crew. Actors Lorne Greene and Gavin MacLeod, amid scores of minor players, were attempting to shoot a scene for "The Love Boat." The TV cast was assembled on the pier in Vancouver, in front of the white superstructure of *Island Princess*. The cameramen had shot the same scene over and over again, but the director was not satisfied with any of the takes.

On the bridge of *Island Princess*, Captain Malcolm Rushan was looking down upon all the action. A reporter stood at his side. The journalist asked the captain how the life of a real master differed from the role of captain on the television show.

Rushan thought for a moment and then replied, wryly, "The basic difference, as I see it, is that I have to get everything right the first time around."

THE SHOW

The partnership between Princess Cruises and Hollywood that has existed since 1975 is one of the most interesting and unique in the seafaring or television world. Since it first blossomed on the tube as a made-for-television movie, "The Love Boat" has been a regular fixture in Nielsen's top-ten-rated shows. Instead of slipping in its later years, "Love Boat's" 1980-81 season was its strongest ever. Greater than 90 per cent of the season's episodes were in the top ten. One rerun, aired on a Saturday night, scored a rating of 55 in Chicago, a figure achieved only by such blockbusters as "Roots."

The show's impact, not only on Princess Cruises but on the

entire cruise ship industry, has been dramatic. The series is thought to have helped trigger the sales boom of the late 1970s. The title of the show is now firmly entrenched in the vernacular of the industry. Every cruise director of every ship at sea welcomes passengers aboard "the love boat." The most requested song in every seagoing cabaret is the "Love Boat" theme, sung on television by Jack Jones.

The show has its origins in a 1960s series, "Love American Style," produced by the fertile minds of the Spelling-Goldberg organization, one of the most successful companies in Hollywood. "Love American Style" offered three completely separate romantic comedy sketches in each one-hour TV show. The program enjoyed success for several years before fading from popularity, but according to Spelling-Goldberg producer Henry Colman, the company and key executive Douglas Cramer never lost faith in the concept. They were convinced that "Love American Style" merely needed a new setting.

Princess Cruises, in the meantime, was demonstrating that cruise ships could make good television. The company's vessels had played host to Hollywood shows, including a major episode of the "Columbo" series. When a book emerged on the market called "The Love Boats," Henry Colman and his associates quickly snapped up the idea. They bought the rights to the title and began planning a TV-movie.

Spelling-Goldberg struck a deal with Princess Cruises and then sold the pilot to the American Broadcasting Corporation, at that time headed by Fred Silverman. Colman says the first effort was just "so-so," but Silverman was intrigued and a second movie was made. That led to "The Love Boat III," which was such a tremendous hit that the regular series was born.

Each of the three movie pilots had been written in the "Love American Style" tradition: three separate, unrelated sketches per show; as one ended, another would begin. Colman says they were "far too jumpy." The producers then decided to continue using three separate stories for each show, but to interweave them into a one-cruise time frame. And so the format has continued for seven years.

When the show began, Princess Cruises had just welcomed *Pacific Princess* into the fleet, the identical twin of the company's *Island Princess*. Because *Island Princess* enjoyed a strong passenger demand, it was decided to feature the name of her new sister on the show. Both ships have been and continue to be used for location filming. At Twentieth Century-Fox studios, where most of the show is created, the set includes identical replicas of the actual pool area and lido deck.

The star of the show, Gavin MacLeod, became known to television audiences in the long-running TV hit, "The Mary Tyler Moore Show." He has since blossomed into a first-rank television star with the success of "The Love Boat." Captain Stubing, now seen on television sets in 62 countries, is better known than any master who has ever sailed the seas. In person, he is an even more ebullient personality than he is on the screen. He calls the show "'Wagon Train' on the water," recalling a hit from television's past. He says the show is "an actor's heaven" because of the steady parade of show business greats who have guest parts. Helen Hayes, Vincent Price, Ginger Rogers and Lloyd Bridges are just a few of hundreds of stars who have made appearances.

"Douglas Fairbanks, Jr. taught me how to salute," MacLeod recalls with a chuckle. "But I have completely forgotten. This is a cruise ship, not a warship."

MacLeod says that before "The Love Boat," the only ship he had ever been on was a "mock gun boat in the South China Sea . . . I had a part in 'The Sand Pebbles.'" Producer Henry Colman was another shipping neophyte. He once became so violently seasick as a child, "I purposely went into the air force during the war."

Critics frequently call the show frivolous and mindless, but Colman unashamedly says that people are tired of programs with depressing social themes. "We are producing good commercial television . . . pure escape, glamor, romance." Adds Gavin MacLeod: "People are tuning in to things that make them feel good." In fact, the only ratings slippage in the program's history came during the 1979-80 season, when the writers deliberately inserted more meaningful themes.

The television set designers have been scrupulous in their attention to detail, matching every item, from the Princess Cruises' logos throughout the ship to the staff nametags. This care has provided at least one engineering benefit to the cruise company. Engineers on *Island Princess* and *Pacific Princess* were having problems keeping mosaic tiles from falling off the sides of pools. Every glue they tried failed to work. The problem continued for months, until someone at head office wondered out loud how the pool on "The Love Boat" set was holding up. The engineers visited the studios and the problem was instantly solved. "Hollywood can do anything," says Princess's public relations director, Max Hall.

At least once a year the entire TV crew books aboard a Princess ship for an entire cruise. Not only is a two-hour television movie shot on these cruises, but location scenes of major ports and general romantic film footage are obtained. A routine episode of "The Love Boat" was budgeted at $500,000 in 1981; when the cast went to sea, the figure increased to $750,000. The show pays Princess for the cruise, but at a discounted rate.

There are many passengers of cruise ships who would resent the intrusion of a cumbersome TV crew, with sections of the ship roped off for filming. For this reason, Princess Cruises advises all passengers long in advance that a given trip is to be a "filming cruise." On the other hand, as the demand shows, there are many passengers who would love nothing more than to be on a filming cruise. Passengers are asked to be "extras" in all the scenes, usually sitting in the background. There is no difficulty in getting people to go before the camera, Colman says. "Our problem is the people who want to be in every scene." The performing passengers sign releases authorizing the use of their pictures, but under Hollywood union rules, they can't be paid. However, every time a passenger is used in a scene his name and a number are placed in a bucket. On the final day of the trip, a draw is held for a color TV set.

On board, Gavin MacLeod says he is under no illusion that he knows anything about the actual role of a ship's officers. "They run a real ship and we run a real hour of entertainment."

In fact, cruise line executives are frequently amused by the literary licenses taken by the show. The real passengers and crews are never quite so young and perfect as their TV counterparts. Ed Holbert, vice-president of Eastern Steamship Lines, pointing out the two stripes on "The Love Boat" bartender's shoulders, says, "He must be the highest-ranked bartender in shipping history."

It was equally amusing to the professionals at Princess when they were advised that "The Love Boat" crew wanted to go to Australia to shoot a 1981-82 two-hour special aboard *Sea Princess*. Formerly the Swedish American ship *Kungsholm*, the vessel is operated by Princess's parent company, P&O Cruises. The Princess people told the Hollywood producers that the Australian ship was remarkably different in design and larger than the "Love Boat" twins, so the show's writers explained that *Pacific Princess* would go into drydock; in the meantime, Captain Stubing would be assigned another ship.

This is another first in the cruise ship industry: a captain moving to another ship, in another hemisphere, for a mere two weeks — and taking his crew. Hollywood was not bothered by petty details — such as what happened to the usual crew of *Sea Princess?*

The television show became one of the most bizarre casualties of the 1982 Falklands crisis. Constantly looking for new locations, "The Love Boat" producers had planned to sail aboard *Sea Princess* in the Mediterranean, a spring and summer venue the ship shares with P&O's *Canberra* and *Uganda*. With both of her sisters called to action in the Falklands, and *Sea Princess* herself on emergency British standby, it was impossible to accommodate the 120 beds required by the television crew. "The Love Boat" cast moved, instead, to the Sun Line flagship *Stella Solaris* for what is believed to be a one time only departure from the Princess Cruises partnership. The Sun Line was so excited by its good fortune that even its Greek owners were aboard during the cruise.

THE SHIPS:
GENESIS OF A CRUISE LINE

The City of Seattle hosted the 1962 World's Fair. The event, while only moderately successful, indirectly gave birth to one of the most famous cruise lines in the world.

A Canadian-born Seattle businessman and entrepreneur, Stanley McDonald, successful in air freight and various industrial activities, saw an opportunity for bringing tourists to the Fair. He purchased an old ship, *Yarmouth*, and marketed package tours of Portland, Oregon, and Vancouver and Victoria, British Columbia, all including several days at the Seattle exhibition. At the end of the season he sold the ship. Pleased with the profitability of the tours, McDonald began thinking about further ventures in the cruise field. More than two years would pass before his ideas were realized.

With amazement, McDonald — a cruise ship novice — observed that while cruise markets of the Caribbean, the Mediterranean, the Aegean and the South Pacific were growing, virtually nothing was taking place on the west coast from Alaska to Acapulco. Small Canadian coastal steamers continued to conduct summer cruises from Vancouver to Alaska, and numerous ships stopped at Acapulco either before or after a crossing of the Pacific Ocean. As cruise destinations, McDonald became convinced, these markets were ripe for exploitation.

At the end of 1964, he negotiated a deal with Canadian Pacific Steamships to charter the Alaskan coastal steamer *Princess Patricia*. The 6,000-ton vessel, built in Scotland during the late 1940s, was used by her owners solely for summertime cruises. McDonald proposed to finance extensive renovations, install air conditioners and keep the ship's Canadian seamen employed during the winter months with cruises to Mexico.

When she sailed in 1964 from Los Angeles, with 400 American passengers aboard, *Princess Patricia* was to launch one of the modern cruise industry's greatest markets: the Mexican Riviera. And when her royal title was adopted for the corporate name, not even Stan McDonald could foresee how famous Princess Cruises would become.

The first trip brought its share of headaches. *Princess Patricia* was the first cruise ship ever to visit Puerto Vallarta. The local population, excited by the prospect, sunk an old barge to create a makeshift wharf. But a storm erupted the night before the ship was to arrive, and the barge floated off the beach. The townsfolk worked with ropes for 24 hours to get the barge back in place. When she arrived, *Princess Patricia* was greeted by fireworks and shoreside celebrations. During that first winter, McDonald paid for the construction of a proper wharf for the town.

The cruise brought other calamities. The new air conditioners, installed above clothes' lockers in the cabins, developed so much condensation that the wardrobes of most passengers were thoroughly flooded. In Acapulco, the ship and passenger laundry was sent ashore for processing, only to arrive back at night, unsorted, in one giant bag. The passengers and crew spent an entire evening in the ballroom sifting through the heaps and trying to find their personal articles of clothing. On another occasion the ship's ballast tanks inadvertently were emptied into the main water supply. Rust-colored water poured from every tap.

But both the ship and the company survived these and scores of other uncomfortable incidents. As *Princess Patricia* sailed to Canada for her 1965 Alaska season, McDonald negotiated a contract to charter her for one more Mexico season. But he was thinking of bigger things.

During the second *Princess Patricia* season, McDonald discovered that, partway through the construction of perhaps the most luxurious small ship ever built, an Italian company had gone into bankruptcy. He flew to Rome and negotiated with the Banco del Lavoro for the right to charter, with an Italian crew, the 12,500-ton *Italia*. The next winter, the ship sailed as *Princess Italia* and was soon joined by a second Princess Cruises vessel, the older and much larger *S.S. Carla C.*, renamed *Princess Carla*.

The two ships were so successful in the Mexican and Alaskan waters that Stan McDonald found himself beating back offers from major corporations to purchase his cruise company. In 1968, the offer from a huge conglomerate was so generous that the Princess founder could not turn it down. With mixed emotions he stepped aside, to focus all his attention on his other business activities.

Carla and *Italia* continued on their successful cruises, but the conglomerate was having difficulties in other business interests. When the corporation decided to unload Princess Cruises, McDonald was waiting to buy it back. His 1970 purchase price was lower than the figure he had been paid in 1968.

With the cruise line again in his control, Stan McDonald wanted a better ship. Two vessels under construction at Emden, West Germany, fitted his plans perfectly. Being built for Norwegian owners, *Sea Venture* and *Island Venture* — 20,000-tonners — were to be the most elegant, efficient and modern ships of their class afloat. He worked with the builders, and was instrumental in planning the ships' interior designs, while trying to negotiate rights to charter both vessels. He was only successful in obtaining charter rights to one, however, and eight months later *Island Princess* became the pride of the North American west coast. Her sister, *Sea Venture*, sailed for a company known as Flagship Cruises.

With his new ship and the no-less elegant *Princess Italia*, McDonald was able to drop the contract for *Princess Carla*. She was returned to her owners, the giant Italian company, Costa Cruises.

The two modern Princess ships dominated every port from Acapulco to Skagway, Alaska, from 1971 until 1973, when the contract with the bankers for *Princess Italia* came to an end. McDonald tried to negotiate a purchase of the ship, but the Italian bankers were completely unrealistic in their price demands. He was sad to see her return to Italy. (Both *Italia* and *S.S. Carla C.* are currently in the Costa fleet.)

During 1974 Princess Cruises operated *Island Princess* only, with her Norwegian officers and Italian service staff. Competition in Mexico and Alaska had grown with the arrival of Royal Viking Lines, Sitmar Cruises and the huge British company, the P&O Line. A one-ship operation is less than desirable; the same overhead is required to manage and market one ship or two. McDonald had to obtain another vessel, or to merge with another company.

P&O's new cruise ship, the 17,000-ton *Spirit of London*, smaller and less luxurious than the *Island Princess*, was competing head-to-head with her on the same runs. It was perhaps inevitable that the two companies would come together. P&O finally made an offer to purchase Princess Cruises, and McDonald accepted. The founder was asked to remain on, for an indefinite period, as salaried president of the wholly-owned P&O subsidiary. *Spirit of London* was renamed *Sun Princess*, and McDonald was given the funds to purchase a third ship. He had but one mind: *Sea Venture*, *Island Princess's* identical sister. In 1974, *Sea Venture* joined the fleet as *Pacific Princess*.

Although P&O installed British officers on all the ships immediately, McDonald convinced the parent company to have Italian staff work the galleys and dining rooms of both *Island* and *Pacific Princesses*. *Sun Princess* retained her Goanese catering staff until late 1981, when Italians replaced them.

Stan McDonald continued to serve as president of Princess Cruises until late 1979. Speculation in the company was that he grew bored working for other masters, but he resigned to pursue his numerous business activities. There are many rumors in the industry that he is exploring the opportunity to launch a completely new cruise company. About this he will say only, "I still love ships and I am interested in any opportunity."

Princess Cruises has thrived under P&O ownership. The chairman of the board is Len Scott at P&O headquarters in London, but the subsidiary is autonomously run from its Los Angeles office by president Joe Waters.

Waters is enthusiastic about the company's expansion into other areas of the tourist business. The firm recently purchased a major resort complex at Oxnard, California; its travel subsidiary, Princess Tours, has become a major force in the west coast package-tour business. But he is no less enthusiastic about the cruise ship business.

When *Island Princess* and *Pacific Princess* were commissioned in West Germany during the late 1960s, the construction budget was $16 million per ship. The final delivered price for each was $25 million. To build each vessel today would require as much as $130 million.

But Princess president Waters says the ships will never be duplicated. He explains that the new vessels under construction make heavy use of prefabricated components, with less attention paid to detail.

"A ship like *Island Princess*," Joe Waters says, "will never be built again." The comment was made a few months before Princess Cruises and its P&O parent announced plans for a $150 million, 40,000-ton new ship, currently under construction. The new flagship, twice the size of the "Love Boats," will be critically compared to the predecessors that determined the image of the company.

11

Current Developments

SHIP NEWS

S.S. United States

The cruise industry was startled by Norwegian Caribbean Lines' announcement to reincarnate *S.S. France*. Richard Hadley, on the other hand, created only mild interest with his plan to bring *S.S. United States* back into business. It is never surprising when an enthusiastic amateur proposes some questionable project.

Hadley, a wealthy Seattle businessman who made his fortune in Hawaiian real estate, had no prior experience in the cruising business. He negotiated a deal with the United States government to buy the 53,000-ton ship for $5 million, and said he would spend $90 million renovating the vessel for modern cruise service. The government attached one condition to the deal: *S.S. United States* must sail under U.S. registry with an American crew.

The Seattle announcement came in 1979. *United States* still sits at her berth in the James River at Norfolk, Virginia, her resting place since United States Lines pulled her from service in 1969 after years of appalling financial losses.

The crowning achievement of America's greatest ship designer, William Francis Gibbs, *S.S. United States* was as much an experiment of the U. S. Navy as it was an ocean liner. The government paid $48 million of her total cost of just over $75 million. Her engine room was built with both patriotism and technology in mind. It was believed that if the U.S. produced the Blue Riband champion, the prestige would pump new life into the entire American merchant marine service. But the Navy looked at *S.S. United States* for practical purposes. Gibbs was instructed to design the ship in such a way that she could convert instantly into a troop transport capable of carrying 14,000 soldiers.

Gibbs was obsessed with fire safety and weight. It is said that the need for every piece of furniture and equipment weighing more than 25 pounds was carefully studied. Much of her hull and superstructure, and as much of the interior as possible, was made of light-weight aluminum and alloys. Gibbs was fond of saying that the only wood aboard was the grand piano and the butcher's block. He told reporters that he had asked the Steinway people to build an aluminum piano, but the company indignantly refused. The architect prohibited oil paintings, choosing, instead, metal sculptures and other noninflammable works of art.

All the military concerns and Gibbs' experiments tended to lessen the elegance of *S.S. United States*. She had an austere beauty about her, yet she paled in luxury against the *Queens* or, ten years later, *S.S. France*.

But she was fast. On her 1952 maiden voyage she steamed the North Atlantic Blue Riband in three days and eleven hours, a mark that will likely stand forever. The engine room of *S.S. United States* remains to this day a U.S. Defense Department secret.

In 1981, Richard Hadley said that he viewed the plans to resail the great ship as, "a fascinating challenge." It may be all of that, or more. In 1979, Hadley and his associates had attempted to sell the ship as a holiday time-share proposal. An expensive advertising campaign encouraged people to buy a one-week holiday for twenty years into the future. There were few takers, and the plan fizzled.

Since then, not much has happened. When critics suggest that the fuel costs alone would make the ship uneconomical, Hadley replies that he plans to remove half her engine capacity. This was done to *S.S. Norway*. *Norway* is still one of the most expensive fuel burners at sea, despite her slow-speed cruising.

What may finally scuttle Hadley's plans is a revitalized interest by the Pentagon in the once proud ocean liner. Navy planners are lobbying the government to spend $400 million to make *S.S. United States* the largest hospital ship in history.

There is speculation in the cruise industry that the Seattle company would only maintain ownership of the ship if the United States government lifts its insistence on American registry. If this were to be done, Hadley would be free to crew the ship with less expensive foreign nationals, or to sell her to others for use in cruising, as a museum, as a hotel, or for scrap.

All the Seattle company would say in late 1981 about the continued debate was; "We are waiting for the government to make up its mind." About what, the company did not say.

S.S. United States still sits quietly in Norfolk waters.

The Falklands Crisis

When P&O's flagship returned to Southampton after her distinguished duty in the Falklands, thousands of British troops and Gurkhas waving from the rails, *Canberra* basked in the glow of her finest moment. Tens of thousands ashore sung "Rule Britannia" with gusto and emotion unseen since the fading era of empire.

Within days of Argentina's 1982 invasion of the Falklands, British government authorities requisitioned *Queen Elizabeth 2* from Cunard, and *Canberra* and *Uganda* from P&O. The ships hastily went into port to have expensive accoutrements removed and rough planking laid over the more valuable deckboards, in preparation for military drills. *Uganda* was outfitted for hospital purposes.

Participation in the campaign by the cruise ship officers was voluntary and, to the last man, they swore themselves into military service. As the three ships made their way toward the South Atlantic, a pall was cast over the P&O contingent by the first casualty of the British Falklands armada. *Uganda* Captain B.J.B.C. Biddick collapsed at the helm of his ship. Surgery at sea diagnosed inoperable cancer and he was airlifted ashore. He died shortly after reaching England. Biddick, just 47, was the long time senior captain of *Island Princess*, and a personal favorite of Gavin MacLeod and "The Love Boat" cast.

The troop carriers *Queen Elizabeth 2* and *Canberra*, and the

182

hospital ship *Uganda,* served with distinction. *QE2,* the most prestigious and potentially demoralizing target, was kept a considerable distance from the action, transferring her troops by helicopter to the warships. But *Uganda* had to be close and *Canberra* sailed many times into the fray, suffering minor hits, cosmetic damage and many near misses.

The British government contracted to remunerate Cunard and P&O for the before-and-after renovation and business interruption, and provided a two-year maintenance contract for future mechanical difficulties that can be traced back to the wear and tear in the Falklands. Shortly after her refit and reentry into passenger service, *Queen Elizabeth 2* suffered a major mechanical breakdown, forcing vacationers to be ferried ashore.

The quick enlistment and valiant service of the ships aptly demonstrated the value of being the nation of registry for passenger liners. Countries such as the United States and Canada, which have largely lost their passenger merchant marine, may well be rethinking their military priorities in the wake of the Falklands campaign.

Long Beach Dumps *Queen Mary*

When it was announced that *Queen Mary* and *Queen Elizabeth* were to be withdrawn from service, Cunard capitalized on nostalgia and, in their final voyages, the royal pair did tremendous business. When the French government, having decided to retire *S.S. France,* tried to follow the British lead, its plans were cut abruptly short. Several expensive final voyages were announced just as the news of the ship's upcoming retirement was made public. On her next trip into Le Havre, *France's* crew refused to bring her into port. The longshoremen, equally hostile, called an instant strike.

The French Line was able to settle the dispute and moor the great ship, but only after it announced cancellation of the final voyages.

Queen Elizabeth perished in Hong Kong, but *Queen Mary* sits today in regal splendor, one of California's leading tourist attractions. The City of Long Beach bought the ship. With its final voyage, from England to California via Cape Horn (she was too large for Panama), came stories of poor sanitation, no air conditioning in tropical climes and poor food. But she did arrive, and Long Beach spent more than $100 million creating the floating museum.

Three of her twelve decks comprise a Hyatt hotel and include numerous dining facilities. The many museum attractions show the grandeur of the ship in her prime and through wartime service. There is a large Jacques Cousteau marine display as well.

Long Beach has lost fortunes over the years operating the *Queen Mary* attraction. There have been millions of visitors, but costs have always exceeded revenues. Recently, the city sold the vessel to a private company that is highly optimistic about *Queen Mary's* future success.

Titanic I, II and III

If the industry is skeptical about Richard Hadley's eventual success with *United States*, it regards the plans of San Diego insurance executive Jim Beardsley as sheer fantasy. Beardsley has announced that he will build three 46,000-ton vessels: *Titanic I*, *Titanic II* and *Titanic III*. He says he has been at work for three years, planning the venture through his Titanic Steamship Lines.

He wants to have the ships constructed in the same Belfast shipyards in which the original *Titanic* and her sister, *Olympic*, were built for White Star Lines. "But if the situation doesn't settle down over there, we may have to go elsewhere for construction," Beardsley says.

The vessels would resemble the *Titanic* on the outside but the interiors would be completely different. On each ship there would be 600 passengers in 300 luxury two-room suites. The crew would number 1,200. (Generally, there is one crew member for two passengers. Beardsley's ratio is the reverse.)

Beardsley says construction will begin in 1983, with the first ship launched in 1985. The projected fare is $15,000 per couple for a five-day crossing of the Atlantic. The vessels will be built for speed. Jim Beardsley says that his ships will regularly beat the Blue Riband record held by *S.S. United States*.

People from around the world have been clamoring for

reservations ever since his plans were made public, Beardsley explains. But the United States government has expressed concern that people are spending money for a highly speculative venture. Beardsley says he is accepting reservations, not money, at this stage.

He is, however, raising investment capital. In late 1981, he claimed to have raised three-quarters of the $1.5 billion he says the ships will cost. At $500 million per ship, the budget is three times that of any ship ever constructed.

When it was suggested that his plans sounded rather farfetched, Beardsley replied, "I can see why you would say that, but I assure you we can do this ... Each ship will do $250 million worth of business each year, without even considering liquor and gambling profits."

THE SAFEST TRANSPORT

There are so few serious accidents at sea that the subject would not be worth mentioning, were it not for the fact that some passengers still express concern. The total number of accidental deaths at sea during the past 30 years is less than the number of traffic deaths that happen on the highways of the western world in just a few hours.

In all aspects of passenger shipping, including harbor ferries, accidental deaths since the second world war number in the hundreds. When *Andrea Doria* collided with *Stockholm* in 1956, there were 51 deaths. When *Yarmouth Castle* burned in 1965, 89 perished. When *Prinsendam* sank off Alaska in 1980, all passengers and crew were rescued safely. The record is the best of any business engaged in public transportation. In more than three decades of passenger service, hundreds of ships, thousands of voyages and millions of passengers have sailed happily and safely.

Fire is, without question, the greatest concern at sea. Ships are built with every fire-prevention and control device imaginable, plus watertight compartments in the event of hull damage. Crews are exercised continuously in fire procedures and boat drills. Every cruise begins with a passenger lifeboat drill.

Most western countries insist that ships entering their ports conform to regulations of safety and sanitation. And to obtain insurance, cruise ships must submit to regular inspection by a reputable independent surveyor.

The most respected surveyor of shipping in the world is Lloyds Register of Shipping, an autonomous adjunct to the Lloyds of London insurance empire. For a fee, a cruise line arranges an inspection of its ships which, if deemed satisfactory, are assigned the prized "100 A-1" Lloyds Register rating. A company with such a rating can expect a beneficial insurance policy. Lloyds is dominant in the field — it also does surveying for 83 governments — but there are other ship surveyors. The Norwegians have a highly respected firm that, for a fee, will perform an inspection and assign a rating.

THE CALM SEAS

Many passengers still worry about rough seas, despite the fact that most cruises take place in waters as calm as a bathtub's. With aircraft carrying travellers to the ship, cruises no longer have to cross rough waters to reach the vacation area.

Every ship in the industry is now equipped with stabilizing fins. Resembling aircraft wings, the stabilizers are eight to ten feet long, and five feet wide. Located one-third the length of a ship back from the bow, they work much like an aircraft's aileron: with a pitch into the waves they adjust automatically to suit the sea condition. The gyro-controlled devices electronically record sea conditions, and through hydraulic systems they dispatch counteracting wing positions against the sea.

Denny Brown stabilizers, named for their Scottish inventor and still manufactured in Scotland, are dominant in the industry, though the American firms Ledgerwood and Sperry have been gaining ground. Stabilizers can eliminate 90 per cent of a ship's roll. They are used most of the time a cruise is in progress, although they require extra fuel consumption and cost a ship about one knot in speed.

PORTS

Cruise lines once searched for world-renowned pleasure spots, then planned cruises to serve them. The destination

186

would make the cruise a success. With the growth of cruising, the pattern has been reversed. When the ships discover a little-known port, it is sure to gain international prominence. Governments of Caribbean islands, mayors of Mexican villages and various officials throughout the rest of the world do everything in their power to attract the passenger cruise ships.

The best example of this situation is the transformation of the island of St. Thomas in the U.S. Virgin Islands. Prior to the arrival of cruise ships a little over a decade ago, this free port was known only to a handful of jet-setters. Today, cruise line promotion throughout the world has turned the tiny island into an international landmark. As many as 14 ships may, on any day, be anchored in the harbor of Charlotte Amalie, capital of St. Thomas. Additionally, the hotels are packed with visitors who did not come by ship. There were few tourists here before the cruise lines made St. Thomas a regular port of call.

CLOSED-CIRCUIT TELEVISION

Ten years ago, many cruise companies experimented with closed-circuit television, if not throughout the ships then at least in the deluxe staterooms. But the lines had so much difficulty obtaining good quality program material that the practice was largely abandoned. With the video boom of recent years, securing top-rate material no longer is a problem. Yet the cruise companies seem reluctant to renew their interest.

The reason now is purely commercial. The ships do not want to encourage passengers to stay in their cabins; they want people to visit the bars, the casinos or some other revenue-producing area.

Some companies are moving back into the video field. *S.S. Emerald Seas* has a black-and-white set in every cabin and uses the closed-circuit facility for ship's announcements, newscasts and some entertainment.

S.S. Norway has moved farthest ahead in the area There is a color television set in every passenger cabin, and sets through-out crew quarters as well. An experienced Los Angeles TV producer works full time on the ship's six-channel station, WNCL (W-Norwegian Caribbean Lines). The station offers regularly scheduled newscasts throughout the day, promotes constantly the program of activities (including the revenue-producers) and features interviews with the ship's entertainers. One camera remains focused at all times on the pool and lido deck area, and passengers tune in to see if the action looks worthwhile. It is presumed that the ship, no less interested than its competitors in keeping passengers in the public areas, will minimize entertainment offerings on the tube. Not surprisingly, the channel carrying the majority of movies and entertainment programs is available only to the crew.

THE BOARDROOMS OF CRUISING

The cruise executives of today have little time for the nostalgia, tradition and emotion that governed the lives of their passenger-liner predecessors. The new industrialists are simply businessmen; it matters little whether they are selling cruises or spaghetti, so long as they are skilled in management, finance, engineering, promotion and market research.

The modern-day shipping executive spends far more of his time in the air than on the sea. He covers the globe — the shipyard in Germany, the insurance agency in New York, the catering company in Genoa, the personnel agency in Paris, the travel agents' convention in Miami Beach. The presidents of two American-based Norwegian companies attend board meetings in Norway every six weeks; not unusual for industry executives.

A modern cruise line of three ships has assets approaching $250 million. The staff numbers nearly 2,000 with a weekly payroll of up to a million dollars. In addition to the crews, there is a battalion of accountants, personnel directors, office managers, promoters, salesmen and secretaries.

The glamor and romance of cruising remain only in the minds of passengers.

FUEL AND OTHER HEADACHES

The meteoric rise of fuel costs has dramatically effected the cruise ship industry. Most of the shipping companies negotiate complicated international agreements with the oil giants (there have been occasions in the past decade when ships were fuelled on the black market). Marketing brochures for a cruise season are prepared a year or more in advance and include rate schedules. But fuel costs have escalated so unpredictably that on several occasions during the 1970s, the companies were forced to impose last-minute passenger surcharges.

As the oil price skyrocketed from $3.35 to more than $40 a barrel, a ship's fuel cost per passenger rose from $10 a week to more than $100. Meanwhile, the costs of food, capital construction, wages and bank interest rates have, of course, assaulted the balance sheets as well.

But fuel has done more than change prices; it has completely reshaped the cruise industry. Ten years ago, a ship could leave Miami and cover most of the Caribbean in a week or ten days. Today, the cruises from Miami don't get much farther than the next-door Bahamas, Puerto Rico and the Virgin Islands. Ten years ago, the companies in Los Angeles marketed ten-day cruises to Acapulco and back, with stops at three other ports. Today, the Mexico cruises generally take seven days each way, and the passengers fly one way. These adjustments are all in the interests of reducing speed and conserving fuel.

The most important technology being built into the modern ships is designed to conserve fuel — from efficient diesels to computers that automatically regulate every device at optimum conditions for fuel conservation.

On a typical crossing of the North Atlantic, the turbine-powered *Queen Mary* consumed 4,500 tons of fuel. She carried 2,000 passengers across the Atlantic in less than five days. Two modern cruise ships would require six days to transport the same contingent, and the two ships combined would burn only 1,000 tons of fuel.

IF YOU CAN'T LICK 'EM, JOIN 'EM

The most important tools today of any cruise company are the aircraft that carry the passengers to the ships. The struggle between jets and ships in the 1950s ended with the death of the ocean liner. Through the 1960s, the two transportation industries had little to do with each other. Then, gradually, the cruise firms began to discover that ships do not need to go to the passengers; the people could come to the ships.

Many cruise lines claim credit for starting the fly/cruise packages during the late 1960s, and all of them are heavily into the business today. The cruise companies negotiate special air fares on the basis of thousands of seats per year, from all over the world. Sometimes, when a ship's passengers come mostly from one large urban area, special charter flights are organized. Passengers can fly free of charge from many cities to the port of embarkation. And from everywhere in North America, for ships sailing from U.S. ports, highly discounted air fares are available through the cruise companies. Regardless of cruise destination, it is usually much more reasonable to purchase the air ticket through the shipping company than directly through an airline.

Airline executives are equally enthusiastic about the trend. Gerry Draper, British Airways' director of commercial operations, says he is anxious to see his company become much more involved in fly/cruise packaging. He sees major opportunities in developing cruise-related air travel from Europe to the Mexico and Alaska markets, and from the United States to the Mediterranean market. British Airways and Cunard have worked out an elaborate package tied in to the trans-Atlantic crossings of *Queen Elizabeth 2*. One-way air fares, including first-class and even the elite Concorde service, are much less than the airline's usual prices.

MARITIME LAW

The law of the sea has evolved over centuries of difficulties among nations. In fact, ongoing conferences continue to take place at Geneva, with countries haggling — sometimes bitterly — over fisheries treaties, 12-mile limits and the conventions for all forms of shipping procedures.

There are numerous articles of maritime law which, over the years, most of the nations of the world have signed. When an accident takes place at sea, the first investigation is conducted by the shipping company, the second is by one of the insurers, and the third is by the ship's country of registry. If an accident occurs within the territorial waters of any major nation, that country will hold hearings according to the conventions of its own maritime law.

When a ship is registered by one of the sophisticated western nations, the maritime tribunals are beyond reproach. There have been occasional difficulties with "flags of convenience." Truthfully, countries such as Liberia and Panama do not have any enforced standards for their ships. When an accident occurs involving one of their vessels, usually the owners accept the verdict of an insurance adjuster; they cannot afford to be banned from ports in the great shipping nations.

Each shipping nation issues certifications to its own ships' officers. The country issuing the papers enforces its own standard, but a captain found negligent in a foreign country will usually have his papers suspended back home.

When all the corporate, insurance, national and coast guard examinations fail to resolve difficulties on the high seas, disputes between countries arrive at Geneva. Participation is voluntary among nations.

12

Pumping the Bilge:
Data and Anecdotes

Those who recall the glory days of the great liners tend to forget how poor the conditions were for most of the passengers most of the time.

Consider a letter from an irate first-class passenger to a shipping company after a dreadful voyage in 1956. He complained about accommodation, cleanliness, entertainment and just about everything else. Describing the food, he added, "The bread, toast, rolls and pastries were most certainly evolved from an old Royal Air Force recipe that many of us had assumed could never be duplicated except under the exigencies of total warfare."

Only the most passionate cruise buff could answer this quiz question: Who were the "Martini Marines?"

In 1973, when *Queen Elizabeth 2* sailed for Israel for the country's twenty-fifth anniversary, there was so much security aboard that the press dubbed her, "the Floating Fortress." British commandos and bomb disposal experts, wearing civilian clothes and blending in with the passengers, circulated over the ship. Cunard paid the British government for their services, and the press named the pros the "Martini Marines."

One ship carries a 25,000-gallon tank of chianti for her crew. On one night during every cruise, this wine is distributed free to passengers in the dining room. The bite is as sharp as a razor blade's, but there are those people who enjoy anything that doesn't cost them money. At the captain's table one night, a couple who had previously distinguished themselves by not buying wine when their turn arrived, remarked that the crew chianti was delicious. A passenger across the table said he thought it was rather poor.

Flustered, the wife turned to the captain for help. "Each to his own taste, that's what I always say. What do you think, captain?" she asked.

"You must understand that we have this wine once every cruise," the captain replied. "Over the years, I've tried it straight, on the rocks, with water and with soda. I haven't been able to get it down yet!"

Imagine the revved-up heartbeat of the passenger, seated in his deck chair and reading a book, who felt a very wet nudge on his hand. He looked down to see a huge pig. A Chinese crew member had bartered for the animal on shore and brought it back to the ship. The porker managed to find its way from crew quarters to the public area, seven decks above.

One chief engineer, taking a group of passengers through the engine room, remarked on the "vital purpose" served by a certain machine.

"Such as booze storage?"

The question came from a passenger at the back of the group. He was holding up a bottle of vodka.

"I found this jammed in behind the machine," the passenger explained.

As the engineer's face reddened, the passengers enjoyed a laugh.

The engine room, accessible only to a few crew members, is an excellent hiding place for contraband. It is so noisy and greasy that inspecting officers and customs agents rarely look too closely.

One night the entertainment featured Madame X, a well-disguised member of the cruise staff. It was announced that this world-renowned psychic had been flown in by helicopter.

Madame X delivered rather vague and general readings to passenger after passenger. What created chuckles among the crew were the passengers who returned to their seats muttering:

"Astounding!"

"Imagine that — flying her in for the evening!"

"How could she possibly have known that?"

And so on.

One of Hollywood's biggest box-office hits is among the few important feature films that have never been show on a cruise ship. The movie, not surprisingly, is "The Poseidon Adventure."

There are always those passengers who express genuine disappointment upon discovering that daily newspapers from major urban centres are not available at sea.

As passengers were filing from a ship to go ashore by launch, the boarding party officer noted an elderly lady standing at the side. He asked if he might help her into the boat. The passenger shook her head. She said she was waiting for her tour bus. The officer patiently explained that the boat would take her to meet her bus on the shore, but she refused to budge.

The puzzled officer walked away, only to return moments later. "Madam, your bus has arrived," he said. The passenger thanked the officer and stepped out the door and into the launch.

FOG, STORMS AND LIFEBOATS

Fog can give a captain nightmares. When visibility is reduced to near zero, the master of the ship suspends all other functions, including attendance in the dining room, to be on the bridge. Radar and navigational equipment cannot spot small fishing boats unless special radar deflectors are being used by the fishermen. The ship's foghorn is switched on to

194

blast automatically every few minutes. Tension on the bridge — shrouded in dark-green lighting — is overwhelming. Officers can only pray that all small craft move out of the way.

Crews find the lifeboat drill a nuisance, but it is one of the most important routines at sea. All members of a ship's company are schooled in emergency procedures. Each person has a precise role to play in time of emergency, and inspections are frequent. At the start of every cruise, passengers are asked to assemble with life jackets for a safety lecture.

Although a ship carries a sufficient number of motorized lifeboats in which to carry all passengers and crew, in the event of an emergency scores of rubber rafts are automatically launched into the sea. All lifeboats and rafts are equipped with first-aid supplies and enough food and water for 24 hours at sea.

Contrary to myth, a captain is not expected to go down with his ship. His duty is to ensure that all watertight doors are closed. This substantially delays the sinking of a vessel, and it ensures that she will go down on an even keel. When a captain is satisfied that everyone is safely off the ship, he then collects the logbooks and boards the last launch.

A few years ago a large liner encountered a tornado. The bow of the vessel was digging deep in the swell and waves were engulfing the ship, slapping high and powerfully into the windows of the bridge. On several occasions the glass was smashed in. The passengers — almost 80 per cent of them ill — were confined to cabins. Ropes were stretched through the inside and outside corridors to assist seamen, who were stumbling from place to place on their rounds.

Every member of the company was given an assignment, ensuring the safety of the ship through the critical period, and on the deck seamen were tightening down facilities. On the bridge, in the radio room and in the bowels of the ship, officers and crew fought the storm. Crew were dispatched to cabins to snap down deadlights, the protective metal screens on older vessels that are pulled down at times of emergency to block the glass portholes. (Porthole glass can shatter viciously.)

The seamen making the cabin rounds usually found the passengers clutching their stomachs as the ship pitched wildly in the seas. The hardy, however, enjoyed the adventure. Occasionally, lovers were caught in their beds. A second team was sent through the ship delivering tea and sausages. A few disgruntled passengers demanded coffee and, on that occasion, the crew were at perfect liberty to speak their minds.

During storms, the ship's galley is the most exciting place, with the huge pots and cauldrons clanging and swaying in all directions. Equipment is bolted down as a matter of course, but the few things that break loose do so in noisy and messy fashion.

CREW MADNESS

One shipping company has a printed warning for crew members who over-extend their bar budget: "Today's Sobering Thought."

Young women in a ship's crew always have an able and willing team of bouncers not far away, to help them out of difficulties with obnoxious passengers. There are stories of large muscular brutes who, to their alarm, find themselves being hustled down a hall by three or four equally strapping seamen.

Brief cruises of three or four days have become popular throughout the industry. Because loading and unloading passengers and supplies make up a significant portion of a crew's workload, these short cruises are generally despised by the ship's company. The so-called "party cruise" is marketed to young people as a three-day fiesta. For many passengers these trips can be wild affairs, with almost nonstop drinking for 72 hours.

Theft among crew members is extremely rare. Even the less scrupulous members of the company recognize the obvious fact that the team has to live together for long stretches. There can be no escape when someone is suspected of theft, and a thorough search is ordered. Police work is generally left to the crew.

A common treatment for thieves, once caught, is to place their fingers on a porthole ledge, then slam down a metal protective door.

On most British ships, one member of the crew occupies the unofficial position of ship bookie. Gambling is a crew pursuit on every ship, but particularly because of the football pool, it is most complicated on a British vessel. Sophisticated arrangements are made with the radio officer to have the scores transmitted. On one ship, a gambling operation involves periodic raffles of stereo equipment purchased ashore.

In the luxury environment of cruise ships, it is not surprising that crew may experience weight or drinking problems. Although dieting on a ship is difficult, stern warnings from the captain soon sweat off the poundage. Controlling alcohol intake is far more difficult. Liquor has brought many seafaring careers to an early end.

A male dancer on one ship is a former bullfighter. His duties, in addition to performing at nightly shows and helping lonely ladies on the dance floor, include giving disco lessons, fencing classes and exercise sessions.

Pursers have more difficulty with crew's requests for cabin changes than they do with passengers'. Because crew members live closely together seven days a week and for six or eight months at a stretch, disagreements, fights and romances happen. These are always followed by reassignment requests.
One trick is to pair two crew members from the same hometown. Fear of one roommate writing home with stories of drunkenness, fights or too much girl-chasing can be inhibiting to the other.

A photographer on one ship married an entertainer who was working on board. Shortly after the wedding, the bride was transferred to entertain on another vessel. They saw little of each other between vacations, but occasionally their ships crossed paths. One time, when they learned that the ships would be passing each other in opposite directions, the couple made arrangements by cable to stand on the decks at the sterns; they would wave when the vessels crossed. But when the moment arrived, it was too overcast for them to see more than the other ship shrouded in the mist. They did manage a brief chat by radio phone.

In the early years of cruising the South Pacific, P&O Lines' bar chits were honored by many shoreside establishments, notably at Yokohama. When the chits came due back on the ship, many crew members discovered that their entire salary had mysteriously disappeared — a hangover from a fine time at shore.

STOWAWAYS

Stowaways are not the problem they once were, but occasionally they do show up. The most frequent stowaway is the guest who got carried away at a bon voyage party. If discovered early, he is simply put ashore on the pilot boat. Caught later, the stowaway is dropped at the first port of call; he is billed for the days spent on the ship and legal means are used to ensure collection. Natives of some poor countries, particularly Fiji, are often a problem. In some ports, thorough ship searches are conducted prior to embarkation. Unwelcome visitors have been found in ship's launches, lavatories and even in passenger cabins, pretending to be a part of the crew. When the stowaway is successful, the cruise line usually must pay the illegal immigrant's air fare home before he can be put ashore into the hands of the authorities.

One visitor who had failed to hear the sailing announcements demanded that the ship return to the pier. She was offered a ride in the pilot boat but adamantly refused. When advised that she would have to pay the fare to the next port, she objected loudly. After an uncomfortable hour the purser was able to make telephone contact with the woman's husband, who told the officer to give her whatever she wanted. The husband cabled money to the ship.

Advised of her husband's arrangements, the woman, with several drinks behind her, muttered, "The sonofabitch wants to get rid of me."

The purser couldn't understand why.

One wealthy playboy, when caught, claimed that he had been getting away with stowing-away for years. The chap's trick was to befriend a young single woman, spend the night with her in her cabin, and then disappear first thing in the morning.

His game finally came to an end when an alert cabin steward discovered him just before the ship arrived at San Francisco (he had boarded at Panama). Not only did the stowaway have to pay the cruise line full fare, he was prosecuted and given a stiff fine.

ALL THE SHIPS AT SEA

Throughout the English-speaking world, ships are always personified in the female gender; even vessels with male names are referred to as "she" or "her." For example: "When *Prince George* reached her final destination, she was greeted by royalty."

The opposite is true in France. It is correct French usage to use the masculine gender. Ships are referred to as "le."

Queen Elizabeth 2 is one of the few ships in the industry with the capacity to carry automobiles. Vehicles — usually an array of Rolls Royces, Cadillacs and other luxury models — are driven on and off the ship. The 1981 trans-Atlantic one-way fare for a vehicle ranged from $1,000 to $1,400 per vehicle, with small discounts offered on return bookings.

Car owners are advised to bring the vehicles aboard with almost empty gas tanks, to avoid spillage on high seas. One passenger, greedy to take advantage of lower U.S. prices,

A New Orleans pilot with the Captain and Staff Captain.

Celebreties find a cruise an ideal location for a Columbo episode.

An officer checks that everything is in order during a popular Lido deck lunch.

Crew's close quarters often result in new friendships.

A few trans-oceanic ships carry cars — a Rolls Royce on QE2.

ignored the warning and topped up his Rolls. A major gas spill cost the ship thousands of dollars to clean up, and presented a fire hazard as well.

During the 1981 Alaska season, Holland America Cruises was in the strange position of competing with itself. The company had purchased Westours, a respected west coast travel packager that for several years has been chartering ships for Alaskan cruises. In 1981, Westours chartered *Cunard Princess*, and was, in effect, competing with its parent company's *Statendam* and *Rotterdam*.

Pilots board passenger vessels at every significant port, but the captain remains in charge. If he is dissatisfied with a pilot's performance, he can assume command; however, in the event of accident the captain's personal liability increases. If a pilot is at the helm and a mishap occurs, the pilot will be reprimanded by his superiors, but legal responsibility remains with the captain.

There are two places where this rule does not apply: the Panama Canal, and the river approach to Calcutta. In these waters, the pilot assumes all legal and financial responsibilities from the captain.

The USSR ship *Odessa* offers not only Russian wines but Russian movies. In 1981, selections included, "Three Plump Men" and "Gypsy Camp Vanishes into the Sky." (American movies are shown as well.)

Cruise lines are extremely conscious of the welfare of their crew members. When a seaman's relative, for example, is seriously ill, the radio officer assists in obtaining regular bulletins on the condition. When an emergency exists back home, it is rare for the company to refuse to pay for an employee's air trip there.

When ships anchor in a bay, passenger complaints about the frequency of launch service to shore are routine. For this reason, an officer keeps a log of departures during the long periods at anchor. When a passenger is shown the log, illustrating that the launches are being dispatched within minutes of each other, his complaint is quickly silenced.

Cruise ships are regularly requested to assist other vessels in trouble. A large liner sailing between Panama and Mexico passed a pleasure yacht. A crew member on the yacht was signalling wildly for the cruise ship to pass on the left. As the ship honored the request, passing the small vessel, a deck officer decided that the yacht was in trouble. The signal given was an incorrect attempt at an SOS.

The cruise ship abruptly turned around, moving at maximum speed, and dishes, books, suitcases and furniture scattered everywhere. The ship, reducing to a dead slow, circled the yacht as a launch was lowered and dispatched for the rescue. Seamen armed with tools, first-aid supplies, food and cigarettes rushed to the yacht. Aboard were three free spirits — two men ignorant of seamanship and a scantily clad young woman — en route from Australia to Mexico. The yacht's rudder had broken and there was a gaping hole in the hull.

The launch towed the craft back to the ship, where the damaged yacht was hoisted aboard. The threesome boarded the cruiser for the comfortable last leg to Acapulco. The rescue mission, the delay and the manpower employed cost the cruise line $10,000.

Various marketing devices are used to encourage passengers to take cruises. One of the most common is to include a "happy hour" in the daily activities — a period when ship's bars serve free drinks. These one-hour daily sessions are a nightmare to the bartenders. Nearly every passenger rushes to the lounges, creating huge line-ups; and with no money changing hands, few passengers are sufficiently conscientious to leave a tip. It is also annoying to passengers who don't mind the cheap shipboard prices but resent the huge line-ups.

Coastal shipping between British Columbia and Alaska has been a tradition since the Klondike gold rush of 1898. Most frequently operated by railway companies, the ships have generated both nostalgia and emotion in B.C. Today, there are but three ships left: the 6,000-ton *Princess Patricia*, her near-identical sister *Princess Marguerite*, and the slightly smaller *Prince George*. All built shortly after the second world war, their mahogany, brass and marble interiors serve as a reminder of an era past.

Of the three ships, only *Prince George* continues to serve Alaska. Abandoned by the giant Canadian National Railway in the mid-1970s, she was rescued by a group of Victoria businessmen in 1981. Despite continuing financial difficulties, *Prince George* keeps the tradition alive.

Sadly, the best of the three ships sits neglected at a Vancouver pier awaiting a buyer who might give her a new life. The first ship and the namesake of the now renowned Princess Cruises fleet, *Princess Patricia*, was retired by Canadian Pacific in the fall of 1981. Captain Ray Hudson's final sailing to Alaska became one of the great civic events of a decade in Ketchikan, Juneau, Skagway, Wrangell and other Alaska centres. Mayors, dignitaries, brass bands and thousands of local citizens turned out to say farewell to "Princess Pat." The tears turned to bitterness when Canadian Pacific, one of the largest conglomerates in the world (resources, aviation, railways, cargo shipping, communication, real estate and hotels), said it couldn't afford to keep the little 6,000-ton charmer alive.

CP had, however, more than paid its dues. The great Empress ships of the past on the high seas, and the Princesses of the west coast, occupy a proud chapter of Canadian history. The company contributed several ships to the allied cause during the second World war. The first *Princess Marguerite* was sunk in the Mediterranean, and *Empress of Britain* was the largest vessel of any kind to be lost in action.

During 1980, the last *Princess Marguerite* became the focal point of a raging controversy in British Columbia and the State of Washington. When Canadian Pacific said she would be scrapped, the B.C. government purchased her in 1974. Converted to dayliner tourist use between Victoria and Seattle, *Princess Marguerite* carried tens of thousands of passengers between 1975 and 1980. But the overwhelming success story was interrupted when the government, acting on misguided engineering information, decided that *The Maggie* was unsafe. Despite top safety ratings from the Canadian and American coast guards and the Lloyds Register of Shipping, she was retired from service. The B.C. government continued the Seattle-to-Victoria service in 1980 with an old ferry and a Boeing hydrofoil.

The season was a financial disaster, and a monumental uproar occurred in B.C. The government's engineering report was consistently attacked in the press and also in shipping circles. Without the charm of *Princess Marguerite*, tourist volume dwindled. The government finally succumbed in late 1980 and, after a $5 million refit, *Princess Marguerite* established volume records in 1981. The episode illustrated the affection coastal shipping history has earned on the west coast. Officials were startled by the emotion and outrage of the public.

Most ships have three complete sets of sheets and pillowcases; one set is on the beds, a second is in the laundry and a third is being ironed and stored. Linen is changed daily.

Every ship loses hundreds of ashtrays with each cruise. Since it is just about impossible to prevent this form of petty theft, company accountants purchase lower-priced items in mass quantities and sit back confident that the stolen ashtrays will have a promotional advantage. A ship's ashtray in a passenger's home serves as a constant reminder of a great vacation, and guests in the home, noticing the ship name, always ask about the cruise.

Larger, more expensive items are also stolen, but the customs clearance at the end of a cruise inhibits major efforts by less-than-honest passengers.

Tours of ships' engine rooms once were standard on most cruises. The passengers would walk through the control room and in among the boilers and propeller shafts. Liability insurance companies have warned repeatedly that accident premiums could be very high if the practice continued; there have been a few accidents. As a result, it is rare for a ship to permit passengers in the area. Engineers never had been very happy about the public intrusion.

Tours of the bridge of ships and through the galleys are conducted regularly.

The cruise industry spends fortunes on the construction of models: large replicas of ships to fill the corporate offices, and also models of passenger staterooms and public areas for ships on the drawing boards. People are hired to live in and use these facilities as ship architects plan passenger comforts.

SANTA CLAUS AND THE KING

Christmas at home is a treat enjoyed by very few career seamen on passenger vessels. The Christmas cruise is always packed with passengers, and the agenda is a busy series of special entertainment and features. The cruise lines try to arrange that all top officers have Christmas off every two or three years, but one captain hasn't had a Christmas with his family in fifteen years. Christmas is always a nostalgic period in crew and officer quarters.

It's not uncommon for the officers to turn things around on Christmas Day and serve the crew of the ship. And it is always the duty of the most portly member of the company to play Santa Claus at the children's party.

On one cruise, the party was preceded by a small but boozy crew celebration. It was quite a sight to see Santa, followed by a group of tipsy reindeer, tripping, stumbling and bumping along, laughing uproariously and occasionally falling as they made their way toward the confused children.

As a ship steams across the equator, King Neptune rises from the deep to welcome the newcomers to his realm. The time-honored ceremony, "Crossing the Line," is performed with gusto by the ship's younger crew members — and the event is enjoyed more by staff than by passengers. Each company has its own approach to the ceremony. On some ships, the crew assemble for cocktails in the officer's mess, where King Neptune, sea nymphs and other participants don costumes for the show. On others, passengers put on the costumes.

When the crew are the performers, passengers assembled on the deck will hear the ship's horn boom overhead. An announcement follows that King Neptune has just emerged from the deep and has come on board. His Majesty leads a procession through the ship on the various outside decks, heading toward the swimming pool, where the captain waits to welcome the King aboard. All people crossing the line for the first time are accepted into the "Order of the Dead Fish."

One or two sacrificial passengers are presented to King Neptune. Caked in meringue, ketchup, fish oil and other colorful and smelly ingredients, they are greeted by the King and tossed into the swimming pool. A few crew members, playing the roles of "bears," catch the victims to ensure that no damage is done.

Safety precautions during the raucous event are unnoticed by the passengers — but they are thorough. Sometimes fences are erected to hold back the crowds. The ship's doctor is always standing close by.

FOOD AND SERVICE

Most ships feature two sittings for dinner. Although many people prefer to eat at 6:30 p.m. rather than two hours later, the late sitting, with captain and senior officers present, is the more important of the two. Passengers indicate a sitting preference by mail, but there are always many who neglect this detail.

On one cruise, on sailing day, a very proper English maître d' sat at a table in the dining room facing more than a hundred passengers waiting to request a sitting and be given a table assignment. One by one, the people filed past and were efficiently processed until, with half the crowd still to go, the maître d' put up a large sign advising that the late sitting was full. One woman would not cooperate, noisily berating the calm and polite dining room captain and holding up the line. The passenger said she was a friend of the president of the cruise line and angrily demanded to be in the late sitting. The maître d' patiently explained that he didn't have any seats available but offered to put the woman's name on a waiting list. He explained that some passengers always want a change of sitting on the second night of the cruise.

The woman stamped her feet and shouted, "I will not go to the early sitting!"

The maître d' stared at her for a moment and, without altering his tone of voice, calmly replied, "Then, madam, you will not eat."

A ship with three or four major nationality groups on staff will have a crew chef responsible for each of the special ethnic diets.

The best dining room stewards learn how to look after the people who assist them. They recognize that payday comes in the form of tips, so they always kick something back as an investment in the future. Some money is passed to headwaiters — to be certain that the best prospects among passengers are sent their way. To ensure speed with the food, some money changes hands in the galley as well.

Two dining room stewards were exceptionally angry when an elegantly dressed lady left a lengthy cruise without leaving the expected gratuities. The stewards complained bitterly to their friends that they had given the woman the best of service.

As the ship left port on its next cruise, the two stewards were paged to the purser's office. The crew purser explained that, courtesy of this woman, two sports cars would be waiting at the pier in New York when the ship arrived there, in a few weeks. The stewards remembered having told the woman that they would be going on leave in New York and that they planned to do some touring.

THE LIGHTER SIDE OF ILLNESS

Regardless of weather conditions, the lounge show must go on. There are times during higher seas when half the passengers skip the show to recuperate in their cabins, but the entertainers — who rarely have much more sea experience than the passengers — somehow seem to recuperate on stage. On one cruise, a male vocalist started a tender love ballad and, as he proceeded, the look on his face became progressively pained. His eyes bulged, his color grew green, and finally he just dropped the microphone and ran off the stage.

One charming female vocalist — actually a crew member participating in a music hall show — developed hiccups as she started a song. Every line was punctuated with the unladylike noises. Her face reddened with each interruption, but she gamely continued her tune, accompanied by ever-increasing levels of applause.

Sometimes the show can't go on. Another female singer, a featured star for a cruise, developed laryngitis on the day of embarkation. She spent 38 days speechless and idle.

Everyone is aware of seasickness. Few people, however, realize that landsickness is an equally interesting phenomenon of the sea. After the first day or so of sailing, passengers grow accustomed to the movement of the ship. When they return to land, the body's equilibrium must adjust. Landsickness produces dizziness and, in some cases, nausea.

The seaman's remedy for seasickness is brandy mixed with port wine.

Medical doctors among the passengers frequently are seated in the dining room with the ship's medic. On one cruise, a businessman named Walter Reed — the name of the famous Washington, D.C., hospital — was seated at the doctor's table. He spent the entire cruise trying to convince people that he wasn't a doctor.

The more gregarious doctors throw a "slap-up" party for all passenger physicians on the cruise. These are always lively affairs. The passenger doctors are intrigued by the style of practice at sea. After a tour of the hospital and a demonstration of the facilities, the party shifts into gear.

The party is good for public relations. In the case of medical emergencies that occur at sea from time to time, the passenger physicians are asked to assist.

If a ship has two doctors, the subordinate has all the night calls. He is known among the crew as "Baby Doc."

A LONG WAY FROM HOME

A gentleman received an invitation to a private party in the captain's quarters at seven o'clock. Shortly after sunrise the next morning, the captain was on the bridge when a duty officer interrupted: "There is a Mr. Smith here, sir, for your seven o'clock party. Shall I show him in?"

Celebrated Los Angeles writer and former policeman Joseph Wambaugh, the author of such bestsellers as *The Blue Knight, The Onion Field, The Black Marble* and *The Glitter Dome,* is a cruise buff. He, his wife, Dee, and their children have been on several cruises.

On one cruise from Los Angeles, the Wambaugh family sailed halfway, disembarking at Acapulco where they checked into the stunningly beautiful Acapulco Princess Hotel. The trip took place about a month after Wambaugh's celebrity status had made it impossible for him to continue as a policeman. At Acapulco, he invited a few of the ship's passengers to spend their day in port at his hotel pool.

When two of the passengers arrived to join him poolside, they were greeted by a Mexican attendant who demanded a payment from the nonresidents for the use of the facilities. The fee requested was 60 pesos; Wambaugh was suspicious. He asked his guests to wait as he charged up the path to the hotel lobby to make inquiries. He was advised that the fee for nonresidents was 50 pesos, not 60, and that payment was to be made at the hotel desk, not to the attendant. As the hotel manager went to find the crooked attendant, Wambaugh returned to his guests.

"I just love being a cop," he said.

Passengers from small towns are usually the most avid moviegoers aboard a ship. New Yorkers, used to being pushed around, closely follow the cruise director's organized programs. More than anyone else, travellers appreciate the live entertainment. Westerners generally are the most active dance-floor and game participants. Easterners are the heaviest guzzlers at the bar. And no one can match the Europeans when it comes to sampling dining room fare.

Americans and Englishmen often experience difficulties with their different approaches to the language. One American lady asked an English ship's officer where the rest room might be.

The reply?

"There are no rest rooms on this ship, madam, but you might try the library."

CUSTOMS

Visits by customs officers pose a series of headaches for ships' crews. All liquor and cigarettes must be sealed in bond when the vessel enters port. But, since the crew members are not supposed to have liquor in their cabins in the first place, it is impossible to ask the senior authorities to seal that stock for customs purposes. Liquor and tobacco are required to remain sealed until the customs officials clear the vessel. When the ship is cleared, the bars can open for service.

A ship reaching its home port after a lengthy period of cruising gives cause for some extensive celebrations in crew quarters. Virtually every cabin brings out assorted spirits that are hidden in various crannies. Before the customs clearance begins, the contraband must be consumed. The final parties are awesome events.

On English ships reaching Southampton, for example, it's common for all the liquor — beer, whiskey and anything else around — to be poured into a few huge dustbins. The potent and no doubt ghastly punch circulates among the entire crew until it is gone, the night before arrival.

Customs procedures at the home port are always wearisome after a long cruising season. The crew members are not only bleary-eyed from the party the night before, they usually have several hundreds of dollars' worth of purchases to declare. The customs officers rarely screen the goods and they tend to be lenient with the duty charges.

Customs officers have been known to throw parties for a ship's crew. It gives cause for speculation when endless liquor and cigarettes appear from nowhere.

When one ship arrived in Los Angeles, the passengers dutifully filled out their customs declarations. Then, after walking down the gangway, they were led to customs booths in the terminal. Here they discovered — many to their horror — that the customs officers had complete printouts of every purchase made on the ship. In making cash and credit card sales, clerks had recorded cabin numbers. Many passengers who had purchased expensive jewellery, crystal or handicrafts faced stiff tariffs and penalties.

X RATED

Movie sessions for a ship's crew are regular happenings. One such event was not quite so regular. A group of crewmen had secured a series of pornographic movies during a port visit. They received permission to use the cinema late one night, although senior officers were under the impression that there would be a normal replay of movies that had been shown earlier to the passengers. And the crew recruited the stage manager as a projectionist.

A swinging drinking session preceded the movie event, and then the films were shown for two hours. By now, the stage manager, who had been sipping beer in his projection booth, was rather drunk. He neglected to put the films back in their containers. One movie was left on the projector.

The next morning a hostess arrived to show passengers a film about an upcoming port. The passengers assembled and, after presenting a lecture, the speaker introduced the film:

"And now, some adventures in Pago Pago."

Remarkable adventures.

A captain, arriving at night to take command of a ship, had a most unusual introduction to his cabin stewardess.

After a long meeting with the captain he was relieving, the new master, in civilian clothes, decided to take a walk in the fresh air before retiring. His stroll took him down to crew quarters, where he followed the noise to a boisterous party. No one took any notice of him; new faces, particularly among the concessions staff, are common on a ship. A seaman put a drink in his hand and the captain started to enjoy his anonymity. When asked what he did on the ship, he replied that he was with the shore-excursions office.

As the music rose to a deafening volume, a beautiful but very drunk young woman jumped on a table and started to dance. Many of the men shouted, "Strip!" And she accommodated them. As her final undergarment sailed into the crowd, she fell to the table and passed out. The captain quietly took his leave.

For weeks afterward, the captain was greeted by curious glances from the crew. One or two remembered his face, and rumblings started to circulate through the ship. The young stripper, the captain's private stewardess, couldn't remember much of the party. She was embarrassed when friends told her of her role that evening, and became horrified when she heard that the new captain might have been there.

A celebrated seaman is renowned for his tattoos. He is painted from head to toe. When dressed, there is nothing extraordinary about his appearance. Undressed, his chest displays two huge bull heads, with rings piercing his nipples. A dragon spits fire down his back, the flames disappearing in the cleft of his buttocks. Even his genitals are adorned.

One crew member went to a cabin occupied by three young women, to assist them with their life jackets for a safety drill. He left the most attractive for last. When the bell sounded for the drill, the first two rushed into the corridor while the seaman struggled with the straps on the third.

"How long is the drill?" the young lady asked.

He replied that it would be fifteen minutes.

She sighed. "There's not much we could do in fifteen minutes."

The seaman, startled, paused for just a second.

"Wanna bet?" he said. "Get that silly jacket off."

13

Planning and Enjoying Your Cruise

The Saltiest Passengers:
Freighter Travellers

There are people who are more interested in the sea itself than they are in vacations at sea. They like the musty smells of a cargo port and the work-life on a ship, and they relish the chance to make their marine fantasies come true. They consider cruise passengers to be softies living in an unrealistic world. To these hearty old tars, a banana port is more exciting than a tropical beach. Aficionados of cargo travel pursue their hobby with an all-consuming passion. They correspond with shipping companies, join clubs and subscribe to special publications. Passenger travel on freighters doesn't fall within the context of cruising, but it's an area that cannot be completely ignored.

Although there are hundreds of freighters that carry passengers, most offer poor standards of accommodation. Nevertheless, there are many vessels that offer a passenger amenities more luxurious and spacious than are found on cruise ships. Research should be done before any travel at sea is undertaken, but it is positively essential in freighter shipping.

Maritime law requires all ships that carry more than 12 passengers to have a fully qualified medical doctor on board. As a result, all but a few of the cargo liners carry precisely 12 guests. Passengers usually have the run of the ship, watching the officers and crew perform their daily functions. Tours of the bridge, engine room and other departments are cheerfully permitted.

Freighters cater to travellers who seek a quiet, uneventful and relaxing voyage, with considerable time for reading.

Unlike cruise ships, they offer few recreational facilities. The better ships offer attractive and comfortable lounges, libraries and card rooms. Passengers are housed in large cabins and suites, all with private bath, air conditioning, closed-circuit radio and telephone.

Cargo officers' quarters are segregated from the passengers, with a private mess for dining and relaxing, but the ship's senior officers join guests for the evening meal. Food tends to be the cuisine of the ship's nationality, but there are usually several main selections to choose from.

The freighters often have unpredictable schedules, frequently adjusting arrival and departure times and even changing ports of call according to the contingencies of longshore labor problems, cargo-handling backups, mechanical breakdowns and unexpected opportunities for picking up profitable loads of merchandise.

There are several things prospective freighter passengers should know. The ships do not have stabilizers, though the bulk of a fully loaded vessel and the weight below the turbulent sea surface tend to make the voyage rather smooth. When empty, the cargo vessels can take a substantial pounding in high seas. Many companies have an age restriction, refusing to carry passengers older than age 69; frequently, passengers over 65 will be asked to produce a certificate of good health. On ships from non-English-speaking countries, there can be language difficulties. Some ships do not carry wine or liquor. Passengers must carry passports and, depending on the scheduled ports of call, immunization certificates for a variety of diseases. The dress aboard ship tends to be relaxed and informal, from blue jeans to leisure suits, but passengers should be prepared for more dressy evenings at shoreside attractions. Cargo officers are trained in first aid, but passengers with medical problems should not expect to obtain treatment or find pharmaceuticals on the ship. Policies on tipping the service staff vary according to company. Gratuities are encouraged on some ships, discouraged on others; occasionally, a company recommends tipping only in cases of exceptional service.

The best companies in the business — and there are many excellent ones — are extremely proud of their ships. Top-rated interior designers are hired to create the guest lounge and cabin facilities. Cargo companies are pleased to outline, by correspondence, all their shipboard policies, fares, routes and facilities. They often encourage prospective passengers to tour the vessels if possible. This is arranged by writing to the company headquarters or to the shipping agent in a specific port.

In 1981, the average cargo ship passenger fare was about $70 per passenger per day — for accommodation, transportation and all food. Wine and liquor, when available, are exceptionally inexpensive. Passengers who are disappointed by freighter travel rarely complain about the quality of amenities or the price. Some find the life too dull, and many find that with schedule changes they miss out on the exciting ports they had looked forward to seeing. Anecdotes are many about people who expected days on the high seas and exotic ports of call, but found themselves limping back and forth between ports not far from home.

There is one unique company in the industry that is neither a pure cargo operation nor a cruise line. Delta Cruise Line's four identical "Santa Magdalena Class" 20,000-ton ships — *Santa Maria*, *Santa Mariana*, *Santa Mercedes* and *Santa Magdalena* — carry 100 passengers each and offer deck sports, heated outdoor swimming pool, cabaret entertainment, a medical doctor, a shopping arcade, a hairdresser and many other amenities found on cruise ships. Formerly sailing as Prudential Line, the Delta ships cruise from Vancouver in the north to Cape Horn in the south, and from Cape Horn to the Caribbean and Panama, across the canal and back to Los Angeles, stopping at numerous ports each way.

The ships are first class, and so are the fares. In 1981, the full 52-day "Circle South America" package was priced between $8,000 and $15,000 per passenger, depending on cabin quality. Although the amenities of a cruise are offered, the four *Santa* ships are cargo vessels, built in 1963 and 1964 under subsidy from the United States government. They are pledged for the U.S. Navy in the event of conflict, created for instant troop-transport conversion.

Two sources for comprehensive information about freighter travel are:

Ford's Freighter Travel Guide
P.O. Box 505
Woodland Hills, CA
91365
U.S.A.

The Freighter Travel Club
of America
P.O. Box 12693
Salem, OR
U.S.A.

The Ford organization publishes superb seasonal guides to freighters and also to cruise ships. In 1981, the Freighter Travel Guide was $5.95 an issue, $11.00 for a yearly subscription (two issues).

The Freighter Travel Club of America charges annual dues of $10.00 (1981), which include an informative monthly newsletter.

The author with best-selling novelist Joseph Wambaugh (The
New Centurions, The Blue Knight)
and with television's famous Love Boat captain, Gavin MacLeod.

14

Planning and Enjoying Your Cruise

EVERYTHING A PASSENGER SHOULD KNOW

The standards of the cruise industry are maintained at such a high level that passengers who don't enjoy their vacation can usually blame only themselves. A great deal of whatever dissatisfaction does occur can be credited to insufficient planning. With proper research, a prospective passenger can learn everything from the square footage of the cabin to the spices used in the galley. The style of entertainment and detailed outlines of the scheduled ports and their excursions are all listed before departure.

Travellers who book onto a Norwegian vessel can expect the officers to be more rigid than their playful Italian colleagues, but they can expect the most luxurious decor afloat. An inquiry into the nationality of a crew can tell much about what the shipboard atmosphere will be like.

The first step in successful cruise planning is to visit a respected travel agent. Scout him out carefully. The good ones have been on cruises themselves, and they have a library of guidebooks at their disposal. They have also spoken with many clients after cruises, to keep abreast of consumer reaction to a given cruise line and its ships and their facilities. Don't let the agent do the selling; make the agent do the work. The agent will earn at least 10 per cent of your fare. (The fee comes from the cruise line. You save nothing by making the arrangements yourself.)

If an agent is not knowledgeable about cruising, it can only be because of laziness, ignorance or incompetence. The cruise lines regularly offer complimentary or exceptionally low-priced cruises for travel agency staff, for promotional and educational purposes. To teach agents about the industry, the industry's public relations arm, the Cruise Lines International Association, conducts comprehensive seminars in many North American cities every year. CLIA and its member companies are eager to help agents plan social evenings for their better clients; movies, lectures and general data about cruising are offered at these sessions. Individual cruise companies sometimes cover the costs of these events.

CLIA and several private companies provide extensive and relatively inexpensive guidebooks listing all cruise schedules, rates, ship deckplans and companies (with firm histories, sample menus, tour offerings). Cruise companies invest fortunes in the publication of glossy color brochures, all freely available to travel agents and their clients. Although the brochures are helpful, a good agent knows that they are published a year ahead of time and are not always up to date. Companies sometimes make changes or offer special bargain packages while a season is in progress. These changes may result from slower-than-anticipated sales, or from unexpectedly heavy competition when a rival company tries to undercut the market.

The cruise industry represents an agent's best source of large commissions; 98 per cent of cruises are booked through agents, as compared with 60 per cent of airline tickets and 11 per cent of hotel rooms. Because a passenger pays all food, entertainment and cruise costs up front, the agent is commissioned on it all, including the air fares, land tours, rental cars and hotels booked along the way. A typical one-week cruise for a couple can net a travel agent a commission of $400 for perhaps half an hour's work. It pays for him to keep informed.

CHOOSE THE PROPER ATMOSPHERE

It is important for a passenger to select a ship that seems best suited to his taste and temperament. Since most of the companies predominantly sell to Americans, menus always feature basic food items in addition to gourmet cuisine. Food will be influenced by a ship's country of registry, but not always directly: British-registry Princess Cruises, for example, has Italian galleys.

Finding the proper atmosphere is important. Norwegian crews tend to be more staid, the British — while ever so polite and proper — are remarkably lively, and the Greeks and Italians are the most high-spirited of all. The industry offers environments that range from the electric excitement of Carnival Cruises to the more tranquil atmosphere of Royal Viking Line and Norwegian America cruises.

If you like to gamble, make sure the ship has a casino. If you want to shop, check to see that the ports-of-call cater to your needs. If you are bored by touristy resorts, there are cruises to more exotic, adventurous locations. Study the land tours available in connection with the cruise. Veteran cruise passengers tend to prefer fewer ports and more days at sea. But since first-time passengers seem to want as many ports as possible, at-sea days are generally kept to the minimum. While the multi-port junkets are viewed with disfavor by experienced cruisers, the current trend and market demand are increasingly moving in that direction; there are rumors that Cunard will soon have its small ships doing two ports a day in the Caribbean. If you prefer intimacy, don't book behemoths like *Norway*, *Queen Elizabeth 2*, *Canberra* and *Oriana*.

WHERE TO CRUISE

Royal Cruise Line senior vice-president Duncan Beardsley is one of the most gracious executives in the industry. Beardsley, active in CLIA, believes that the companies should work in concert to recruit the 95 per cent of potential customers who have never taken a cruise, not fight among themselves over the 5 per cent who have.

Beardsley, a P&O Lines veteran who has been with Royal Cruise Line since it was founded in 1974, says his greatest beef with passengers is that they have unrealistic expectations about how much geography can be covered in one cruise. Some years ago his company financed the publication of a booklet with maps, "Cruise Ships of the World and their Itineraries." Royal's own *Golden Odyssey* was on the cover, but the booklet (now out of print) was remarkably unbiased.

From Miami and Port Everglades

Three- to seven-day cruises to: an area from Bermuda to Puerto Rico, with stops at points in the Bahamas, Cuba (for Russian ships), Jamaica, Haiti and the Virgin Islands (St. Thomas).

Ten-, 14-day and longer voyages to: the entire Caribbean; Central America; Los Angeles via the Panama Canal and Mexico.

From New York

One-week cruises to: Bermuda; New England; Nova Scotia; the St. Lawrence River and Montreal. (Two-week cruises include return to New York.)

Two-week cruises to: several Caribbean points; the Canary Islands across the Atlantic (occasional).

Trans-Atlantic sailings (to Southampton): five-day crossings by *Queen Elizabeth 2*; six-day crossings by other ships.

From San Juan, Puerto Rico

Seven-day cruises to: the northern Caribbean (Jamaica, Bahamas, etc.) or the southern Caribbean (Trinidad, Barbados, Curacao, etc.).

Fourteen-day trips (various itineraries) similar to those offered from Florida.

From New Orleans

Sixteen-day cruises (occasional) to the Caribbean and Central America.

From Los Angeles

See: **To Alaska**; **To the Mexican Riviera**.

To Alaska

Seven- and eight-day cruises from Vancouver. Glacier Bay, Alaska, is the breathtaking highlight, but environmentalists have forced the U.S. government to curtail the number of ships permitted into the bay during each summer season. Study the brochures.

Fourteen-day cruises from: Los Angeles and San Francisco

To the Mexican Riveria

Three- and four-day cruises from Los Angeles do not touch port at the Mexican Riveria; some go only as far as Ensenada, Mexico.

Week-long cruises travel one-way from Los Angeles to Acapulco, with stops at some of the following ports: Cabo San Lucas, Mazatlan, Puerto Vallarta, Manzanillo, Zihuatanejo. (Passengers fly one way.)

Two-week packages are Los Angeles – Acapulco return trips or cruises via the Panama Canal to the Caribbean.

To North Cape (Norwegian Fjords)

Twelve- to 16-day cruises from Southampton or Oslo, with stops at North Cape and some of the following ports: Leningrad, Helsinki, Stockholm, Bremerhaven (Hamburg), Copenhagen, Amsterdam, Trondheim.

To the Mediterranean, the Aegean and the Baltic

The entire area from the Canary Islands to Yalta in the Black Sea, offers a dizzying array of cruises of all lengths.

Cruises from three to seven days out of Piraeus (Athens) cover the Greek Islands and sometimes go as far as Istanbul.

Fourteen-day and longer cruises out of Piraeus, Naples, Genoa or Venice stop at some of the following ports: Toulon, Catania (Sicily), Malta, Dubrovnik, Corfu, Rhodes, Istanbul, Odessa, Yalta, Alexandria, Haifa.

Full-length Mediterranean cruises (14 to 39 days) sail from Las Palmas (Canary Islands), Lisbon or Gibraltar; to Piraeus or Istanbul. Ports of call include points in: Northern Africa, Spain, France, Italy, the Middle East, the Aegean.

From Southampton

Trans-Atlantic sailings (to New York or Florida): five-day crossings by *Queen Elizabeth 2*; six-day crossings by other ships.

One- and two-week packages cover a range of destinations from North Cape to the Canary Islands. Longer cruises to the Mediterranean are available.

South Pacific

This cruise region has faded in significance over recent years because of the vast distances between the beauty spots of Australia, New Zealand, Singapore, Bali, Penang, Hong Kong, Taiwan, Yokohama, Hawaii, Tahiti, Rarotonga and Fiji.

P&O Cruises maintains a high profile in the area. Sitmar Cruises operates the economy ship, *Fairstar*.

Most cruises from Sydney, covering a range of South Pacific destinations, are 14 days or longer. One-week cruises from Sydney sail to Hobart, Australia, or to Noumea in New Caledonia. Sitmar has departures from Singapore or Darwin, as well as from Sydney, but most are long cruises.

P&O's 41-day cruises from Australia to England feature a range of South Seas ports, Mexico, the Panama Canal and the Caribbean.

There are occasional 30-day and longer cruises from Los Angeles across the South Seas.

Miscellaneous

Oceanic Independence conducts one-week cruises through the Hawaiian Islands.

Costa Cruises and Karageorgis Cruises offer cruises from Rio de Janeiro to other South American destinations (various durations), and across the Atlantic from Rio to Africa.

Cruises from Southampton to Capetown, South Africa, with several points in between, are two-weeks-plus, one way.

Several companies offer world cruises.These range from 80 to 96 days.

THE COSTS OF CRUISING

Most ships today advertise "all one class," but the phrase is misleading. All passengers enjoy the same food, entertainment and recreation services, but cabins vary widely — from tight inside bunks the size of a closet to the grand veranda-and-penthouse suites. The quality of cabin service usually improves with the class of accommodation.

In 1981, the poorest cabin on an economy ship cost about $80 per passenger per day, including all food and amenities; the best staterooms and suites on the luxury ships cost $400 per passenger per day. The average cabin, based on industry figures, was about $160 per passenger per day. Because of a mild slump in sales during 1981 plus considerable new tonnage now entering the market, it's anticipated that fares will remain reasonably stable in the foreseeable future.

There are traditionally few bargains in the cruise ship industry, though the determined head-to-head competition in Miami makes that market the best dollar-for-dollar value in the business. It is generally true that you get precisely what you pay for. Passengers interested in cutting costs should realize that very little time is usually spent in the cabins. Many staterooms have third and fourth upper bunks that can be pulled down from the bulkheads. Travellers who don't mind sharing accommodation will find that fares for extra passengers are very modest. Children under three usually travel free of charge. On the older ships, there are still rooms without private bath. These cabins have a wash basin and possibly a toilet, but bath and shower are down the hall.

It is wise to book a cruise as early as possible. The most expensive and the least expensive accommodation on a ship tend to sell out first. When a reservation is made, the cruise line requires a 25 per cent deposit; the balance is due 60 days prior to embarkation. (It is one of the accounting joys of the cruise industry to have millions of dollars of passengers' money on deposit long before any service is rendered.) Most companies will not refund the entire amount if a passenger cancels after full payment has been made. Some firms will refund part of the fare; some will refund it all only if they are able to sell the space to another passenger. It is wise to check the company policy at the time of booking and to purchase inexpensive trip-cancellation insurance.

The travel agent should carefully explore the air/sea packages associated with any cruise, comparing the savings offered from company to company. No matter how far from home the cruise area is, it is almost certain that the shipping company will know the cheapest and most efficient route between a passenger's home and the ship's port of embarkation/disembarkation.

The recession of the early 1980s, which has generated ulcers in the industry, has produced substantial bargains for cruisers who shop around. While passenger shipping is going through one of its greatest building booms ever and thousands of new passenger beds are coming into service, customer demand has weakened. Companies have been offering myriad incentives: free airfare, Canadian dollars on a par with the U.S. dollar, third passengers in a cabin free of charge and sharp discounts. The bonanza is not expected to last very long. Despite the poor financial balance sheets, no one is cancelling orders for new ships.

TIPPING

Nothing seems to produce so many passenger questions and so much anxiety as the business of gratuities to be paid to the service staff. It is not at all a complicated matter. The payment should be about two dollars per passenger per day ($28 per week for a couple) for the pair of dining room attendants, and a similar amount for the cabin stewards. Passengers in more deluxe accommodation are expected to tip a little more generously. If a dining room headwaiter renders special services — they usually do — such as tableside flambés, he should be rewarded with five or ten dollars per week. If the maître d' has been friendly and helpful, five dollars to him is normal. Lounge and wine stewards are tipped 10 to 15 per cent of each purchase made through them.

It should be remembered that the average standard of service is expected to be "excellent." Service that is merely "good" deserves smaller gratuities. Similarly, exceptional work and special requests merit a higher amount. On longer cruises, tips should be paid at the end of each week. Officers and entertainment staff are never offered a tip. It is common to reward hairdressers and hostesses who do special personal services. Winners in the casino usually toss a chip or two in the direction of the croupier or dealer.

When a poor tip is offered, the tendency of a steward is to fault a passenger's stinginess and not his own performance. Therefore it is wise, in a friendly and unantagonistic way, to advise the maître d' if you are disappointed. He will then tell the steward why the tip was poor (or nonexistent). It is fairer to the maître d', however, to inform him of such a problem early in a cruise, giving him an opportunity to correct the flaw.

Veteran cruisers sometimes use a clever device to enhance service. On the first night of a cruise, they will invent a special request of a cabin steward (ice bucket, glasses, extra pillow, extra blanket). This is done by leaving a note on a bed, with five or ten dollars attached. The steward is thereby alerted that the passenger is a good tipper. Similarly, following the first meal in the dining room, a passenger can ask the headwaiter to prepare a fruit basket or some other item to be taken back to the cabin. It is surprising what a five dollar bill will do for the balance of a cruise. A ten dollar tip, discreetly passed to a maître d' at embarkation, can do much to improve a passenger's assigned dining room seating; sometimes it even leads to an invitation to the captain's table.

Although the Russian ships and Holland America Cruises advise that no tipping is required, the gratuities are always gratefully received.

GROUPS

Cruise lines enjoy booking large groups aboard vessels, and they are only too willing to provide every assistance possible. The larger the group, the greater the likelihood of astonishingly fine service . . . or of immediate rejection. If a couple of hundred members of the "Loyal Fraternal Brotherhood of the Wild Crow" try to book passage for their annual hoot, chances are they will have difficulty finding a ship to take them (unless they are willing to charter an entire vessel). Too large a group can cause a great many problems among the general passenger population, unless, of course, it is a very sedate bunch.

For group bookings, usually for a dozen or more people, many special deals may be offered. It could be that one free cruise will be given for every eight doubles booked at full fare. Travel agents put together groups with these deals in mind, on a regular basis. If a hundred people book, a flat negotiated price will be arranged.

If group travel is planned, the best advice is to start negotiating a year in advance with a competent travel agent at your side, and drive a hard bargain with several companies. They will offer special fares, group social events, air travel rebates, and a variety of ship's facilities and staff to assist with the needs of your party.

Chartering an entire vessel is an extravagant business. The wife of then West German chancellor Willy Brandt chartered *Island Princess* for a private party on a ten-day cruise to Mexico in 1972. The ship was filled with her friends. At today's prices, the charter would cost about one million dollars, plus all liquor and sundry purchases made on board.

CLOTHING

The first thing to consider when packing for a cruise is that you will be with the same people for its duration. Those who pack heavily, rarely regret having done so. Ships allow almost unlimited luggage, though the aircraft used to reach the ship will have stipulations. Remember, once the airport hassles are over with, a cruise passenger unpacks only once; the hotel floats from destination to destination.

Southern routes are substantially more casual than cruises to the north or the still very formal trans-oceanic crossings. A typical seven-day cruise will feature two formal nights, three casual evenings and two evenings that are billed as informal. Casual means sports shirts and slacks for the men, and just about anything short of swimming suits for the women. On the night of embarkation and any night in port, the dress is always casual. By informal, the ships mean jacket and tie for the men, and cocktail wear for the women. When ships request formal attire, they hope the men will show up in dinner jackets or black tie, and many do, but dark business suits are acceptable. Women should plan to wear their best evening gowns and outfits. On some cruises to the Caribbean, a man may feel out of place in a tuxedo; on the North Atlantic, he will feel shabby in his best business suit.

Common sense should be the key to packing. Remember, it can be quite chilly in Bermuda during the winter, and it is rarely hot enough for swimming in Alaska in the summer. (But note if the ship has an indoor pool.) Regarding valuables, all ships offer safety deposit box services free of charge.

A full range of cosmetics, suntan lotions and sundries are sold on the ships, but favored personal brands may not be available.

PREPARATION AND EMBARKATION

Tickets for a cruise arrive in a package, usually a month or so before the sailing date. The package is full of information: a map from the airport to the dock in the port city; possibly information regarding baggage check-in at the airport of arrival, from where luggage is taken to the ship by truck; parking arrangements for passengers who will arrive by car; baggage tags for the ship; advice on passports, vaccination certificates and any other needed documentation; order forms for bon voyage parties; boarding passes for guests who are to see you off; and the all-important dining room seating selection card.

Your dining room and bon voyage cards must be returned by mail immediately. State your preference for early or late sittings in the dining room. Bon voyage parties, held in passenger cabins, can rarely accommodate more than three or four guests at a time. Most companies can handle larger groups in public rooms, but arrangements must be made far in advance. (The passenger will pay for all liquor, food and staff provided.) The card enclosed with the ticket is an order form for the small cabin parties; check off the champagne, liquor and food you need to purchase, and it will all be waiting when you reach your cabin.

The standard currency at sea is the United States dollar; only on rare occasions is any other currency listed. The pursers' offices will convert the more common international currencies, but the rates of exchange, though fair, may not be as attractive as those offered by banks. All major credit cards and traveller's checks are acceptable on the ships. Purchases made aboard are usually signed to the cabin account, with settlement made during the final 48 hours at sea, when the ship reverts to a cash-only policy. Casinos operate on a cash basis.

When you arrive at the ship, your bags will be whisked away by a well-paid longshoreman. (The ships have no choice here.) You are not expected to tip him, though gratuity will never be refused. You won't see your bags again until you are in the cabin. When you reach the gangway, a photographer will record the moment. A steward will greet you, accept your hand luggage and lead you to the cabin. A small tip is in order.

Your cruise has begun.

MARRIAGE AND PREGNANCY

Marriages are no longer performed aboard ship, and engaged couples are encouraged to get married ashore and have their reception on the ship as a bon voyage party. Then follows the honeymoon at sea. In some cases a clergyman is brought aboard to perform the ceremony, but he leaves the ship before it embarks.

If you sail on S.S. Emerald Seas out of Miami, you don't have to bring your own clergyman aboard to perform a marriage ceremony. Corporate secretary Helen Cohen, who works at the Miami head office of Eastern Steamships, is a Florida justice of the peace. She has performed many weddings on the ship. When she's not handling marriages, she works for one of

Miami's best-liked cruise executives, vice-president Eleanor Esser.

Captains stopped performing marriages at sea after scores of embarrassing incidents occurred, not to mention a growing number of court cases in various jurisdictions challenging the validity of the papers; different governments have different marriage laws. One chap, off on a lark and drinking far too much, married a ship's hostess. When bride and groom marched down the gangway, the man's real wife was waiting. He had thought it was just a laugh. The hostess was serious. The affair resulted in formal charges of bigamy, a conviction and fine, and a divorce with hefty alimony payments. But the story ended happily. The passenger and the hostess were re-wed ashore, and they took their honeymoon on the same ship.

If consulted, a cruise line will rarely accept women passengers who are more than six months pregnant. An obviously long-pregnant woman may be sent immediately to the ship's physician and put ashore at the point of embarkation, with or without refund. If her advanced condition is detected too late, she may be sent ashore at the first port of call. Ships, like aircraft, have fine print on the back of their tickets, giving them the right to bounce any passenger; the captain's judgment is supported by international maritime law.

ENJOYING YOUR CRUISE

The first thing to forget when you step aboard a ship is how much you paid for the privilege. It is difficult to put thousands of dollars out of one's mind but, if you don't, the cruise can't be successful. As the cliché goes: "If you have to think about it, you can't afford it."

For liquor, budget between one and one-and-one-half dollars per shot and, for wine, about 30 per cent less than you would pay at home. Allow an appropriate amount for tips, and establish a ship-and-shore shopping budget.

Too many people go on cruises determined to get their money's worth. They eat far past the point of possible enjoyment, drink too much, play too hard and sleep too little. Many guests scurry so frantically, trying to enjoy all the activities the cruise offers, they have time to enjoy none. The cruisers who derive the most make the ship work for them; they don't make themselves work for the ship's agenda.

Take things as they come. Scan the day's activities. If a shipboard activity conflicts with a movie, the movie will likely be shown again. If you decide to sleep in, don't worry about missing breakfast. There is always room service. And if that isn't appealing, the next meal is never more than an hour away. Sometimes a stroll on an abandoned moonlit deck is more fun than the show in the nightclub.

If you don't exercise, a vacation is hardly the place to start. If you don't normally go to the movies, why bother on a cruise ship? If you don't like pickled octopus, why not order steak and potatoes?

Make the ship cater to your moods. There are hundreds of people aboard whose jobs depend on delivering that service.

DISEMBARKING

Passengers should allow at least two hours for getting off the ship. When a vessel docks, customs officers come aboard to clear the ship for unloading. That completed, the luggage is removed and placed in long lines in the shoreside terminal. At this point, the passengers start to leave the ship. Clearing customs is the last obstacle before hitting the street and the awaiting taxis.

For the purposes of airline connections, it is important that passengers allow adequate time between ship disembarkation and flight departure. A rule of thumb is: three hours plus travel time between dock and airport (two hours to get off the ship and clear customs, one hour at the airport before the flight). It is very important to know the time it takes to travel from the ship to the airport.

Passengers cause themselves unnecessary trouble by not studying customs regulations before leaving on a cruise. They return loaded down with purchases made ashore, declaring more than their legal entitlement. Then they complain about the duty charged.

With expensive items that you take along, such as cameras and jewellery, it is wise to carry with you proof of ownership and documentation of the place of purchase. If that is not possible, then such items should be cleared by a customs officer before you depart on the cruise. The officer will tag the items or issue a signed chit indicating ownership. The burden of proof in these cases rests with the traveller, not the customs agents.

Few things amuse a ship's officers more than the sight of hundreds of travellers lined up before the vessel is at the berth. People paid a small fortune for the cruise, and waited eagerly for months. Now they are desperate to escape.

Relax. A ship is not like an airplane. Customs and immigration clearances take a long time. Have a final champagne breakfast or lunch, savor every moment, and then leisurely stroll ashore.

ODDS AND ENDS

Many travellers experience jet lag after rapidly crossing numerous time zones in an airplane. The experience at sea is rather different. When *Queen Elizabeth 2* dashes across the Atlantic to England, she does so in five 23-hour days. The return (westward) trip is in five 25-hour days. The latter is especially recommended. Consider having five daylight-saving clock adjustments in a row. That is precisely what happens on ships. You lose an hour's sleep every night that you sail in an easterly direction. You gain an hour a night on westerly trips.

Many ships have a chapel on board (*Queen Elizabeth 2* also has a synagogue), often with a clergyman along on the cruise. When no priest, rabbi or minister is aboard, the captain conducts an interdenominational service.

Policies for purchasing bottled liquor aboard ship vary from company to company. Some ships will not sell it at all (hoping to keep you in the public rooms), some sell it at a reasonable price over the bars, some have special liquor shops and others sell it at an extortionary rate (the equivalent of 26 shots at the bar). Best to check in advance, or to pack a bottle of your favorite potion. Duty-free shops at the ports will look after later needs.

Passports are almost always required. There is rarely any need for customs clearance at ports of call, only when the cruise ends. In the event that a port immigration official chooses to do an inspection, the ship may request that all passports be kept on file with the purser. Depending on the port itinerary, you may need a valid vaccination card and, for some exotic places, proof of immunization against tropical diseases.

It once was common for cost-conscious travellers to reserve single accommodation in a room housing four or more passengers, taking their chances that the company would be pleasant. Firms sometimes still accept such bookings, but the practice is discouraged.

Most, but not all modern ships are equipped to handle both European and North American appliances, and the matter should be checked with the line. Voltage, currents and cycles can vary from ship to ship and may cause damage to the appliances. Women with hair dryers and men with electric shavers may be in for a disappointment. (The ship's beauty parlor can satisfy the women's needs here.)

Some appliances, such as electric blankets and irons, are strictly forbidden aboard a ship. There have been too many accidents over the years.

It is rare that a ship will accept a pet of any kind. Giving in to the wishes of one passenger causes too many difficulties with the rest of the population — including the crew. Ships that make longer voyages, however, will often include a kennel in the cargo areas of the vessel.

Passengers with medical conditions that require monitoring should have a discussion with the family physician before leaving on a cruise. The physician may wish to write a letter to the ship's doctor. Most common pharmaceuticals are available on ships, but it is wise to bring along a supply of a current prescription. Special diets should be requested and confirmed by correspondence prior to embarkation, but most ships are prepared, at a moment's notice, to provide salt-free, diabetic, kosher or other special but not unusual requests.

Today's ships' stewards often have an easy time because passengers rarely know how much service the staff really is prepared to render. In addition to carrying out the usual bedroom services, stewards will shine shoes, cook breakfast, maintain a fresh supply of mix, deliver a bucket of ice or basket of fruit — and run any errand a passenger wishes.

In the dining room, every special wish becomes an urgent assignment, and nearly all reasonable requests can be accommodated. The most common service above the norm is to provide passengers with box lunches free of charge, for days at shore. In some less-than-sophisticated ports, it is a wise idea to take the meal along.

One group of passengers, arriving at Skagway, Alaska, planned to spend the day driving the breathtaking White Pass Highway to Whitehorse, in the Yukon. They asked the headwaiter to prepare box lunches: a selection of sandwiches, including egg salad. The Italian headwaiter was perplexed, and the passengers repeated the order. The headwaiter, shaking his head, disappeared into the galley. Later that day, at a picnic table in Whitehorse, the passengers opened the box lunches to discover a variety of sandwiches — and cute little plastic bags filled with wet and dripping egg salad.

BON VOYAGE!

THE SHIPS OF THE WORLD

The passenger cruise ship industry is constantly in a state of change and adjustment: new ships are launched, old ones are retired; ancient vessels get luxurious facelifts; assets are sold from one company to another; old companies fade away; and, new ones are born. Any list of ships and companies is, therefore, subject to change. The list here is in alphabetical order and includes country of registry. It is as complete an outline of the industry as is possible. There are many vessels, from riverboats to Chinese junks, that claim to be cruise ships.

NOTE: Years in parentheses indicate major ship reconstruction.

AMERICAN HAWAII CRUISES, One Embarcadero Center, San Francisco, Calif. 94111, U.S.A.

> *S.S. Independence:* 20,300 tons; 1951 (1980); 750 pass., 300 crew; United States.

ASTOR UNITED CRUISES, P.O. Box 13140, Port Everglades Station, Fort Lauderdale, Fla. 33316, U.S.A.

> *M. S. Astor:* 18,800 tons; 1981; 638 pass., 220 crew; Germany.

BAHAMA CRUISE LINE, INC., 61 Broadway, New York, N. Y. 10006, U.S.A.

> *S. S. Veracruz:* 10,595 tons; 1957 (1975); 736 pass., 280 crew; (formerly *Freeport,*) Panama.

BALTIC SHIPPING COMPANY
BLACK SEA SHIPPING COMPANY
(Passenger ships of the Soviet Union)

M. S. Alexandr Pushkin: 19,860 tons; 1965 (1975); 600 pass., 340 crew; U.S.S.R.

T.S. Maxim Gorki: 25,022 tons; 1969; 750 pass., 375 crew; (formerly *Hamburg,*) U.S.S.R.

M.S. Mikhail Lermontov: 19,860 tons; 1971; 600 pass., 340 crew; U.S.S.R.

M.S. Kazakhstan: 16,600 tons; 1976; 350 pass., 240 crew; U.S.S.R.

M.V. Odessa: 14,000 tons; 1975 (1979) 464 pass., 260 crew; U.S.S.R.

M.V. Turkmenia: 5,035 tons; no information available.

CARNIVAL CRUISE LINES, 820 Biscayne Blvd., Miami, Florida 33132, U.S.A.

T.S.S. Carnivale: 27,250 tons; 1956 (1976); 950 pass., 550 crew; (formerly *Empress of Britain,*) Panama.

T.S.S. Festivale: 38,175 tons; 1961(1978); 1,146 pass., 580 crew; (formerly *Transvaal Castle, S.A. Vaal,*) Panama.

T.S.S. Mardi Gras: 27,250 tons; 1962 (1973); 906 pass., 550 crew; (formerly *Empress of Canada,*) Panama.

M.S. Tropicale: 36,674 tons; 1981; 1,200 pass. 600 crew; Liberia.

Carnival Cruises is currently constructing a 45,000 ton ship to be named *The Holiday.*

CHANDRIS INCORPORATED, 666 Fifth Avenue, New York, N.Y. 10019, U.S.A.

S. S. Britanis: 25,245 tons; 1932 (1970); 1,000 pass., 450 crew; (formerly *Monterey,*) Greece.

238

S. S. Ellinis: 18,564 tons; 1932 (1965, 1977); 1,200 pass., 500 crew; (formerly *Lurline*) Greece.

S. S. Fiorita: 3,523 tons; 1950 (1979); 350 pass., 80 crew; (formerly *Amsterdam,*) Panama.

S. S. Italis: 26,353 tons; 1940 (1977); 1,100 pass., 475 crew; (formerly *America, Australis,*) Panama.

S. S. Regina Prima: 10,153 tons; 1939 (1965); 600 pass., 250 crew; (formerly *President Hoover,*) Panama.

S.S. Romanza: 7,638 tons; 1939 (1971); 832 pass., 250 crew; (formerly *Aurelia,*) Greece.

The Victoria: 14,917 tons; 1939 (1971); 500 pass., 280 crew; (formerly *Dunottar Castle,*) Panama.

COMMODORE CRUISE LINE, LIMITED, 1015 North America Way, Miami, Florida, 33132, U.S.A.

M. S. Boheme: 11,000 tons; 1968 (1979); 440 pass., 220 crew; West Germany.

M.S. Caribe I: 23,000 tons; 1953 (1971,1983); 980 pass., 480 crew; (formerly *Olympia*)Panama.

COSTA CRUISES, 733 Third Avenue, New York, N. Y. 10017, U.S.A.

S. S. Amerikanis: 19,377 tons; 1952 (1971); 614 pass., 250 crew; (formerly *Kenya Castle,*) Greece.

M. S. Andrea C: 8,600 tons; 1942 (1976); 400 pass., 180 crew; (formerly *Ocean Virtue,*) Italy.

M. S. Carla C: 20,477 tons; 1952 (1976); 748 pass., 370 crew; (formerly *Flandre,*) Italy.

M. T. S. Danae: 15,560 tons; 1956 (1976); 404 pass., 250 crew; (formerly *Port of Sydney,*) Greece.

M. T. S. Daphne: 16,330 tons; 1955 (1975); 406 pass., 250 crew; (formerly *Port of Melbourne,*) Greece.

T. S. Enrico C: 16,000 tons; 1950 (1976); 700 pass., 300 crew; (formerly *Provence,*) Italy.

T. S. Eugenio C: 30,500 tons; 1966; 1,000 pass., 475 crew, Italy.

T. S. Flavia: 15,465 tons; 1947 (1976); 654 pass., 240 crew; (formerly Media,) Italy.

T. S. Frederico C: 20,416 tons; 1958; 700 pass., 280 crew; Italy.

M. S. Italia: 12,200 tons; 1967; 514 pass., 240 crew; Italy.

CUNARD LINE LIMITED, 555 Fifth Avenue, New York, N.Y. 10017, U.S.A.

M. V. Cunard Countess: 17,495 tons; 1976; 752 pass., 300 crew; Britain.

M. V. Cunard Princess: 17,495 tons; 1977; 752 pass., 300 crew; Britain.

R M. S. Queen Elizabeth 2: 67,140 tons; 1969; 1,766 pass., 930 crew; Britain.

NORWEGIAN AMERICAN CRUISES, 29 Broadway, New York, N.Y. 10006, U.S.A. (As of 1983, a subsidiary of *The Cunard Line.*)

M. S. Sagafjord: 24,000 tons; 1965 (1980); 513 pass., 300 crew; Norway.

M. S. Vistafjord: 25,000 tons; 1973; 677 pass., 370 crew; Norway.

EASTERN STEAMSHIP LINES INC., 1220 Biscayne Blvd., Miami, Florida, 33101, U.S.A. (Subsidiary: Western Cruise Lines)

S. S. Azure Seas: 20,000 tons; 1955 (1975, 1980); 800 pass., 325 crew; (formerly *Southern Cross, Calypso,*) Panama.

S. S. Emerald Seas: 24,458 tons; 1944 (1979); 800 pass., 400 crew; (formerly *Richardson, President Roosevelt, Leilani, La Guardia, Atlantis,*) Panama.

EPIROTIKI LINES, INC., 551 Fifth Avenue, New York, N. Y. 10017, U.S.A.

M. T. S. Apollo: 6,000 tons; 1948 (1970); 228 pass., 139 crew; (formerly *Irish Coast,*) Greece.

M. T. S. Argonaut: 4,500 tons; 1929 (1965); 176 pass., 102 crew; (formerly *Orion, Vixen,*) Greece.

T. T. S. Atlas: 16,000 tons; 1951 (1973); 568 pass., 297 crew; (formerly *Ryndam,*) Greece.

M. T. S. Jason: 5,200 tons; 1965; 268 pass., 112 crew; Greece.

M. T. S. Jupiter: 9,000 tons; 1961 (1971); 372 pass., 212 crew; (formerly *Moledet,*) Greece.

M. V. Neptune: 4,000 tons; 1955 (1972); 190 pass., 97 crew; (formerly *Meteor,*) Greece.

M.S. World Renaissance: 12,000 tons; 1966 (1978); 426 pass., 235 crew; (formerly *Renaissance,*) Greece.

HAPAG-LLOYD A. G., Postfach 107947, Gustav-Deetjen-Allee 2/6, 2800 Bremen 1, West Germany

M. S. Europa: 33,819 tons; 1982; 600 pass., 290 crew; West Germany.

THE HELLENIC MEDITERRANEAN LINES CO. LTD. Pan Am Building 200 Park Avenue, New York, N. Y. 10017, U.S.A.

M. S. Acquarius: 4,800 tons; 1972; 280 pass., 125 crew; Greece.

M. S. Castalia: 9,000 tons; 1975; 360 pass., 220 crew; Greece.

HOLLAND AMERICA CRUISES, Two Pennsylvania Plaza, New York, N.Y. 10001, U.S.A.

> *M. S. Nieuw Amsterdam:* 32,000 tons; 1983; 1,210 pass., 559 crew; Netherlands Antilles.

> *S. S. Rotterdam:* 38,000 tons; 1959 (1969); 1,111 pass., 550 crew; Netherlands Antilles.

> *S. S. Veendam:* 23,500 tons; 1957 (1973); 713 pass., 325 crew; (formerly *Argentina, Monarch Star,*) Panama.

> *S. S. Volendam:* 23,500 tons; 1957 (1973); 717 pass., 325 crew; (formerly *Brazil, Monarch Sun,*) Panama.

> Holland America plans to welcome to the fleet in 1984, the 33,00 ton *Noordam.* .

HOME LINES CRUISES INC. Suite 3969, One World Trade Center, New York, N.Y. 10048, U.S.A.

> *M. V. Atlantic:* 33,500 tons: 1982; 1,050 pass., 400 crew; Liberia.

> *S. S. Oceanic:* 39,241 tons; 1965 (1979); 1,034 pass., 600 crew; Panama.

'K'; LINES-HELLENIC CRUISES, Olympic Tower, 645 Fifth Avenue, New York, N. Y. 10022, U.S.A.

> *M. T. S. Atlantic:* 5,500 tons; 1965 (1978); 296 pass., 130 crew; (formerly *Adonis,*) Greece.

> *M. T. S. Constellation:* 12,500 tons; 1962 (1980); 392 pass., 190 crew; (formerly *Anna Nery,*) Greece.

> *M. T. S. Galaxy:* 5,500 tons; 1957 (1971); 286 pass., 130 crew; (formerly *Scottish Coast,*) Greece.

> *M. T. S. Kentavros:* 2,500 tons; 1944 (1964, 1968); 206 pass., 100 crew; Greece.

> *M. T. S. Orion:* 6,200 tons; 1952 (1969, 1979); 243 pass., 130 crew; (formerly *Achilles,*) Greece.

LAURO LINES, One Biscayne Tower, Miami, Florida, 33131, U.S.A.

> *M. S. Achille Lauro:* 23,629 tons; 1964; 900 pass., 400 crew; Italy.

> *M. T. S. Oceanus:* 14,000 tons; UA* (1979); 540 pass., 230 crew; Greece.

> *Original construction date unavailable.

LINDBLAD TRAVEL, INC. 8 Wright St., Westport St., Westport, Ct. 06881, U.S.A.

> *M. S. Funchal:* 10,000 tons; 1961 (1981); 395 pass., 185 crew; Portugal.

> *M. S. Lindblad Explorer:* 2,300 tons; 1969; 92 pass., 60 crew; Panama.

> *M. S. Lindblad Polaris:* 2,150 tons; 1960 (1982); 76 pass., 35 crew; (formerly *Oresund*) Sweden.

NORWEGIAN CARIBBEAN LINES, One Biscayne Tower, Miami, Florida, 33131, U.S.A.

> *S. S. Norway:* 70,202 tons; 1962 (1980); 1,900 pass., 800 crew; (formerly *France,*) Norway.

> *M. S. Skyward:* 16,264 tons; 1969 (1974); 725 pass., 306 crew; Norway.

> *M. S. Southward:* 16,607 tons; 1971 (1974); 730 pass., 308 crew; Norway.

> *M. S. Starward:* 16,000 tons; 1968 (1976); 742 pass., 325 crew; Norway.

> *M. S. Sunward II:* 15,000 tons; 1971 (1977); 718 pass., 279 crew; (formerly *Cunard Adventure,*) Norway.

FRED OLSEN LINES KDS, Vestre Strandgt 42, P.O. Box 82, 4601 Kristiansand S. Norway

M. S. Black Watch: 9,000 tons; 1966; 330 pass., 150 crew; Norway.

M. S. Blenheim: 13,800 tons; 1970; 380 pass., 180 crew; Britain.

P&O; INCORPORATED: London, Southampton, Los Angeles and Sydney

P&O CRUISES, Beaufort House, St. Botolph Street, London EC3A 7DX, Great Britain.

S. S. Canberra: 45,000 tons; 1960; 1,800 pass., 900 crew; Britain.

S. S. Oriana: 42,000 tons; 1959; 1,860 pass., 900 crew; Britain.

M. S. Sea Princess: 27,670 tons; 1966 (1978); 844 pass., 400 crew; (formerly Kungsholm,) Britain.

S. S. Uganda: 16,907 tons; 1952 (1967); 300 pass., 900 crew & students*; Britain.

*P&O marine educational ship.

SWAN HELLENIC CRUISES (a P&O subsidiary)

M. T. S. Orpheus: 6,000 tons; 1952 (1969); 300 pass., 139 crew; (formerly Munster,) Greece.

PRINCESS CRUISES, 2029 Century Park East, Los Angeles, Calif. 90067, U.S.A. (P&O's North American Subsidiary)

M. V. Island Princess: 20,000 tons; 1972 (1979); 626 pass., 350 crew; (formerly Island Venture,) Britain.

M. V. Pacific Princess: 20,000 tons; 1971 (1979); 626 pass., 350 crew; (formerly Sea Venture,) Britain.

M. V. Sun Princess: 17,370 tons; 1972 (1979); 686 pass., 370 crew; (formerly Spirit of London,) Britain.

P&O's Princess Cruises division will be taking delivery of the 40,000-ton *Royal Princess* at the end of 1984.

PAQUET CRUISES, 1370 Avenue of the Americas, New York, N. Y. 10019, U.S.A.

M. S. Azur: 11,600 tons; 1971; 800 pass., 240 crew; (formerly M. S. Eagle,) France

S. S. Dolphin: 12,500 tons; 1956 (1973); 565 pass., 280 crew; (formerly *Ithaca,*) Panama.

S. S. Mermoz: 13,800 tons; 1957 (1970, 1976); 550 pass., 230 crew; (formerly *Jean Mermoz,*) France.

S. S. Rhapsody: 24,500 tons; 1957, (1972, 1982); 880 pass., 280 crew; (formerly *Statendam,*) Bahamas.

POLISH OCEAN LINES, 410 St. Nicholas Street, Montreal, Quebec H2Y 2P5, Canada.

T. S. S. Stefan Batory: 15,024 tons; 1954 (1969); 550 pass., 335 crew; (formerly *Maasdam,*) Poland.

PEARL CRUISES OF SCANDINAVIA, Pier 27, San Francisco, Calif. 94111, U.S.A.

M. S. Pearl of Scandinavia: 12,400 tons; 1967 (1979, 1982); 488 pass., 220 crew; (formerly *Finnstar,*) Bahamas.

M. S. Princess Mahsuri: 7,940 tons; 1980; 300 pass., 140 crew; (formerly *Berlin,*) West Germany.

ROYAL CARIBBEAN CRUISE LINE, 903 South America Way, Miami, Florida 33132, U.S.A.

M. S. Nordic Prince: 23,000 tons; 1971 (1980); 1,038 pass., 400 crew; Norway.

M. S. Song of Norway: 23,005 tons; 1970 (1978); 1,040 pass., 400 crew; Norway.

M. S. Sun Viking: 18,559 tons; 1972; 728 pass., 320 crew; Norway.

M. S. Song of America: 1982; 1,414 pass., 500 crew; Norway.

ROYAL CRUISE LINE, One Maritime Plaza, San Francisco, Calif. 94111, U.S.A.

M. S. Golden Odyssey: 10,500 tons; 1974; 454 pass., 200 crew; Greece.

S. S. Royal Odyssey: 25,300 tons; 1964 (1976, 1981); 725 pass., 425 crew; (formerly *Doric, Hanseatic,*) Greece.

ROYAL VIKING LINE, One Embarcadero Center, San Francisco, Calif. 94111, U.S.A.

M. S. Royal Viking Sea: 28,000 tons; 1973; 500 pass., 320 crew; Norway.

M. S. Royal Viking Sky: 28,000 tons; 1973; 500 pass., 320 crew; Norway.

M. S. Royal Viking Star: 28,000 tons; 1972; 725 pass., 400 crew; Norway.

SITMAR CRUISES, 10100 Santa Monica Blvd., Los Angeles, Calif. 90067, U.S.A.

T. S. S. Fairsea: 25,000 tons; 1956 (1970); 925 pass., 500 crew; (formerly *Carinthia,*) Liberia.

T. S. S. Fairstar: 24,000 tons; 1957 (1964); 1,600 pass., 650 crew; (formerly *Oxfordshire,*) Liberia.

T. S. S. Fairwind: 25,000 tons; 1957 (1970); 925 pass., 500 crew; (formerly *Sylvania,*) Liberia.

Sitmar's new flagship, the 36,000-ton *Fairsky,* is due to enter the fleet in 1984.

SUN LINE CRUISES, Suite 315, One Rockefeller Plaza, New York, N.Y., 10020, U.S.A.

M. S. Stella Maris: 4,000 tons; 1960 (1967); 178 pass., 100 crew; (formerly *Bremerhaven,*) Greece.

M. S. Stella Oceanis: 6,000 tons; 1965 (1967); 300 pass., 140 crew; (formerly *Aphrodite,*) Greece.

S. S. Stella Solaris: 18,000 tons; 1973; 640 pass., 310-crew; Greece.

SUN WORLD LINES LTD., Suite 1424, Marquette Building, 314 North Broadway, St. Louis, Mo. 63102, U.S.A.

M. V. Regina Maris: 5,813 tons; 1966 (1980); 200 pass., 175 crew; Singapore.

WESTERN CRUISE LINES: See Eastern Steamship Lines Inc.

WORLD EXPLORER CRUISES, P.O. Box 2428, Laguna Hills, Calif. 92653, U.S.A.

S. S. Universe: 18,100 tons; 1953 (1976); 570 pass., 260 crew; U.S.A.

A Glossary of Nautical Terms

Aft — toward the rear or stern of a ship
Afterdeck — open deck area at the stern
Amidships — middle of a ship
Astern — movement toward the stern, or as in aft

Beam — width of a ship
Below — lower than main deck;
one goes "below," not "down"
Bow — front of a ship
Bridge — the control room, topside and forward
Bulkhead — wall

Companionway — corridor

Deck — floor
Deckhead — ceiling (see also "overhead")
Disembark/Debark — leave a ship
Draft — bulk of ship below the water line

Embark — begin a voyage

Forward — toward the bow

Galley — kitchen (small kitchens are "pantries")
Gangway — ramp to board a vessel

Heel — leaning to one side (same as "list")
Helm — steering mechanism on the bridge

Keel — the centre rib on a ship's bottom from bow to stern
Knots — nautical miles per hour
(5 knots equal 6 land miles per hour)

Ladders — stairways
Lee — ship side sheltered from wind
Lines — ropes (never say "ropes")
List — leaning to one side (same as "heel")

Main Deck — the longest deck stretching from bow to stern

Overhead — ceiling, roof (see also "deckhead")

Pier — wharf, berth (never say "dock")
Pitching — forward motion, bow rises and falls
Port — harbor, or to the left

Rolling — side to side movement

Starboard — to the right
Stern — rear end of a ship

Topside — outside or decks above main deck

Underway — when a ship is moving

Wake — ruffled water at the stern
Windward — side toward the wind

Seamen's jargon contains a veritable lexicon of words, expressions and unique terminology. This list contains only some of the more common words a passenger might encounter. *The principal gauchery to be avoided is the reference to your ship as "boat."* Boats hang on the side in the event of emergencies.

REFERENCES

GENERAL BOOKS

Coleman, Terry, *The Liners: A History of the North Atlantic Crossings.* London: Allen Lane, 1976.

Hoffer, William, *Saved!* London; Macmillan, 1980.

Miller, Byron S., *Sail, Steam and Splendour.* Montreal: Optimum Publishing, 1977.

Wall, Robert, *Ocean Liners.*Collins, 1978.

TRAVEL GUIDES

ABC Shipping Guide. (London: ABC Travel Guides.)

Cruise Ships of the World and Their Itineraries. (Royal Cruise Line.)

Cruises Everywhere, 1978. (New York: Fodor's Modern Guides.)

Ford's Deck Plan Guide. (Woodland Hills, California.)

Ford's Freighter Travel Guide. (Woodland Hills, California.)

Ford's International Cruise Guide. (Woodland Hills, California.)

In-Cruise Network. (New York: TL Enterprises.)

Travel Agent's Manual. (San Francisco: Cruise Lines International Association.)

Worldwide Cruise & Shipline Guide. (Oak Brook, Illinois: Official Airline Guides.)

Other sources include hundreds of cruise line brochures, newspaper articles and magazine articles.

INDEX

Names of ships are in *italic* type. Names of lines are in capital letters. For ports of call, embarkation points, and cruise destinations, refer to pages 25-53 and 237-47.